AMERICAN CRITICISM
1926

American Criticism
1926

Edited by
William A. Drake

Essay Index Reprint Series

REMOVED FROM
E.S. FARLEY LIBRARY
WILKES UNIVERSITY
COLLECTION
EUGENE SHEDDEN FARLEY LIBRARY
WILKES COLLEGE, WILKES-BARRE, PA.

BOOKS FOR LIBRARIES PRESS, INC.
FREEPORT, NEW YORK

PN710
D68

First published 1926
Reprinted 1967

REMOVED FROM
E.S. FARLEY LIBRARY
WILKES UNIVERSITY
COLLECTION

LIBRARY OF CONGRESS CATALOG CARD NUMBER:
67-28734

PRINTED IN THE UNITED STATES OF AMERICA

To
the Memory of
STUART SHERMAN
1881-1926

Ἄρτι λοχευομένην σε μελισσοτόκων ἔαρ ὕμνων,
ἄρτι δὲ κυκνείῳ φθεγγομένην στόματι,
ἤλασεν εἰς Ἀχέροντα διὰ πλατὺ κῦμα καμόντων
Μοῖρα, λινοκλώστου δεσπότις ἠλακάτης.
σὸς δ' ἐπέων, Ἤριννα, καλὸς πόνος οὔ σε γεγωνεῖ
φθίσθαι, ἔχειν δὲ χοροὺς ἄμμιγα Πιερίσιν.

159622

INTRODUCTION

In presenting *American Criticism, 1926,* the editor wishes to disclaim all the pretensions of superlatives. These arc emphatically *not* the best critical essays of the year. Scholarly excellence had, in fact, very little to do with their selection. They are merely those essays which, out of the large number appearing in American periodicals between July, 1925, and July, 1926 (the period fixed for the first volume of our probable series), have given the highest degree of pleasure and the most definite impression of general appeal and permanence of interest.

Guilty as our eclecticism may appear to serious thinkers, I am not sure that this arbitrary selection of taste is not more reliable in the long run than a more sober consideration of academic merits—certainly in a book which, like this, is directed primarily to the "common reader," and intended rather for his entertainment than his edification. This implies an obvious practical consideration which in the present instance we have not found embarrassing. That it can be read with pleasure need not stand in prejudice of any work. It is the happy quality of almost all masterpieces that they are eminently readable; and this quality is hardly accidental. A classic example of the expert winnowing of taste is seen in the way that the half-wild, untaught little Circassian ward of Baron d'Argental, Mademoiselle Aïssé, found the story of *Manon Lescaut* in the dreary morass of the Abbé Prévost's interminable romance: "A new book entitled *Mémoires d'un Homme de Qualité Retiré du Monde* is going the rounds here. It is of little consequence, but I read a hundred and ninety pages of it, weeping all the time." The world would not let *Manon* perish. It could not bury the rest of the *Homme de Qualité* quickly enough.

Indeed, now more than ever before, it seems that the instinctive selection of cultivated and sensitive taste is more surely to be trusted than any prescribed and anciently proven dicta. An epoch was born out of the travail of the Great War, and many of the criterions which were valid for the old are not valid for the new age. It is necessary that this disconcerting fact should be understood. The modern world is involved in a situation comparable to that of the medieval world when the Roman Empire collapsed. Our physical forces are morbidly exuberant; our spiritual forces are woefully spent. Exactly those ideas which we had formerly deemed the most secure have been the quickest to fail in the general ruin. Geographical, political, and economic demarcations have been shifted again and again with an amazing dexterity. The very nature of patriotism has changed, becoming critical rather than jingo, broadly humanitarian and internationally aspiring (to some, at least) where it was formerly dogmatically nationalistic. Science has usurped the place of religion in the ethos of the modern world, and the discoveries of scientific criticism have shaken the fundamental conceptions of every department of knowledge.

We stand today in the center of a vast disintegration. In America the situation is complicated by the peculiar problems of our own culture. Our forces and problems must be organized before the artist can do his work. Perhaps the reason why the creative spirit has never (in literature) experienced a full flowering in America, and is at present enervated in Europe, is that the artist exhausts his creative energy in a squandrous and unavailing struggle before this synthesis can be reached. Perhaps because our general skepticism no longer allows us to take literature seriously, and because most of us are lacking in the courage for long endurance. But ferment is at work. Feeble and sporadic as is our creative spirit in its manifestations, our critical spirit is prodigiously fecund. It is unquestionably more sensitive, more searching, more revealing, more democratic, in an abused word, more *creative,* than it has been at any time in the memory of our generation. Thus the criticism of today, in its diverse ways, is striving to localize the point of synthesis in which alone superior creation can be achieved and man may possess his soul. Criticism, says Matthew Arnold, "tends to make an intellectual situation of which the creative power can profitably avail itself." It is precisely this that contemporary criticism, in its uncertain and prodigal way, is actually accomplishing.

But it is the native vigor of the critical spirit, rather than its actual performances or apparent direction, which gives us hope for this desideratum. It is at this point that Croce's theory of intuition as a concept becomes valuable. For at first view it would appear that criticism in America is generally inept and trivial, that journalism has wreaked too grievous havoc on it, and that wholesale distributors, consulting circulation experts, and querulous advertisers have in turn ruined journalism. It seems at first view unlikely that a set of more consummate ignoramuses have ever assembled for the professional practice of literature, until we look beyond our own shores and descry on every hand their fellows in sublimity—amiable and eager, to be sure, but ignoramuses none the less. In America pure scholarship—knowledge of comparative literatures, history, philosophy, and the theoretical sciences—has seemingly twittered its last breath beneath an almost unparalleled neglect. In the view of our nation-builders' ideal of utility, it has become distinctly disadvantageous, in the terms of mundane success, even to possess such knowledge; and to be actually learned is an affront to democracy which expiates itself with heavy penalties of isolation and neglect.

The generality of our critics are certainly untainted by such culpability; they appear to know extraordinarily little. The present tendency of journalism, which provides too few vehicles for serious essays, discourages their composition, and prefers light and topical reviews which do no more than trace the contours of a single book, forces the acquiescence of the younger men who depend on their writing for their livelihood. Our universities, with their inexhaustible genius for laying desolation on the scanty knowledge they dispense, complete the cycle of forces which in America enshrine the commonplace. One wonders what has become of the ancient passion for learning in this age when the average boy on the street knows more facts than Plato, yet grows up to toil at an office desk, read *The New York Evening Journal,* and buy a radio. The lofty aspiration of Israel's high-priests for the *urim* and *thummim* of existence is not really extinct. But none of us knows enough to be deeply moved by it, and our knowledge is not even sufficient to help us formulate our quest. It is not in the spirit of our age to cherish or accomplish learning in a universal sense. We have communized knowledge and isolated its departments in a way which has entirely obliterated the creative inner significance of the whole subtly merging stream of human experience. We have resorted to that ineffably short-sighted refuge of small and lazy minds, specialization. But universality and a proportioned synthetic conception of knowledge are prerequisites of superior creative accomplishment, and also of superior creative criticism, which partakes of exactly the same nature. We have forgotten this. We have forgotten that either everything is important or nothing at all is important, since life is immanent in no single thing, but indeed in the intermingling of all things. And the tragedy of it is that we do not know enough to know how much we have missed.

Another prerequisite of creative criticism, the absence of which in America is still more difficult to explain, is that of a definite esthetic conception. It would appear that long disuse of the reflective faculties has incapacitated us for esthetic thinking, so that a radically different (and usually unassimilated) standard exists for every critic who pretends to one, while the praise or blame of most of our reviewers signifies merely that he has found a particular book interesting or tiresome, as the case may be. A promising approach to an American esthetic conception was made by Emerson with his expressionistic conception of beauty as "its own excuse for being" and "an ultimate end," and by Poe with his definition of poetry as "the rhythmical creation of beauty." An approach to a critical platform was made by Poe when he wrote that "true criticism is the reflection of the thing criticized upon the spirit of the critic," a doctrine which has been very ably elaborated by Mr. J. E. Spingarn. The late James G. Huneker, a critic whose activity and superb sensitiveness answers the feeble alibi of the difficulties of journalism, perfectly exemplifies this school. Mr. Mencken, whose unproclaimed but admirably regulated scholarship is not less praiseworthy than the vigor and heresy of his intelligence, has done a valiant work in discountenancing what Huneker terms "the naughty boy theory and practice of criticism" and in introducing a novel ideal of honesty.

Rock-bound esthetic requirements may be more pernicious in their effects on a growing literature than their lack, it is true, but a little sound esthetic thinking at this point would do us no harm. It might help us to a clearer conception of *why* we like what we like, and it might serve to eradicate some of the balderdash of our intellectual critics and the familiar triviality of our popular reviewers. In recent years, since the advent of the American realistic-satirical novel and especially since Mr. Van Wyck Brooks designated the social background of American literature in his all-too-meager early writings, we have endeavored to plumb the complicated mazes of American social character, American history and biography, and the nature of the prodigy which we call the American tradition. Herein we strike bedrock. Here is something vital, something living, something personal, something evocative, in a deep and stirring sense. By searching these mysteries, we release them. By exposing the causes why so youthful and so rich a nation as America should have been so tardy in expressing itself artistically, we break the seal of our muteness. This national identification, this accurate and candid national comprehension, both somewhat perilous in an older culture, is preëminently necessary in one still so diffuse and callow as our own. It is the best pledge that we can make for the future of American literature that we have come to it so soon and with such an unabashed avidity for the truth.

We come, then, to the matter of taste, of emotional recognition, which is the ultimate crucial point of contemporary American criticism. "Criticism," writes Mr. Spingarn, "is essentially an expression of taste, or that faculty of imaginative sympathy by which the reader or spectator is able to relive the vision created by the artist. This is the soil without which it cannot flourish; but it attains its end and becomes criticism in the highest sense only when taste is guided by knowledge and rises to the level of thought, for then, and only then, does the critic give us something that the artist cannot give." In the same provocative essay he writes: "The greatest need of American criticism is a deeper sensibility, a more complete submission to the imaginative will of the artist, before attempting to rise above it into the realm of judgment. The critic is not a man seated on a block of ice watching a bright fire, or how could he realize the full force of its warmth and power? If there is anything that American life can be said to give least of all, it is training in taste. There is a deadness of artistic feeling, which is sometimes replaced or disguised by a fervor of sociological obsession, but this is no substitute for the faculty of imaginative sympathy which is the heart of all criticism. By taste, I mean, of course, not the 'good taste' of the dilettante or the amateur collector, or taste in its eighteenth-century sense, but that creative moment of the life of the spirit which the artist and the enjoyer of art share alike. For this the ardor of the reformer, the insight of the historian, even the moral passion of the saint, is no substitute; for taste, or esthetic enjoyment, is the only gateway to the critic's judgment, and over it is a flaming signpost, 'Critic, abandon all hope when this gate is shut.'"

There is no need to elaborate these statements. Taste, then, is the touchstone; but a much more highly cultivated, surer, and better-informed taste than, for example, we have been able to employ in selecting the articles in this book. Guided by the knowledge, the social conception, the theoretical background, and the quasi-creative consciousness which we have indicated as desirable in a critic, this taste is likely to function very much as an esthetic criterion. The assumptions being similar, its judgments will be consistent; and its latitude, and the hospitality which it offers for the encouragement of the new, render it an infinitely valuable ally to a literature still in the making. One could wish American literature no better fortune than such a criticism; and slowly but certainly, beneath the pattering accents of the trivialists and the vacant thunderings of the pedants, such a spirit is arising. We are coming no closer to scholarship or to theory, but we are coming very close to the basic currents of the American spirit; and in that spirit there is life. There are only two nations in the world today where the eternal accent of life arises brightly from the very soil: in the new Russia, so lately born, it rises in a robust shout of triumph; in America, which only now has found the life-giving stream of its virgin genius, it rises as a clear, strong voice that promises loftily for the future. It is a voice which by its virile timbre suggests Milton's prophetic vision: "Methinks I see in my mind a noble and puissant nation rousing herself like a strong man after sleep, and shaking her invincible locks. Methinks I see her as an eagle mewing her mighty youth, and kindling her undazzled eyes at the full midday beam."

For all our crudeness, our ignorance, our materialism, for all of the faults of the rawness of our culture, we bear within our national fiber the stuff of a great literature. In our culture and our society, in the exuberance of our materialistic life and our deep need for spiritual employments, an intellectual situation is arising which, if wisely grasped, will inevitably result in such a literature. It is the high obligation of our criticism to precipitate that situation, to expose its hidden causes, and to accomplish its appointed results.

WILLIAM A. DRAKE.

New York, July 20, 1926.

CONTENTS

CONTENTS

CONTENTS

AMERICAN CRITICISM

1926

ANON IS DEAD[1]

By Henry Seidel Canby

I

ONE famous author has sunk into oblivion. His name, once the best known of them all, is scarcely intelligible to our generation. Title pages of famous periodicals printed it not once but a dozen times, anthologies recorded it and readers were always asking, Who is he? The raciest writing was often over his signature, and if the great ones of the social or political world condescended to literature, he was their representative. In old newspapers and magazines his masked brilliance stirred our curiosity in childhood. Now he is unfashionable, if not altogether forgotten. Anon, alas, is dead.

The mind of a man who, like Keats, wrote burning poetry, or, like Hazlitt, pungent criticism, or, like Washington Irving, excellent stories, and printed them anonymously, is as alien to Broadway or Greenwich Village, or to Bloomsbury or Fleet Street as the character of a Quaker who went to prison rather than raise his hat. The thing is simply incredible to editors who buy names and sell names to their subscribers, or to newspapers which head every other column with a name. Even advertising

[1] From *The American Mercury,* May, 1926.

with us has become personal. If there are no moral sentiments in the founder of a big business, there will be a write-up by his advertising agent in the best short-story fashion. More, the advertiser is offered a choice of names well known in literature, which, for a handsome fee, will be signed to almost any blah about himself or his goods that he specifies. A name will carry anything, and many a sweating hack makes a good living by writing articles that become important when they appear over the signature of some one great in the movies or Wall Street. Anonymity, in brief, is now an inhibition that every one tries to escape.

All this is so common, and the reasons for it seem so obvious, that we do not remember how recent the practice is, nor realize its significance. Medieval work was usually anonymous, and much of it remains anonymous in spite of laborious investigation. Who wrote "Beowulf" or the "Chanson de Roland"? Who composed "Gawayne and the Green Knight"? Anonymity was common until modern times, although a willingness to be discovered becomes more and more evident. Consider the famous pseudonyms in English literature: Gulliver, W. S., Boz, Junius, George Eliot, Geoffrey Crayon, "The Author of *Waverley*," Christopher North, Elia. Note that even the intensely personal R. L. S. published most of his earlier sketches as Anon and that the brilliant egoisms of Edgar Allan Poe appear among the critiques of *Graham's Magazine* with no name attached. As many important books, essays and poems before 1850 were first published anonymously or over a pseudonym as with the name of the author attached. We have come in a few generations from

The Pickwick Papers
By Boz

to what would be nationally advertised as

Charles Dickens
writes in the current
Green Book.

This increase in egomania must have impressed the least observant, for it is by no means confined to journalism and the arts. Signboards now display individuals who gesture urgently to the passer-by and speak by exclamatory captions. Most of these are already familiar types—the banker, the lumberman, the druggist. Soon they will be pictures of well-known persons, who will gladly consent to lend their faces for the publicity value: Harold Bell Wright with lifted finger will warn us, from the roadside, to read only moral fiction, and John Barrymore, in the blaze of an electric sign, will be pointing at the springs of an automobile that solves the traffic problem.

And yet it cannot be proved that the columnists, the dramatic critics, the feature and sports writers, who are leaders of this modern exhibitionism, are vainer or more egotistical than their predecessors, when they had predecessors. Read the "Noctes

Ambrosianae" of Christopher North for such a display of personal whim and effrontery in criticism as would be hard to find today. Nor are short-story writers and novelists and playwrights more willing to be self-assertive than when Anon was in power. Such instances of colossal egoism as may be collected from Pope and his age or Dr. Johnson and his circle cannot be exceeded even in New York. Pope was incredibly vain, Southey clamored for publicity, the young men of the *Edinburgh Review* were possessed by a kind of sadism and they fed their egoes with cruelty. Sterne pulled wires for a reputation with a shameless assiduity that a modern publicity agent may well envy, and through the aristocratic ages, from Chaucer down to Tom Moore, writers bootlicked their patrons with an unblushing vulgarity that is more offensive than the noisy appeals of moderns to their new master, the crowd. There has been no general decline in virtue, and a shrinking rather than expansion of the ego. But now "everybody is doing it." When Pope exploited his malicious personality one got something worth the pains; but when every one flings, not only his opinions, but also his name and idiosyncrasies in your face, there is a phenomenon worth discussing. If this be vulgarity, then vulgarity has become fashionable.

II

It may often be vulgar, but this glorification of the capital *I* is not explained by calling it vulgarity.

What we are encountering is a panicky, an almost hysterical, attempt to escape from the deadly anonymity of modern life, and the prime cause is not the vanity of our writers, but the craving—I had almost said the terror—of the general man who feels his personality sinking lower and lower into a whirl of indistinguishable atoms, to be lost in a mass civilization.

In village life every one knows every one else, and knows about them, which, for the ever sensitive ego of man, is even more important. The villager moves and has his being in the consciousness of others. They realize him or her, not as a clerk, stenographer, or salesman, but as George, Mary, or Jim, with such a background of manner, experience, and temperament as one gets in a novel. That this consciousness is often unfavorable does not change the argument. Dislike is better than disregard, and unpopularity preferable to loneliness. Only matured and self-sufficient personalities or those beaten and crushed by life prefer the anonymity of an impersonal, unfriendly environment. A familiar word in passing, a gibe, a recognition of that ego which we are always cherishing, is the stimulant that humanity craves.

City living, however, as we know it, is essentially impersonal. The I-that-am-I lives for most of its day among strangers, and comes home at night to the unhomely environment of an apartment in a beehive—and the personality of a newspaper. In the modern university, instead of a family of like-minded students all nicknaming each other, there are two thousand strangers in a class; instead of a dozen professors in familiar rivalry there is a great teaching machine, in which the units are solitaries, drifting in and out, as impersonal in their relationship as the employees of a steel mill. Clubs, since Prohibition, have lost their social values and become places to eat and run. For writers there is now no Grub Street even. A few of the lonely youngsters take refuge in Greenwich Village, where tradition says they will meet their kind, but most of them are scattered in lodging-houses, small jobs, farms, newspapers—anywhere, everywhere.

Once out of the family, if there is a real family, or that enlargement of the family which only the fortunate get in school or college, the struggle against anonymity begins in earnest. The crowd draws us under and we become mere units: a job with a name that is no more than a number, a wife indistinguishable from ten thousand others waiting in line in the delicatessen stores. We struggle against the tug of the current in ways that are pathetic in their triviality. We put the name of our town on the crossbar of our automobile—"Granton—the Athens of Florida"—as if to say, "At least you can tell where I come from." We thrill at the sight of our names in print, until a front-page reference has become a synonym for success. We join associations where "brother," "comrade," or "good fellow" is the label and chief excuse for being. We are like those pathetic remainders from the great anonymous civilization of the later Roman Empire, whose names are found upon scrolls and monuments with the additions of a race or a country, as if that might serve to give them passing identity—Heliodorus the Phoenician, Polycrates of Attica.

The city dominates our way of living whether we are in town or country, and the modern city is inevitably standardized and anonymous. The individual is sinking day by day nearer to the conditions of nobody. This fact, inescapable for the vast majority, has its influence even upon dress. Never was there such a widespread striving by both male and female to be correct in hat, coat, rouge, earrings, cigarettes, shirt, cuff buttons, width of trousers, color of shoes. The noon hour in New York is a dress inspection, in which the stenographers and clerks are so busy with discoveries and comparisons that some of them forget to eat. Every office boy, secretary, and minor executive is busy testing how well he measures up to the fashion, which means that he is trying to feel himself a visible part of the one great personality he knows—the city's—New York's.

More and more society comes to resemble a school of fish, marked alike, moving alike in drifts and dartings, so spontaneous in the mass that one would say there was a group soul. Songs, jokes, slang, dances, opinions appear and spread and disappear with the rhythm of an epidemic or a cyclone. Thanks to the radio, the mass thought and mass emotion are instantaneously communicable everywhere. There is a difference in tempo but not in kind between the effect upon individuality at the Podunk corner store and its cracker box, and at New York.

And yet man himself is just as he always was: a self-sympathetic person, craving authority, expression, recognition, and a sense of being somebody. In all probability he is much more personal in his desires, because they are now more complex, than the epic heroes whose names served for nations and whose actions were history. Because I am insignificant among a hundred millions of people, because what I say never gets beyond my family or my office, because no one has need or opportunity to discover what I think, because I am not Roland, or Francis I, or Dr. Johnson, or William Jennings Bryan—all this does not mean that I crave any the less the position of the "old man" of the savage tribe, whose words established custom, or the intense personal expression of Mary Queen of Scots. It is impossible that my ego should impress a nation, it is difficult to make a hundred people aware of my existence as differentiated from the society in which I live, yet while my rational self accepts this conclusion, my emotions balk at it. I must at all costs feel myself to be intensely personal, and if not myself, then my little world in which I move.

III

The answer, of course, is vicarious experience, and

this intense desire is responsible for most of the caperings, the name callings, the exhibitionism described above. In literature we always give our masters what they want; and since the crowd, not the patrons, is now master, we give them personal journalism. Watch the girl swaying at the strap in the subway crowd, a mere fiber of the impersonal mass, and see how eagerly she sinks herself in the blazing personalities of the paper she holds, in which everything from the fashions in stockings to international news is told by a Tom, Dick, Harry, or Ann speaking intimately, familiarly to her. Or note in an apartment home, as like to ten thousand other apartment homes as one cell is to another, how the magazine on the table with its intensely personal style seems to radiate the familiar and the individual like a new kind of electrical toy.

This craving for the friendly, familiar voice is responsible for the success of the column: for the impressionistic personal criticism, where "I like" and "I hate" are the dominants; for photographic illustrations of short stories that are themselves romantic; for the astonishing success of the popular lecture in America; and, finally, for the blazoning of names, as if to say, it is Frank, Don, Mary, Kathleen, not a great remote Author, above all not Anon, that is writing for you. It also lies behind the vogue of the popular magazines' "true stories" and "confessions," which are actually fiction made so personal as to satisfy the craving for individual experience. Furthermore, this rush of the anonymous ego to take refuge in rich, glaring personalities that write of the world as if it were still intimate, is an escape from science which has pervaded education with a consciousness of abstract, immutable physical laws that take no account whatever of wish and ignore individuality completely. How lonely is the very sound of words like force, atom, ion, degeneration, subconsciousness, behaviorism! No wonder that we who live in a civilization made by science should desire its opposite.

And hence, what I have called the universal exhibitionism of modern journalism is undoubtedly good for the crowd. It heartens them. It searches out the individual and speaks to him. The columnist is an agent of humanism as much as the dramatist of the Renaissance was, and the novelist who writes his autobiography for a novel is medicining the need of personal experience in the reader. Fiction and, especially, criticism often suffer from the vulgarity of too much egoism, but more often they suffer because one feels a dramatic temperament standing between the reader and the truth, and is annoyed precisely as the early Protestant was annoyed by the priest who stood between himself and God. But let the fastidious hesitate before they condemn the capers of the public's favorites. The publicists of today are simply Shakespeare's clowns come to outnumber all the rest of the cast. Their display of personality is often a mask, like the clown's cap and bells. When they assume their copyrighted ego, which is advertised by night on the electric signs, they are free to be shrewd, critical, and expressive, because they know that their audience craves the human name, the human intonation, the human idiosyncrasies and prejudices that are rapidly becoming mere words. Bernard Shaw has not hesitated to expose his similar methods, and there is no shame in them. Who that is hopelessly anonymous himself—and that is the permanent condition of most of us—will regard Anon if he can hear an authentic personal voice? Even savages give names to the natural forces they worship.

So much for an honorable and deserved defense of the egomania of our times. But what of the intellectually fortunate, that remnant in whose hands culture must persist, the cultivated minority? Are they yielding to exhibitionism? Is it not true that they seek the same stimulation of the ego that the masses more justifiably ask for, and that when they write they throw reticence to the winds?

Criticism, which is always written for the cultivated, is shot through today with capital *I*'s. The delicate art of a Walter Pater, that suffuses its subject with a glow from the writer's personality and yet establishes general principles and makes subtle interpretations, is almost impossible of general influence in our times. There are men and women capable of it, but they do not practice it, except in holes and corners. The audience for it is very limited. The tiny minority that can digest thoroughgoing criticism is interested chiefly in its own quarrels over recondite or esoteric literature, and the generally cultivated are impatient of so unspiced a dish. What they wish to know is what Walter Pater did on the afternoon when he discovered the Renaissance, and how he lit his gem-like flame. Even university pundits with a record of sober expositions of Arnold-like dignity loosen up when they come to town and begin to pat young authors on the head and tell what happened to their complexes when they first read James Joyce. It is a sociable, merry, vivacious society, this community of the modern literati, and preferable to the solemnities of research in the sources of Chaucer and the language of the "Ancren Riwle," but one begins to wonder what will become of criticism that is *not* autobiography, and to wonder if the end will not be some painless process by which culture comes from inoculation. "Know me," says the critic, "hear what I think, see how I am moved, and you will become inevitably a person of taste."

Anon had to give his reasons, for otherwise no one would believe him. His opinions were no good unless he could back them up. Now that he is dead, emotion does seem to be taking the place of reason, opinion is driving out principle, and impressionism has made off with the art and science of criticism, taking the garage with the car. It is all very jolly and very good for the lonely atoms that we're beginning to believe that there was nothing intimate left for them outside their own ego, but must we all be given a celebrity's private emotions every time we ask for critical nourishment?

IV

The passion for non-anonymity is not likely to decrease. As clothes, food, transportation, language and emotion become increasingly standardized, inhibitions begin to enfeeble the ego. It becomes actually more difficult to think and feel personally, to be a husband, a citizen, a servant, a soul in an individual sense. Formulas exist for everything, even for an expression of gratitude, a laugh, a scream, a faint. We live in such formulas. Eccentricity is notably declining, especially in America, and eccentricity is one of the indices of personality. All the more will the colorless seek color, the conventionalized mind crave spontaneity, the anonymous and impersonal desire a vicarious indulgence in egoism. Novels are already biography to an extent never reached before. Novels have always been made up very largely from the personal experience of the writer transmuted into typical adventure, but the modern novel of the familiar kind depends to a dangerous extent upon trivial happenings which gain their only significance from the ordinary but very personal individual who experiences them. Taking a bath, hugging a sweetheart, dictating to a stenographer, getting drunk—all these things are described with what the author thinks is realism, but which actually provides only the same satisfaction of egoism as may be had from looking at the pictures of familiar individuals in the rotogravure sections of the Sunday supplements.

The art of fiction may have gained access to inner recesses of the personality hitherto kept private, but it has lost its detachment and its sense of the really significant. As Henry James said of the disease in the mild form which he studied, in his notes on the modern novel, what we have in many new novelists is more often material for fiction than fiction itself.

I repeat that all this trotting up and down of the ego is as inevitable as transportation and lighting, and if the popular emotions are exploited by the vulgar and the cynical, nevertheless the jolly fellows who scatter vitamines where they go and put rouge on the pallid cheeks of routine existence are blessing their generation. Yet too much genius has gone into clowning. We are not all of us Buddhists to make the Name a sacred formula which, repeated often enough, will satisfy every want. There should be some precincts of the temple of literature where critics especially will leave their ego in the subconsciousness where it belongs and look at the object rather than their own reactions.

It is not necessary and it is not advisable to relapse into the impersonality of Anon. The stiff formalities of the old form of address were largely due to the dignity of the caste system. The remote third person has no value in a democracy, but it is surely possible to say "I" and "me" without transforming a critique into an autobiography. And precisely because we are democratic in our casual relations and because, like the Missouri frontiersman in Parkman's narrative, we say, "Howdy, stranger. What's your name? Where do you come from? What's your business?" to every writer we meet, the rich personality in literature has an opportunity never equaled before. Let a man make a name for himself and by print and by lecture, as well as by radio, he can broadcast everywhere. What advertisers call buyer resistance and publishers are beginning to name reader resistance does not exist for him. His audience, knowing him by name, are ready to listen. It is a crime against opportunity, then, if he always talks of himself.

Not less of the personal, but more responsibility in the personal, is what we need. Those who break through this shell of anonymity that so oppresses us should do more than shout "I am I" from the apartment windows. Subtle things wait to be accomplished in criticism; a finer touch is needed there. Beauty has been almost lost from poetry. Humor is broader than it is long. The American, even more than other moderns, lives without principles and without plan. It is only the rare person who can do the rare thing needed, but what a chance today if he has a name and can keep his head! He is known among the anonymous, and whether he talks sense or nonsense he will be heard. The London passion for the theater gave Shakespeare a like opportunity. He could write gorgeous and none too intelligible poetry and wise and subtle philosophy in prose so long as his drama held. The analogy with our day is close. Personality is now at a premium and the personal touch is a necessity for crowd-weary men. There is no need to resurrect Anon, but Ego should take some reducing exercises before we weary of his grossness.

THE POETRY OF CHARLES MONTAGU DOUGHTY [1]

By SAMUEL C. CHEW

TO THE generality of readers Mr. Doughty is *homo unius libri;* and even the *Travels in Arabia Deserta* remained till lately one of those "broad expanses" of literature of which most adventurers among books were content to be "told." Now at length they are breathing its "pure serene"; but meanwhile Mr. Doughty's poetry is still neglected, and it seems worth while to attempt to redress the balance which has been so heavily overweighed by his great prose masterpiece.

The author of *The Dawn in Britain* springs from the strength of ancient English blood.[2] The Doughtys are traced far back in the annals of Suffolk and Lincolnshire, and the Hothams (his mother's family) were large landowners in Yorkshire from a period shortly after the Norman Conquest. Charles Montagu Doughty was born in 1843. His mother died shortly after his birth, his father when he was but a little boy; and he was left almost alone in the world. After a full eighty years the sense of be-

[1] From *The North American Review,* December, January, February, 1925-26.

[2] Mr. Doughty has confirmed the biographical facts herein recorded for the first time.

reavement still remained with him, inspiring the lines in *Mansoul* which begin—

> Death cannot dim thy vision, in my heart,
> Dear Lodestar bright; whereby I daily·set,
> My shallops course, in Life's solicitous voyage.

Ambitious to enter the navy, the boy received his early education at the Portsmouth Naval School; but his health was insufficiently robust for the arduous career of his choice, and from Portsmouth he passed about 1860 to Caius College, Cambridge, where in 1865 he took an honor's degree in the natural sciences. His life at the university was interrupted for a year of wandering in Scandinavia. Here he collected material for a monograph on *The Jöstedal-Brae Glaciers in Norway* (1866). These geological studies were of value to him during his later travels in Arabia. A botanist also of no mean quality, his sensitive love of flowers imparts a fragrance to many pages of his verse. From this early time dates also his interest in popular superstitions and folk-lore. His knowledge of Scandinavian languages and literature brought ingredients to the strange and individual style, both in prose and poetry, which he molded from many and diverse materials.

The year 1866 Doughty passed at Oxford in private study. Since the past cannot but exert a strong attraction upon the geologist and folk-lorist, it was this perhaps that drew him now to the study of

Anglo-Saxon. Very evident is the influence of early English poetry upon his own verse: the heavy beat of the accents, the abundant alliteration, the strong, clashing epithets, the harsh yet stately march of the rhythm, the heroic view of life—these characteristics of Doughty's poetry have their far-descended historical justification. It was at Oxford, too, that he made a happy acquaintance with Chaucer and Spenser, in reading whom, as he has told me, he, a lonely man largely dependent upon his own guidance, found his true vocation and came to know that in their art lay his future, near or far off. In the Muses' Garden (described in *The Clouds*) there walks with Cædmon

> Dan Galfred; in whose worthy hand, a book,
> With golden leaves, his Muses song; whereon
> He looketh, oft pensive smiling; whiles he goeth.

There, too, is Spenser, "the Prince of Britain poets," meditating "his laurel verse." Of later poets—even Shakespeare, Milton even—there is no mention in Doughty's verse; indeed, invoking Spenser, he exclaims—

> Dear Master Edmund, since from thy pined flesh,
> Thou wast unbound; is fallen thy matchless Muse;
> Alas the while! on many evil days:
> Wherein, as waxed untuneable; can mens ears,
> Now, no more savour thy celestial lays!

The first fruits of these benign influences were not to ripen for forty years. Meanwhile, with frail health overtaxed by study, he determined to seek the help that might come from change of climate. Behind this physical need was the desire to learn foreign tongues and become acquainted with alien modes of thought. And behind these incentives was the impelling motive of all his wanderings—a yearning to grasp any clew to the mystery of life. He would prove all things and would hold fast that which is good. He would escape from "the busy-idle cares which cloud upon us that would live peaceably in the moral desolation of the world." When the nomads of the Arabian wilderness with persistent curiosity inquired of him: "Art thou not come to spy out the country?" or: "Art thou not some banished man?" it was Doughty's wont to reply that he was a *Saiêhh,* "a walker about the world," "God's wanderer, who, not looking back to his worldly interest, betakes himself to the contemplative life's pilgrimage." *Mansoul* is the record of this life-long spiritual quest.

So it came about that he took his long departure from England, and having sojourned a year's time in the Low Countries, turned southward; and on the Riviera found a paradise of warmth and earthly beauty and happiness. Thus began his devotion to the "summer lands." He passed through Italy and was at Naples, and actually upon the volcano's summit, during the great eruption of Vesuvius in 1872, an experience of which he tells in the *Arabia Deserta.* Whether the narrative of an eruption of Etna, found in *Mansoul,* is based upon a similar adventure, I do not know. From Italy he went westward, spending part of a year in Portugal and Spain. Thence he crossed to Algiers. The relics of Moorish civilization in these countries were his introduction to the culture of the races among whom he was soon to pass the most eventful years of his life. He came to Egypt and then to Asia Minor, where, after a hesitation which led him to retrace his steps some way homeward, he again set his face to the East. Greatly desiring to travel in Bible lands, he came to Damascus some time in 1874. In the Peninsula of Sinai he ascended the two holy mountains; and following in the footsteps of Burckhardt, he penetrated as far as the great Nabataean monuments of Petra. Of Sinai and of Petra he has recorded his impressions in *Mansoul*. With native guides he journeyed through Moab and Ammon; and at Maan his imagination was fired by reports of the rock-hewn monuments, unknown to Europe, at Medain Salih (or El-Hejr; the Hegra of Ptolemy), three hundred miles farther along the pilgrim way. He resolved to take the hazard of visting them—an adventure not to be assumed lightly. For two years he remained in Syria, perfecting himself in Arabic; but when at length he attempted to make interest with the British consul and the Ottoman authorities at Damascus, the boorish consul rebuffed him and the Turkish officials were politely discouraging. Persevering nevertheless, he discovered that the Damascus-Mecca yearly pilgrim-caravan passed by El-Hejr. It was a simple matter, unnoticed at first among the thousands of pilgrims, to join the *haj;* and when the Pasha discovered his presence he accepted the *fait accompli* and even granted Doughty some protection. Thus, in November, 1876, Doughty began his travels in Arabia.

An outline of his itinerary would be a dull and useless substitute for his own magnificent narrative. It suffices to say that though the monuments at Medain Salih were perhaps a bit below his expectations, he there, while waiting for the returning *haj,* caught the fever of further exploration, and from the benevolent Pasha he obtained letters of commendation to the nomad chiefs and a supply of drugs, for he had now to depend for a livelihood upon chance opportunities to dispense medicines. This Christian European leech was left to his own resources among the fanatic nomads. In various places he suffered indignities; at one town he was long held prisoner; from Hail he was ignominiously expelled. Elsewhere, especially at Aneiza, he was treated with rough kindness. Through twenty months increasingly frail health multiplied the burdens of the way. The last part of his wanderings provided the severest hardships, for near the coast he experienced that violent harshness which the nomads seldom fail to exhibit on the confines of settled government towards any unprotected stranger. The Prince of Taif, however, rescued him from his fanatical and bloodthirsty tormentors, and he was given safe conduct to Jidda, where he arrived sick and penniless in August, 1878.

Doughty was not the first European wanderer in the interior of Arabia. Several explorers, chief among them Burckhardt and Burton, had traversed the arc of the circle whose points rest upon Yambu and Jidda; Palgrave had crossed the country from northeast to southwest; and other men had penetrated one district or another on political, commercial, or scientific missions. A full account of these adventurers is given by Dr. D. G. Hogarth in his fascinating book, *The Penetration of Arabia*. All Doughty's predecessors had traveled under the protection either of disguise or of strong official endorsement. Such endorsement had been denied him; and with fine intrepidity he never considered even the possibility of native disguise or of the pretense of religious conformity; his sense of the honor due alike to his family and his country forbade. Confronting the twin perils of Arabia—"famine and the dreadful harpy-face of their religion"—he maintained his Christian character, not hesitating, when alternately threatened and cajoled, to reveal a certain contempt for "the solemn fools' paradise" of the Moslem religion. This unswerving avowal of his race and faith is the highest testimony to the courage which enabled him to accomplish his unique journey. With this endurance were mixed the elements of gentleness, humaneness, and sympathy. He had to exercise shrewdness and to keep a watchful eye upon the fluctuating moodiness of the Arabs. When despitefully used he was moved to indignant protest but never to base supplication.

To his mild nature the humanity of the nomads often responded with hospitality and "God-speed." More often they regarded him as a curiosity to be questioned during the illiterate idleness of the tents. He observed their heavy cares and pathetic pleasures, and during halts of the caravans and in the long evenings he set down what he saw and heard in little note-books, making no concealment of his records though alarmed protests were often voiced against the "magic" which he was concocting.[3] Very frequently, when drooping upon his camel beneath the intense heat or when, leaving the clustered tents, he lay out alone under the stars, his thoughts turned to the problem—

> What were indeed right paths of a mans feet;
> That lacking light, wont stumble in World's murk.

And never was he mindless of his true vocation as a disciple of the Muse of Britain.

More than forty years later he described Arabia in lines as hard and rugged as her volcanic rocks:[4]

> An upland Plain and desolate wilderness;
> Far from the paths of men. . . .
> One of the great waste places of the Earth.
> In Winter chill, in Summer the Sun's Hearth.
> Whereon there falleth seld a life-giving rain:

[3] These note-books, the basis of the *Arabia Deserta,* are now in the Fitzwilliam Museum at Cambridge.

[4] Another admirable evocation of these far-off memories may be found in the review of Dr. Hogarth's *Arabia* which Doughty published in *The London Observer,* March 19, 1922. This review has been reprinted privately in an edition limited to 25 copies.

A weary ground, which seldom shadowed is,
Of any cloud; which stiffened lies as bronze:
A glowing grit, under Sun's fervent gaze;
Or scalding sand. The lean Inheritance;
Of men that dwell, disherited of the World,
In wand'ring Tribes: sith World began, remained
Unsown; wherein the locust is brought forth.
Void silent solitude: Like unto a Strand,
By day and the clear starry night alike;
Of the everlasting Gulf of Heavens Height.
A dewless Coast, whereas few rusty ribs;
Craigs of wild goats be seen, of shapeless rocks.

These memories of "the tented Children-of-the East" inspire the poet's prayer—

Remember them for good: and fill their mouths,
For Want their portion is, from year to year.

Having returned to England, Doughty's "incessant labor" during the decennium 1879-1888 was the composition of the *Travels in Arabia Deserta* (1888). It is not my present purpose to attempt any "appreciation" of that incomparable record. The pleasant task has been accomplished by Dr. Hogarth, by Mr. Edward Garnett, by Colonel Lawrence, and by various other critics. More profitable, did space serve, would be some indication of the relation of the book to other narratives of travel—Burckhardt's *Travels in Arabia,* Burton's *Personal Narrative,* Palgrave's *Narrative,* Warburton's *The Crescent and the Cross,* Curzon's *Monasteries of the Levant,* and Kinglake's *Eothen.* Considered more broadly, Doughty's work might serve as the culmination of the entire history of the influence of the Levant upon English literature.

One pictures the poet-traveler, conscious of a vocation as yet unfulfilled and meditating the theme of a long poem as he lay out upon the desert sands beneath the stars. His championship of Christianity among the Moslems may have suggested a Christian subject; association with the nomads directed his thoughts to life in primitive society; pride in England impelled him to choose an English theme. These three motives—Christianity; Primitivism; England—are intertwined in the story of the bringing of Christianity to Britain. Years passed while the travel-book was written. Then the idea of his epic poem took shape slowly in his mind. The assembling of materials was the work of several years, and the actual writing of the epic, Mr. Doughty has told me, occupied nearly a decade. In 1906 *The Dawn in Britain,* an epic poem in six volumes, was published.

The reception given this long, ambitious, and difficult work resembles that accorded to *The Dynasts;* but whereas Mr. Hardy's epic-drama has won its way to recognition as the greatest English poem of this age, *The Dawn in Britain* remains little read and seldom spoken of. There are serious stumbling-blocks in the reader's path, for Doughty makes no concessions to ignorance of semi-legendary British history. The involutions and contortions of the style, the archaistic vocabulary (for which he had the great precedent of Spenser), and the syntactical peculiarities, have alienated benevolent readers who are, moreover, irritated by the suppression of the apostrophe in the genitive case and by similar eccentricities. The abundant use of secondary ictus necessitates the employment of accents as guides to the proper scansion of the lines. An additional difficulty is the punctuation, which is not grammatical or syntactical but rhythmical and elocutionary, following a system not very logically worked out.[5]

The details of *Quellenstudien* are happily beyond the scope of this essay; but it may be said that the primary "source" of *The Dawn in Britain* is probably the outline of British history which Spenser introduces into *The Faerie Queene* (Book II, Canto x). The poet has also drawn upon Holinshed and his fellow chroniclers, upon Geoffrey of Monmouth and other older native sources, and upon Dio Cassius and the rest of the Roman historians.

The stately monotony of the blank verse, like the tread of unnumbered hosts, harmonizes with the remorseless and monotonous passing of the human generations who appear and vanish again during the vast epoch (from the taking of Rome by Brennus to the revolt of Bonduca) covered by the story.

[5] Doughty's system is analogous to that which, according to modern scholarship, was employed by Elizabethan poets and printers. And it may not be amiss to note that Baudelaire, in one of his letters, objects to changes in punctuation made by his printers, insisting that his purpose is to indicate pause and stress, not the grammatical interrelations of the parts of his sentences.

An effect is gained of vague grandeur, but there is confusion in the reader's mind as the narrative wanders on, as king gives way to king, as now Briton and now Roman triumphs, and as the new faith out of Syria wins converts from the ancient religion of the isle. An ill-defined allegory of the struggle of the forces of light, symbolized by the meek Syrian missionaries, with the forces of darkness, symbolized by the woad-stained devotees of Druidism, may be read into the poem; but in general it is singularly objective, without hidden meaning and with no purpose save the grand one to tell the tale of the dawn of civilization in the poet's well-loved land.

Defective in the larger matters of composition, the epic is rich in striking and beautiful episodes. The following is a characteristic example of Doughty's manner. At a time when mighty Julius had become "an handful of common cinders," in far-off Syria a new Light dawned upon the world:

Pass other years: and seemeth that her first peace,
Returned to earth; and truce in weary hearts!
Then, in a night, which lightsome seems as day,
Sounded in Mona's temple-cave, divine
Voice, saying; Him worship, all ye Briton gods!
  Dear Muse, which from this world's beginning, was
Seated, above, in heavenly harmonies;
Reveal that Radiance to mine hungry ears,
Thine eyes behold; what sacred Light, far off,
Like new wide Dawn (for which, men's eyes have watched,
From age to age) now kindled on the earth!
Whiles Night lies, as a cloak, whelmed on our Britain;

Tell me of Land, under East bent of heaven;
Wherein, is born, the Everlasting Prince
Of Peace, Sun of night-darkness of our hearts!

I would gladly quote a score of passages from this poem; but it must suffice to send my readers to such episodes as that of the first meeting of Brennus and Fridia (Book ii); the descent of Brennus's armies upon Italy (Book iii); the story of the nymph Agygia (Book iii); the coming of the second Brennus to Delphi (Book v); the voyage of Joseph in Mauson's ship (Book vi). In Book vii there is a tremendous vision of Hell where fiends gather in council how to prevent the coming of the saints to Britain. "Disdain, tiptoe-stalking demon," "blind blasphemous Despair," "heart-nipping Envy" and other devils gather with a rabblement of—

Skrats, woodwives, goblins, of earths forlorn night;
Punks, spectres, bugs; earth, well and mountain sprites,
In guise of werewolves, fitchews, and strange shapes.

In Britain battles innumerable are fought and "sounds of insult, shame, and wrong" echo through the poem. The characterization of the Emperor Claudius (Book xiv), though not confirmed by modern research, is a remarkable revitalization of tradition. The harangue of Caractacus to his "blue barbare host" before the battle (Book xvi) is a fine example of Doughty's rugged eloquence; and the picture of the same chief, a prisoner in Rome (Book xx), reflects the poet's own large-hearted patriotism. In the end, there sounds again the motive of the gentle human love which has been brought to war-worn Britain by the Syrian saints—

> Love is here lowest stair to the Infinite Good,
> Love-labour easy is: is aught so hard,
> But will attempt it love? with panting breast!
> For love, love lightly would forsake the world!

There is much evidence in the *Arabia Deserta* of Doughty's interest in folk-traditions, especially such as, possessed in common by various branches of the Semites, illuminate the Old Testament narrative. One such legend, picked up from the nomads, tells how Adam and Eve, "cast forth from the Paradise, fell down in several places of the Earth: whence they, after age-long wandering, meet together again, upon a Mountain." This is the theme of *Adam Cast Forth,* a sacred drama published in 1908. The simple story is told in rude and unadorned fashion, yet with much of primitive nobility. The rock-strewn wilderness through which our first parents move and the smiling oasis to which they come are alike suggestive of Arabian landscape; and the unquestioning obedience to the will of God is characteristic of "the tented Children-of-the-East." But the drama is too remote from Occidental ways of thought and life ever to be popular or widely read. And equally alien to our lives is the narrative poem of *The Titans* (1916), the opening lines of which are typical of Doughty's austere grandeur—

Neath Heavens high stars, whereof we some see cease,
To shed their light, whilst other some increase;
There nothing is at any stay. This House
Of Middle-Earth, which Time brought lately forth;
Our Inn, in bosom of Gods Universe;
Is full of variance, tiding ever forth.
Alone the everlasting Throne stands stedfast.

But this Dantesque sublimity of utterance is not sustained throughout. The Titans, defeated in warfare with gods and men, are cast into a pit. In after ages the "living corse" of one "great Eothen-statue" is found by men who remove it to their market-place, where buried loin-deep the Titan returns to life and, as a yoked laborer, is subdued to the service of man. There is an allegorical suggestion of man's gradual conquest and utilization of the forces of nature; but it is not clearly realized and the general impression is confused. Despite passages of power and beauty, *The Titans* is the least excellent and most difficult of Doughty's poems.

Meanwhile Doughty's intense patriotism and love of England—her past, her traditions, her greatness, her countryside—were leading him to take anxious thought for her immediate future. In politics he had adopted an idealistic Toryism which attributed to other Conservatives a high-mindedness and disinterestedness equal to his own. Of mere blatant imperialism there is no trace in his thought; but, for all his long dwelling in the East, he does not see eye to eye with such opponents of British policy as his fellow traveler in Arabia, Wilfrid Scawen Blunt.

Doughty viewed with increasing alarm the growth of German power and accepted as sincere, and as bound before long to be put into practice, the enunciations of German world policy. He came to believe that his mission was to arouse England to an awareness of her imminent danger and to utter a call to national service. In 1909 he published the dramatic poem *The Cliffs,* and in 1912 its sequel, *The Clouds.* The first of these was written while the earliest German dirigibles were circling above Lake Constance. Doughty voices a passionate prophecy of war's imminence and of the terrible part to be played in it by the new astounding inventions of science. Few things are stranger in literary history than the fulfillment of this vision; not merely in such details as the actualities of submarine and aerial warfare but in the clairvoyant sense of the spirit of a people threatened with immolation—the horrors of invasion, the confusion of an undisciplined country, the realization of the world-shaking ambitions of the foe, the kindling consciousness of the necessity of self-sacrifice. The theme is the secret landing of German spies upon the coast of Kent on the eve of war; the drama ends with the warding off of the danger from overseas. The poet seems to have felt that the warning was not sufficiently drastic; and in *The Clouds* he depicts "War, invading war! in England's midst." With scathing satire he attacks in both poems the bungling and selfish politicians in charge of England's destiny. Intense moral indignation and austere patriotism are combined with a naïve belief in the absolute justice of his country's cause and the utter malignity of her enemies. In both poems are many passages of great eloquence, such as the magnificent soliloquy of old John Hobbe with which *The Cliffs* opens (perhaps the finest lines in all Doughty's poetry); or the chant of the Sacred Band with which the same poem closes; or the vision of the Muses' Garden in *The Clouds*. Both poems are lightened and varied by quaint and charming interludes in which, during the night while the human actors sleep, the gnomes and dapper elves come from their hiding-places to disport themselves and to play their part in the protection of England. A whimsical and tricksy fancy which one might not have associated with Doughty save for odd hints in the *Arabia Deserta* creates in the fantastic play of these sprites the very atmosphere of *A Midsummer Night's Dream* and of *Nymphidia*. The scene of the elfin wedding is as pretty a bit of fairy poetry as is to be found in our literature.

It remains to say something of the latest and noblest of Doughty's poems—*Mansoul; or the Riddle of the World* (1920); though the less need be said since it has secured comparatively wide recognition. All Doughty's life has been a spiritual quest, a ceaseless groping for light through the murkiness of the world. At home, as in Arabia, he has pursued (in Pater's words) "a dimly discerned mental journey." The sense of this is one of the many impressions made by a perusal of the *Arabia*

Deserta, for, as Dr. Hogarth well says, "reading Doughty's personal adventures, one feels him to be less an individual than a type of all his kind undergoing a certain trial of spirit." Joseph of Arimathea and his companions are upon such a journey in which the blindly groping, woad-stained Britons join them. Adam, cast forth from Paradise, pursues his quest, as do the Dawn-Men who wage war against the Titans. Through the centuries Britain, ever groping, has followed the same quest; and the two prophetic war poems are appeals to the younger generation to persevere upon the path. *Mansoul* is yet another and more definite allegory of the way of the soul. The poet, Minimus, traveling in the company of Mansoul, enters the world of the dead and confronts the old prophets, sages, and founders of religions with the persistent question: "What were indeed right paths of a man's feet?" Zarathustra, Buddha, Confucius, and Socrates give answers characteristic of their thought, but all the sages bow in ignorance before the final mystery of death; and the words with which the poem closes and which "abide, a Perfume, in our hearts," are those of Jesus: "Fear ye not, little flock; God is Love."

Mansoul contains many other elements. There are grand passages of Syrian and Arabian landscape. The elves and gnomes reappear at their graceful sports. And there is a vision of Man's City, a City which hath foundations, towards which humanity is painfully making its way. . . . It was in his lovely

Kentish garden that I last saw Mr. Doughty; and as I call to mind the old poet's kindly eyes, his gentle voice, and serene bearing, and majestic head, he assumes the dignity of a type or abstract of all humanity, a stranger and pilgrim upon the road.

STUART SHERMAN [1]

By MARY M. COLUM

ALTHOUGH Stuart Sherman is not a new voice in criticism, he is a new sort of voice in American criticism which has spent so much of itself in yearning over the gods of Europe. He is not much concerned with Europe, except and so far as it abuts, so to speak, on America. He does, of course, occasionally write about European authors, but he, somehow, writes about them in a provincial sort of way which reminds one of nothing so much as the Chinese manner of depicting a lion, or the Japanese manner of depicting a shamrock as the leaf of a wide-spreading tree. He does not really know how to measure them up, and, with the whole Rocky Mountains to his back, supporting his spine, as it were, and keeping it from bending, he decides that Sinclair Lewis is better than Flaubert, or as good, anyway. Starting out as a critic without any particular literary principles, except the conventional academic ones, he carried into both life and literature two strong prejudices—a prejudice against the alien-minded and a prejudice in favor of the

[1] From *The Saturday Review of Literature,* June 26, 1926. The specification of date observed elsewhere in this volume has been set aside to permit the inclusion of this consideration of a famous critic whose tragic death, on August 21, 1926, ended a praiseworthy career in, as it were, the hour of its beginning.

Puritan, and with a firm conviction that these two sorts of people were peculiar to America.

The Puritan and the alien-minded are, of course, indigenous to every healthy country, and they affect the rest of the population as does a catfish in a tank the other fish—they keep them on the move all the time. In other countries, as a matter of fact, the Puritans are far more puritanical and the aliens more alien-minded, but both stand in a peculiar relation to American life. In the old countries the Puritan is merely an ascetic or a suppressed sensualist, who, although he makes himself strongly felt in the general life of the country, is rarely very vocal; he belongs to whatever branch of the Christian religion the majority of his countrymen adhere to, and he is commonly of the middle-classes, for neither the peasantry nor the aristocracy have much stomach for being ascetics or suppressed sensualists. But here in America the Puritan is a different creature altogether. Because the Pilgrim Fathers were Puritans, Puritanism does duty for an aristocracy. The Puritan Fathers have to play the rôle that in England is played by the Norman conquerors—the rôle of supplying pedigrees and ancestors to the upper classes, and Puritanism in some form or another supplies the incitement for Jingoism and hundred-percent patriotism which monarchies and imperialism do in other countries. The alien-minded in this country are mostly foreigners, while the alien-minded in old countries are native sons who, with soured and disillusioned dispositions, or else critical and enfranchised intellects, keep the traditions, civilization, and government of their country all the time under the fire of censorious observation.

Mr. Sherman carried his two prejudices everywhere with him until he got tremendously confused himself as to what they really were and where they were leading him. He finally cleared his mind about the Puritan by writing an essay called "What is a Puritan?" in which he included as Puritans every sort of person that he really liked, such as Christ, Buddha, Socrates, Zeno, Confucius, and the first monkey who decided to walk upright on his hind-legs. He published this in 1924. The essay might almost as well have been called "What is a Nordic?" "What is a Celt?"—I have read essays on both these subjects which contained exactly the same arguments and almost exactly the same examples. In the previous year he had published an essay entitled "Mr. Mencken, the *Jeune Fille,* and the New Spirit in Letters," in which he writes out his feelings about the alien-minded. He got equally confused here, and he attacked people who were as genuine Americans as himself, if of somewhat different racial sympathies, and he turned off an untidy jumble of disordered ideas and shot a few pointless arrows in the air. Having delivered himself of these two essays, he somewhat seemed to have lost the more virile if more splenetic side of his prejudices, and, as literary editor of *The Herald Tribune,* he has evolved into a critic so fair-minded, so sympathetic to every manifestation of talent, that at the present time he is one of the most unprejudiced of American critics.

His pair of biases made him the butt of many of our intellectuals, but it always seemed to me that a very good case could be made for them in a country which intellectually had not yet learned to stand on its own legs. If he had elevated his prejudices into a sort of principle and a sort of philosophy instead of almost making them a plea for Colonialism, a very great deal indeed could be said for them. Had he been quite definitely anti-European, quite definitely an isolationist, he would have been a very powerful influence in contemporary American letters, for he would have been the intellectual leader of an instinctive national movement which, at present, has no leadership.

We have the curious spectacle in this country of the intellectuals mocking at the crude and awkward efforts of the people to shake off their spiritual and intellectual dependency upon Europe. The blind instinct of the people is all making for the same goal—the anti-emigration laws passed by the law-makers, the interest in everything genuinely American, from early American furniture to the great personalities the country has produced—even to the formation of the Ku Klux Klan and the determined attempts of politicians to isolate the country from Europe.—Ignorant and vicious some of the manifestations of the instinct may be, but the instinct itself is sound and splendid. It is the pitiful plight of the country that the very men who ought to be its leaders in this movement are so meager, emotionally and psychically, that they are behind-hand rather than in advance of the people. There is nothing meager, emotionally or psychically, about Stuart Sherman, but he lacked the power to intellectualize an instinct in himself which was the instinctive feeling of large masses of the people, or perhaps it was that he allowed himself to be intimidated by the hostile criticism of the cosmopolitan-minded.

There is about him the air of an intellectual leader far more than the air of a purely literary critic, and perhaps for the sake of being an unprejudiced critic he lost his chance of being a powerful intellectual leader, by turning his back on his prejudices. For the leader, whether an intellectual or a Mussolini, is the man who has the power to intellectualize in himself the desires of the people, and who has the force to satisfy and to drive others to satisfy these desires. As a purely literary critic, Mr. Sherman has two perilous ideas which inform every article in his new book, *Critical Woodcuts* [2]—one of these is that it is the function of the critic to be engaged in the quest of the "Good Life," and the other is that he has to justify literature to the average man as a utility which is capable of assisting him in the performance of his duties. The first he took over partly from Matthew Arnold and partly from the old Latin philosophers and orators. Now a

[2] Critical Woodcuts. By Stuart Sherman. Charles Scribner's Sons. New York: 1926.

critic cannot set out with the consciousness that he is in search of the "Good Life" without getting himself inextricably involved in moral laws, and the moral laws are often merely regulations invented for the convenient conduct of life. When a critic gets himself involved in what is merely convenient his search for reality becomes seriously impeded. The second idea, that of justifying literature as a utility to the average man, is really dependent on the first. It may be the business of priests, politicians, and law-makers to consider the average man, for they can justify what they profess as a utility which will help him in the performance of his duties, but the less literature considers him, the better for both. I fear seriously that the record literature has for making the average man forget his duties is greater than its record for helping him in the performance of them.

As a literary critic, Stuart Sherman has, however, one great quality without which criticism is merely a sort of esthetic grammar and with which it can include all the qualities which are in high poetry and high philosophy—this is, a profound response to life and a profound interest in it, so that his criticism, even when it is poorest as an evaluation of literature, and even when the literature it evaluates is of as poor a quality as Don Marquis's poetry, has a richness of thought and feeling which give him the air of the great critics. Much of the literature on which he wastes his rich feeling for life will not live as long as its authors. Of this he is well aware, for he explains in his preface to *Critical Woodcuts* that, after all, his business in writing his weekly article is to be a commentator on the passing show. The best of all ways for a journal to achieve a high critical standard is to have the same critic week by week write out his opinions on literature. This is what Stuart Sherman does in *The Herald Tribune,* and *Critical Woodcuts* is a reprint of his critical articles. It is hard to believe that a collection of weekly articles by any other contemporary critic could stand up against these without suffering.

Of course, the defects of *Critical Woodcuts* stand out clearly enough: Stuart Sherman has but little sense of artistry; it is often a defect of Anglo-Saxon, as opposed to Continental, criticism, that critics have either no sense of artistry, or merely a sense of artistry and no sense of life; he has, perhaps, but little understanding of poetry; he confounds vigor and clarity too often with distinction. But, in the last analysis, he knows the first and most important thing about a book—*Is it alive?* And very few people know that. The literary reviews are full of appreciative notices of books that are not only dead to start with because they come out of dead souls, but are deadening to their readers. He may not bother greatly in his literary causerie about how long the writers he deals with are going to live, but all of them are alive with at least the life of the rose—*l'espace d'un matin.* In addition, he has that sort of vital scholarship which, without being finicky, is rich enough and extensive enough for the practice of criticism. I am old-fashioned enough to believe that in the practice of that no one can be a good critic of literature in English without a certain training in Greek and Roman literature, particularly in Latin, the language of clarity and criticism, and without that sort of knowledge of English literature which embraces the *Anglo-Saxon Chronicle* as well as Oscar Wilde, and *Piers Plowman* and *Gammer Gurton's Needle* as well as *The Waste Land* and *Ulysses.* Few of the critics writing in America have this sort of scholarship, and it is very distinctively Stuart Sherman's.

DREISER [1]

By Robert L. Duffus

I

Twenty-five years have passed since Theodore Dreiser wrote, and in a manner published, a first novel called *Sister Carrie.* The qualifying phrase is necessary, for, as is well known, the publishers took alarm when they reflected that Carrie had been a very bad girl and had not been adequately punished for it, at least in this world, and so, after sending out a few review copies, they withdrew the book. Here, then, was an ambitious youngster—he was only twenty-nine—with bitterness in his heart and hopes of fame deferred, driven to earn his bread by hack writing and hack editing. Had America broken another butterfly on the wheel? Certainly, the Younger Generation of the intelligentsia, had they known of it, would have cast their nursing bottles upon the floor and reiterated their intention to go and live in Paris when they grew up.

Since then Dreiser has been the recipient of countless other uppercuts, solar plexus jabs, rabbit punches, and left hooks to the jaw. No other American writer, except, maybe, Whitman, has received so many thumps upon his obstinate head, so

[1] From *The American Mercury,* January, 1926.

many kicks upon his stubborn shins. He has endured the snobbery of campus critics, the prudishness of publishers' maiden-aunt readers, and the earnest resentment of multitudes of honest, God-fearing, law-abiding, right-thinking men and women. He has been impaled upon the Comstocks' grotesque lance; he has been ejected by indignant moralists from the Hall of Fame. He has even been apologized for by his friends, who have complained sadly about his style. In brief, few roses have strewed his path, and those few have been plucked late in the season.

Yet his head is not only unbowed—it is not even bloody. Far from being extinguished by that environment which proved so damaging to Mark Twain and Henry James, he has thriven upon it. He has not found it necessary to compromise or to listen to what is called reason, but has gone on being grandly and solemnly himself. Today he stands up like some ancient oak or craggy mountain, austere, unyielding, and unmoved—at once a sort of a poet and a sort of grizzly bear, with a skin as tough as an elephant's and a heart as soft as butter. He is a romantic, a realist, and a mystic all in one; a man pretending no faith in the good intentions or sanity of the universe, or any feeling of responsibility to a Moral Order, or any belief in rewards and punishments, yet one moved by an innner compulsion as real and strange as that which sent John Brown to Harper's Ferry; a man ferociously critical of his country and his countrymen, yet one with an understanding, pitying, and forgiving love for it and them that makes the orthodox patriot seem almost like an apologist.

How did he contrive, not merely to live, but even to reach fruition, in this America that received him so badly? Not easily, one may be sure, and not without some desperate quarter-hours. He entered upon life, and continued for a long time, as sensitive and defenseless as an oyster without a shell. He was, and still is, a sentimentalist—even a kind of Sentimental Tommy. It is only necessary to glance into *A Hoosier Holiday* or *A Book About Myself* to be convinced of that. He "reveres James Whitcomb Riley with a whole heart," "feels a little lump in his throat at 'Auld Lang Syne' and 'Dixie,' " mends his grief at parting from a sweetheart by turning it into a poem, and writes the chorus of his brother's maudlin song, "On the Banks of the Wabash." Pity runs like a golden thread through every paragraph he has written, though it is not, it seems, an emotion he respects. There is still encased in him, to this hour, the wandering, wide-eyed child who was reared in that pious German household in Warsaw, Indiana. He might be a newspaper man for a hundred years, make love to a thousand women, walk a million miles of vicious streets, and yet never be thoroughly sophisticated. Freshness and ingenuousness are still in his view of life; he never gets tired of it; he is always finding out things that he never knew before, and they fascinate him even while they disgust him.

II

But, as in every sentimentalist who survives being weaned, there is also a metallic, unbending streak. Though he is less Nietzschean than he thinks, and is incapable of trampling other people under foot, he does resist, with the placid firmness of a steam-roller, the attempts of others to trample him. The quality which enables him to do this is not mere obstinacy. It is a perception, which he seems to have developed very early, that if he does not do a thing in his own way he cannot do it at all. No doubt its development was hastened by the efforts of his father to make him a docile Catholic. He resisted, and out of that resistance sprang a lifelong hatred of authority, of fixed institutions, of congealed routine—in brief, of all those depressing influences which cramp and oppress the individual, and seek to make a mere number of him.

The young Dreiser was shy, innocent, and emotional, and if his instructors had been sufficiently imaginative they would have caught him, perhaps, in their celestial mouse-trap. He spent his earlier years, as he recalls them, in a nebulous dream, scarcely dispelled until he had passed out of his 'teens. Very early he was on fire with the sweet mysteries of sex, though his bashfulness long kept him virginal:

> Girlhood ravished me. It set my brain and my blood aflame. I was living in some ecstatic realm which had little

if anything in common with the humdrum life about me, and yet it had. Any picture or paragraph anywhere which referred to, or hinted at, love lifted me up into the empyrean. I was like that nun in Davidson's poem to whom the thought of how others sinned was so moving. I never tired of hauling out and secretly reading and rereading every thought and sentence that had a suggestive, poetic turn in relation to love.

He was like one imprisoned in a little room, beating vainly against windows opening upon a vast prairie. He was poor, he was without influential friends, he thought himself unattractive to women, and yet he was poignantly conscious of the great and vivid flood of human passion which was roaring all about him. "Indeed," he says, "I was crazy with life, a little demented or frenzied with romance and hope. I wanted to sing, to dance, to eat, to love." This was not, at first, the yearning of the artist. He did not want so much to picture the whirling scenes he saw about him as to play a part in them. Self-expression through the written word was the last thought he had in mind when, being lucky enough to find himself in the mad city of Chicago just before the World's Fair, he resolved to become a reporter.

"I think," he confesses, "I confused reporters with ambassadors and prominent men generally. Their lives were laid among great people, the rich, the famous, the powerful; and because of their position and facility of expression and mental force they were received everywhere as equals. Think of me, new, young, poor, being received in that way!" Shades of Horace Greeley! But this was not a mere ambition, as if he were a farmer boy hoping to become a merchant prince or a log-splitter contemplating the presidency. It was a pain, a desperate hunger. He saw happiness eddying past him in a fierce torrent, and clutched wildly at every straw. Youth, youth! It throbs like a refrain. "Youth would come no more! Love would come no more!"

Obviously, a depth of emotion, a strength of desire, quite as formidable as that which gave us our lords of railways, mines, steel mills, and finance. How well, later on, he understood Yerkes, Harriman, Carnegie, Rockefeller! Spiritually, in those days of dreaming, he was one of them. When he became a novelist he did not need to invent his supermen and quasi-supermen, for he had lived their lives vicariously. That fact accounts for much that is otherwise mysterious in his fiction—its elephantine bulk and plodding style as well as its overwhelming reality. You ask for rhythm and the balanced phrase, for restraint and a neat sense of structure. "But, good God!" you seem to hear him cry, "I am not playing with building-blocks. This is real!"

III

Some artists escape from reality, some into it. Dreiser was necessarily of the latter group. He had seemed to himself a prisoner of religious and moral delusions, which stood between him and that terrible and enchanting wilderness of the world in which he longed to set foot. As he became aware of himself, therefore, he swept aside romance—at least what passed as romance among the literary gentry of the day—as though it were an embattled enemy. He took fierce delight in recognizing politics as "a low mess," religion as "a ghastly fiction," commerce as "a seething war, in which the less subtle and the less swift or strong went under," and woman as "nothing more than a two-legged biped like the rest of us." He faced, with a kind of joy, "those sterner truths which life itself teaches—the unreliability of human nature, the crass chance which strikes down and destroys our finest dreams, the fact that man in all his relations is neither good nor evil, but both." Beyond the wrecks of his illusions lay freedom, and freedom was for the valiant and the great lovers. The art he served, as solemnly and devoutly as any meager priest kneeling at dawn between his wavering candles, was "the stored honey of the human soul, gathered on wings of misery and travail."

Yet freedom came late and came hard. He had worked on newspapers in Chicago and St. Louis, seeing plenty of horror, foolishness, and corruption, but until he read Balzac, Huxley, Tyndall, and Herbert Spencer, in Pittsburgh about 1893, he retained "some lingering filaments of Catholicism—faith in the existence of Christ, the soundness of His moral and sociologic deductions, the brotherhood of man." These threads of faith suddenly snapped under the hard blows of Huxley's logic, and the stars danced inanely in the sky.

This was, in short, a kind of conversion. He was as miserable as Bunyan or St. Paul. He wandered the streets of Pittsburgh and later of New York in a mood of despair hardly rendered more profound by the fact that he came to know want and got close to what seemed utter failure. He did not care for a time whether he was poor or rich, or whether he died or lived. For him no light shone on the road to Damascus.

He clambered out of this pit of darkness by a kind of plodding peasant strength inherited from his forefathers. He allowed himself to be convinced that the mere fact that successive generations consent to be born, and that the young and vigorous are hungry to live, is evidence of at least the physical integrity of life. Though never again could he be "frenzied with romance and hope," he could see that human existence was worth while, if only for its amazing dramatic quality. "Life was intended for the spectacular, I take it," he concluded. "It was intended to sting and hurt so that songs and dreams might come forth." The theme recurs again and again—"the ache of life"; "life at bottom, in spite of its seeming terrors, is beautiful"; "the long, strange tangle of steps or actions by which life ambles crabwise from nothing to nothing"; "life is a strange, colorful, kaleidoscopic welter."

Five years after this wrestle with despair he wrote *Sister Carrie,* and from that time forth, regardless of the ups and downs of fortune, the Theodore Dreiser of the present moment is recognizable in him. He has grown a shell of comfortable thickness now. He has also acquired some of the defensive properties of the stickly-prickly hedgehog. You would look twice, as Browning remarked of the young soldier at Ratisbon, ere you saw that his breast was all but shot in two. Nor would it be easy to recognize in him today that "dreamy cub of twenty-one, long, spindling, a pair of gold-framed spectacles on his nose, his hair combed *à la pompadour,* a new spring suit, a brown fedora hat, and new yellow shoes," who set out in 1892 "to force his way into the newspaper world of Chicago." Gone, too, beyond recall is the St. Louis stripling who stood six feet, one and one-half inches in his socks, weighed one hundred and thirty-seven pounds, and shuddered at the doctrines of Nietzsche.

IV

This does not mean, of course, that the sentimental boy is dead. At fifty-four he is still capable of such sentences as this: "There is in me the spirit of a lonely child somewhere, and it clings pitifully to the hand of its big mamma, Life, and cries when it is frightened; and then there is a coarse, vulgar exterior which fronts the world defiantly and bids all and sundry to go to the devil." Or: "It seemed a great, sad, heroic thing to me then—common day-labor. I have the feeling that the poor and the ignorant and the savage are somehow great artistically. I have always had it." Is it Lincoln speaking? And again: "Yet for the dream's sake . . . I would like to see . . . this Republic live on. It is so splendid, so tireless. Its people, in spite of their defects and limitations, sing at their tasks. There are dark places, but there are splendid points of light, too. One is their innocence, complete and enduring; another is their faith in ideals and the Republic. A third is their optimism or buoyancy of soul, their courage to get up in the morning and go up and down the world, whistling and singing. Oh, the whistling, singing American, with his jest and his sound heart and that light of humorous apprehension in his eye! . . . Dream on! Believe! You may vanish as have other great dreams, but even so, what a glorious, an imperishable memory!" Whitman would not say it much better, or differently.

In another mood he is sure that "no nation has ever contributed less philosophically or artistically or spiritually to the actual development of the intellect and the spirit"; charges us, or at least our revered ruling classes, with a "financial and social criminality . . . regularly accompanied, outwardly, at least, by a religious and sex Puritanism which would be scarcely believed if it were not true"; and describes America as "the land of Bottom the Weaver." But the sum of it is that, despite their long ears, Americans fascinate him. He finds their gay, childish energy intoxicating. His drumming fingers keep time, whether he will or not, to the swing of their dancing and marching. This is a puppet-show, and meaningless, and an indifferent showman pulls the strings, but what a wild and captivating drama it is, after all, that these grotesque figurines enact—these wistful, struggling Americans!

Life, then, is a parade to him, impressive chiefly in its tumult and variety. He sees a beginning and, far off, across a troubled interval, an end, and he marches solemnly, resolutely, from one to the other. He is deliberately serious. Of his style the critics have said more than enough; though he can be profoundly moved, even to tears, by music, he is plainly indifferent to the music of words. Not for him do they sing exquisite little songs, quite apart from their meaning. They are but stepping stones, across which he strides as he passes toward his destination. There are dull stretches in life; why should there not be dull and unmusical stretches in books? Along these stretches his words march—the phrase is his own—like soldiers.

Yet in the height of emotion he is capable of a rhythmic, almost heart-rending, beauty. It is in his autobiographical pieces, curiously enough, that the style is best. Perhaps the reason is that here he is most consciously the literary man; in his fiction, which is more autobiographical than his autobiographies, he is too much the eager actor. But how poignantly he can move you, as in the last scene in *Jennie Gerhardt,* when Jennie goes to the station to see Lester Kane's body put on the train! And how those gargoyles, meaningless carvings, and dingy gray walls of his style do soar at times, and take on the spirit of loveliness!

If he had a keener feeling for words he might be able to have his say in fewer than the 300,000 which seem to make up his latest novel, *An American Tragedy*. He revises, indeed, writing, rewriting, and correcting proof painstakingly, but it is of the edifice of incident and situation that he thinks, not of the verbal straws and mortar of which it is composed. But his prolixity is not entirely a matter of style. The fact is that he has the painter's eye. Perhaps he should have been a painter himself, an Inness or a George Bellows—he admires both men tremendously. A feeling for color and line stands out on almost every page he writes. He observes minutely, is blessed with a tenacious memory, and has a good reporter's conscientiousness in getting his details right:

> There are city-scapes that seem some to mourn and some to sing. This was one that sang. It reminded me of Rops or Vierge or Whistler, the paintings of Turner and Moran. Low-hanging clouds, yellowish or black, or silvery like a fish, mingled with a splendid filigree of smoke and chimneys and odd skylines. Beds of golden-glow ornamented and relieved a group of tasteless low red houses or sheds in the immediate foreground, which obviously sheltered the heavy broods of foreign miners and their wives. The lines of red, white, blue and gray wash, the honking flocks of white geese, the flocks of pigeons overhead, the paintless black fences protecting orderly truck gardens, as well as the numerous babies playing about, all attested this. As we stood there a group of heavy-hipped women and girls (the stocky peasant type of the Hungarian-Silesian plains) crossed the foreground

with their buckets. Immense mounds of coal and slag, with glimpses of distant breakers, perfected the suggestion of an individual and characterful working world. . . . In the middle distance a tall white skyscraper stood up, a prelude, or a foretouch to a great yellowish-black cloud behind it. A rich, smoky, sketchy atmosphere seemed to hang over everything.

A man who can compose a picture like this ought to be handed some brushes and a box of paints.

V

In the exact sense he describes, rather than creates. His characters are all near enough alike to have been members, or at least near relatives, of the Dreiser family. His autobiographical volumes enable one to trace the origin of many of his plots. For instance, his love affair with Alice, as related in *A Book About Myself*, is plainly the same affair which Eugene Witla had with Ruby in *The Genius*. He even reproduces a peculiarly touching passage from Alice's final letter, addressed in the one case to Eugene and in the other to Theo. In short, he kisses and tells—with infinite advantage to his fiction. His great achievement is less in creating character than in making real the predicament in which it finds itself and in giving that predicament a symbolism that makes it represent a nation and an age.

William Marion Reedy once remarked: "Thank God, Dreiser hasn't got style. If he ever gets one it's good-by." It should now be obvious that he is not a man who can be presented with one. He is not arrogant about this, for it springs from some inner prompting over which he has little control. In 1893 and 1894, when he was fumbling desperately for some future outside journalism, he tried to unravel the art of the short story, as it was then being practiced. It seemed, he found, "to deal with phases of sweetness and beauty and success and goodness such as I rarely encountered." A more facile person, with only a smattering of Dreiser's talent, might have adapted himself to the market and flourished like an oil-well promoter. Many did. But Dreiser did not because he could not. He sent a short story to Robert Underwood Johnson of *The Century*. Johnson not only sent it back, but wanted to argue about it. But Dreiser could not argue. That story was as much a natural phenomenon as a flea in a carpet or a wind on the prairie. The world, Johnson included, could take it or go to the devil. That was and is Dreiser.

Whether *An American Tragedy* indicates any alteration in his philosophy or his technique, or not, is a question best left to time and the critics. He says, not without pride, that he is not aware of any change. Yet his theme changes. The period of the Titans is passing. No longer does New York, or any other American city, present the extremes of poverty and wealth, of power and servitude, that he marked in the early 'nineties. The supermen and superfools are gone, and a new generation is making money, not as a rule by piracy or violence, but by investing it at a safe return in sound securities. Wall Street is now a Sunday-school. The population of the slums, whose chief reason for existence once seemed to be to invent and commit new offenses against decency, has floated into Kingdom Come; the Bowery is now as safe and moral as a country lane.

Life is more interesting than it used to be for nearly everybody, and so fewer people have to be wicked in order to avoid boredom. Here and there comes a stirring toward artistic expression. Half the people you meet, says Dreiser, want to write; at least one in every hundred is bent upon becoming a playwright. The new generations are palpitating with energy, and since the economic structure is being mechanized and stabilized, and there is less hope of adventure, the result may be a sound contribution, soon or late, to the more decorative aspects of civilization. Dreiser does not have much faith in progress. The sum total of good and evil remains about the same. But the character of the human performance keeps up with the times, and programs are changed every year or so.

In Dreiser there is no visible flagging of energy or enthusiasm. He is full of novels, plays, essays, memoirs, poems, which he will produce in his own way, in his own time and without regard to publishers, critics, or readers. He lives inconspicuously, and does not frequent literary circles. He is wistfully fond of his friends, wanting to be liked and approved by them. He enjoys automobiling, but he can still do his twenty-five miles a day on foot. Before Prohibition he was almost a teetotaler; now, as an advocate of liberty and fraternity, he feels that he should wet his whistle now and then, and does. In congenial company he is a very amiable and even merry fellow, but strangers, especially if he feels they are wasting his time and have no claim on him, find him brusque.

You may imagine him sitting, of a late fall afternoon, at an eastern window of a tall office building in Manhattan, fifteen flights above the street. There is white in his hair, a slight relaxation of the lines of the face, in the eyes an expression of philosophical calm that may not always have been there. Some of the fire and fury, perhaps, are gone with the old despair. The fear of want and failure has departed, like his youth—perhaps it *was* his youth.

Yet, as the lights come out in the swift darkness, spreading far away across a dark river, he speaks with a kind of awe of all the mysterious forces that move the world and all the strange lives they fashion, and you see the creative fervor blazing up. In a way he is just starting. His mind is full of things he intends to do. He has one complete, new, unwritten novel, he tells you—as tangible as the chair you are sitting on, though not one word has been put down. With *Sister Carrie, Jennie Gerhardt, The Titan,* and now *An American Tragedy* behind him, he may yet have greater things ahead. Perhaps, in the autumnal days, when he has finished writing and rewriting *Hamlet,* he will give us a *Tempest.*

PSEUDO-LITERATURE [1]

By Waldo Frank

The term, I believe, is Schopenhauer's. He declared that there are two streams of writing, for the most part indistinguishably merged save for a very few. One of these, the effect of creative thought and of creative vision, he called literature; and all the rest, however pleasant and respectable, he outlawed. To go back to any flourishing epoch is to be convinced that Schopenhauer was right and that our present status is not essentially unique. The modish ladies of Weimar forsook Goethe for the "more modern" Kotzebue. Pradon and Quinault outbid Racine for favor. Alexandria, Rome, Athens, Jerusalem had swarms of writers who were so close to the contemporary clamor that they have died with it into as whole a silence. The printing press and the mock crowning of Demos have merely aggravated an immemorial condition. Where only a minority could read, of course only a minority could be idle readers. Now that every one is forced to read, the flood of words without creative source is stintless, and there are organized for it great armies of "distributing agents," of which an unconsciously servile group call themselves reviewers—even critics. The swollen plethora of pseudo-literature has perhaps

[1] From *The New Republic,* December 2, 1925.

lowered the visibility of the real through its sheer mass. But if this be argued an increased deterrent to the life and health of literature, it is more than overcome by the increasing of the potential public for what is good. The more persons who can read at all, the more may read what is authentic.

There is then no good ground for the friend and writer of literature to complain. He has traditionally addressed a minority in a minority; and it exists for him today. The new presence of hawkers and bawlers purveying printed goods to the mob has not altered his position any more than has the deformation of the democratic doctrine into the myth that everybody is as good as everybody else. If the writer hungers after enormous sales, he is the victim of confusion: unconsciously, he desires to leave his true domain. If he feels that he is entitled to the royalties of a Michael Arlen or to the popularity of a Fannie Hurst, the urgence of his vision must be very weak. For it is the glorious compensation of the wooers of beauty and of truth that all other of life's guerdons are by contrast dull. To have heard clear, even once, the word of God is to hear it forever in all the calls of life.

More serious and more concerning is another phase of this mutual attraction between the real with its rigorous isolation and the false with its populous cordialities. The purveyors of pseudo-literature are so many that they fall into classes. They have their snobs too, their social climbers. And there is among their readers an ample group sufficiently emerged from the rest to desire culture even at the cost of thrills. These persons are aware of the term literature and want their share in it. Their conception, of course, is derived from shallow study of the past. Incapable of recognizing the essence of an art, they dwell on its external traits and manners. And the contemporary writers who most flatter them are the emulators of these imitable parts. Such authors are competent in style, they are elegant, they reproduce in terms of up-to-dateness the forms and virtues of previous pioneers. Most of them will be novelists, dramatists, even poets. But they must have their critics. And to them falls the dangerous task of establishing a rationale for their kind; an aggressive apologia for all their sterile wares.

The creative, the heroic, the religious spirit of true literature is by such critics utterly ignored; and by repeated omission comes to be regarded as non-existent. The novel which flows well, the tale which is pleasing, the construction which reflects current thought or current passion, is hailed as *good,* and the more reflective, hence passive it is, the higher is rated its importance. Unconsciously, it is assumed that literature has no independent body: that its real substance is the public taste. From this fallacy it follows that criticism becomes a solemn discussion of secondary traits—timeliness, grace, and color. The primary creative stuff of literature, without which these secondary qualities can have no true existence, is forgotten. The terms of what is genuine are borrowed for what is false. And the confusion grows.

What hungry common reader could dream, from contemporary criticisms of Mr. Hergesheimer, of Mrs. Wharton, of Miss Cather—supply your own names from the current columns—that these are makers of books with an essential lack: a lack as crucial as that which parts organic death from life? The books of such novelists are competent in so far as they are elegant reflections of styles in form and thought and language. As contributions to the creative life of the mind and of the spirit, they are inept. Their source is neither a luminous vision nor an authentic knowledge; but rather the shrewd perusal of past masters and present moods. Neither their purpose nor their substance adds one iota to the experience of man. To call them literature is to degrade the name.

And it is precisely urgent that the name literature be not degraded. For there is much in a name: much directing of intelligence, much shaping of powers. And we possess an age in which intelligence is not small, but confused; in which powers are lavish, but debauched. A critic of our day as aware as were Abelard and Anselm would be as concerned as they were with the pragmatic virtues of the Name. He would know, as they did, that a confusion in words is the symbol of confusion in continents and souls. Much of the dangerous condition of our time springs from the fact that in the readjustment of social and spiritual forms, names have become the prostituted playthings of any fool or knave who wishes to mouth them.

Thus, the gigantic reaches of pseudo-literature from the Hearst papers to Harold Bell Wright, being allotted their proper place, do no great harm. They touch only the senses they appeal to; they convince only minds incapable of conviction; there is no formidable claque to name them other than they are. Far more pernicious is the snob class of pseudo-literature; for it sails under false colors, and of late it proceeds almost unchallenged.

The challenge of other days was a competent tradition. Pseudo-literature has always thrived on pretension. But an audience to whom the classics, holy or profane, were valid had an incessant standard to protect it. If a French academician extolled Quinault, there was Euripides to answer. If an Alexandrian put out a bad pseudepigraph of Ezra, the Chronicles could face him. Our situation is more arduous. In the general liquidation of old forms, the esthetic tradition has dissolved. We must build up a new critical standard not only within, but from the current chaos.

ALLOTROPES [1]

By ZONA GALE

AT INTERVALS a new word, long known to every one else, emerges for one and sounds above other words. For me such a word is allotrope. That whose constituents, identical with those of something else, yet have a different molecular arrangement, so that the two present quite different aspects. We know that the diamond is loosely spoken of as the allotrope of coal—both carbon, but one a child of earth and the other kindred to the sun. We know that oxygen and ozone are allotropic. It is Mr. J. A. Thomson, in his English laboratory, who has lately announced that there exists an allotrope of water.

Now it may be that this allotrope of water will prove to be a substance denser than water, and a baser thing, as coal is baser than a diamond. The lay account of this which was given to me did not specify. But I like to think that the new substance will be more delicate, more exquisite, harder to imagine. Something as much finer and lovelier than water as a diamond is lovelier than coal. Imagine such a substance. How bright, how transparent, how shining! What undivined properties might it not have—what colors, what powers, what fra-

[1] From *The Yale Review,* January, 1926.

grances! It may be acted on by emanations and so open a whole corridor of new experience in perception. "And think," I heard a man say reverently, "think what it will do to us when we drink it." Perhaps the new race will some day be relating how we ancients brewed a strong and fiery and deathful fluid, from which we had to be restrained by law, when all the time there was awaiting us this possibility of entering upon new areas of most delicate experience by tasting the allotrope of water. As we creep about in this primordial ooze, with our faint toys of radium and radio and aeroplane, we can begin to dream what they will be perceiving and feeling when finer and fairer allotropes of other things have been discovered: of air, of fire, of earth, of ourselves. And we can beat the materialists on their home field, for in order to enter into all such wonder it will not be necessary to change human nature, which they are so sure cannot be done. It will be necessary only to arrange our molecules a little differently—or it may be a good deal differently. Orville Wright and Langley did not change human nature when they put it in a plane. The figurative application is beyond words engaging, and brings us inevitably to the allotropes of art.

Loosely used to flash a meaning, without being more particular than is lightning at its business of revealing both earth and heaven, the Elgin marbles and the scratching of the Aztecs are allotropic. And an allotrope of—shall we say?—*Clarissa Harlowe* is *Ethan Frome.* Of what divinable use are some physical facts save to permit us to make figures of them?—

When the stranger enters Ethan Frome's bare kitchen and you understand that the withered, bright-eyed, piping crippled woman, sitting there by the cold hearth with Ethan Frome's old wife is Mattie Silver, the vivid girl with whom you have watched him share the hour when they tried to die together, you have in a glare the black bulk of the years in which these three beings have lived together under one roof; Mattie, made lame and helpless by that catastrophe which was to have dealt death to her and to Ethan—Ethan's wife taking her in—Mr. and Mrs. Ethan Frome hosts to Mattie down the thirty years in which she grows ugly and querulous—without a comment the horror of those years is hurled before you in a page, and by them you are shaken as by experience.

There is no need to go back to *Clarissa Harlowe*. Go back merely to *Jane Eyre*. To that night of horror when Jane, on the eve of her marriage to Mr. Rochester, wakes to see in her room his crazed wife trying on the wedding veil. Between the birth of that terrible visage in the mirror, with the crude affirmation that "the maniac bellowed," which used to keep one awake nights, and the writing of that single line, "This is Miss Mattie Silver," there has been a rearrangement of the molecules of the novel, resulting in hardly less than the discovery of a new substance. We have the same ingredients, the same emotions, the same relations—

but the one result is density and the other is a diamond.

Consider the types of men and women who are appearing in our novels, not as "comic reliefs" or in any form of secondary rôle, but as primary characters, as, if you like, "hero and heroine." For example, Adrienne Toner, in the important novel of that name by Anne Douglas Sedgwick. But before we look upon Adrienne, shall we look back upon an earlier "heroine," upon Lucy in the moment of her meeting with Richard Feverel in the celebrated chapter called "Ferdinand and Miranda":

"She was indeed sweetly fair and would have been held fair among rival damsels. The wide summer hat, nodding over her forehead to her brows, seemed to flow with the flowing heavy curls, only half-curls, waves of hair, call them, rippling at the ends, which went like a sunny red-veined torrent down her back almost to her waist; a glorious vision to the youth who embraced it as a flower of beauty and read not a feature. There were curious features of color in her face for him to have read. Her brows, thick and brownish against a soft skin, showing the action of the blood, met in the bend of a bow, extending to the temples, long and level; you saw that she was fashioned to peruse the sights of earth, and by the pliability of her brows, that the wonderful creature used her faculty and was not going to be a statue to the gazer. Under the dark thick brows an arch of lashes shot out—giving a wealth of darkness to the full frank blue eyes, a mystery of meaning—more than brain was ever meant to fathom; richer, henceforth, than all mortal wisdom to Prince Ferdinand. For when Nature turns artist and produces contrasts of color on a fair face, where is the Sage, or where the Oracle, shall match the depth of its lightest look?"

Here is the introduction to the character of Adrienne Toner:

"Miss Toner's was an insignificant little head, if indeed it could be called little since it was too large for her body, and her way of dressing her hair with wide braids, pinned round it and projecting over the ears, added to the top-heavy effect. The hair was her only indubitable beauty. . . . It was cut in a light fringe across a projecting forehead and her mouth and chin projected too; so that, as he termed it to himself, it was a squashed-in face, ugly in structure, the small nose, from its depressed bridge, jutting forward in profile, flat yet prominent. Nevertheless he owned, studying her over his tea-cup, that the features, ugly, even trivial in detail, had in their assemblage something of unexpected force."

And then, if one is looking for a heroine, what bewilderment to follow! Adrienne is the cultivated Dulcy. She is the apotheosis of Dulcy. She utters spiritualized bromides. She doesn't say: "I never read a story serially. I always wait for it to come out in book form." But she says: "I'd rather say my prayers out of doors in the sunlight on a day like this, than in any church. I feel nearer God alone in His great world than in any church built with human hands. But we must all follow our own light." She doesn't say: "I've just washed my hair and can't do a thing with it." She says: "With all its excesses and errors I have always felt the French Revolution to be a sublime expression of the human spirit." Infinitely removed from the Dulcy of the 'bus top, she is the well-bred Dulcy of the best people, uttering the inanities of her kind. She speaks always of a "fine deep-hearted woman," of a "gifted girl," of a "rare sweet being." In moments of crisis her way of dealing is to quote with sweetness and light in her voice: "Heartily know, when half-gods go. . . ." She meets Roger Oldmeadow for the first time at a house-party and sees him cynical and bored. So after breakfast, as she is leaving, she engages him for a moment by the fireplace in the dining-room, and says: "Try to trust more; will you? Try to trust."

Religious, patriotic, and spiritual cant make up her talk. She sings the terrible Me-first of a young civilization: My ideas first; my religion first, better than anybody else's ideas or religion or country. The cultured internationally-minded mellowed folk of an older civilization, with whose exponents she comes in contact, find her far more subtly amusing than that earlier American in Europe, Daisy Miller. In fact, Adrienne Toner is to a later day, a day which measures its subjects by psychological tests, what Daisy Miller was to that Rome which judged alone by standards of society and its etiquette. Adrienne is the exponent of the unrecognized Absurd in the talk of the informed, the well-bred. She is to the sensitized what Dulcy is to the sophisticated. She is of those called "finished," who utter themselves forth day after day in hand-me-down thoughts. If you see no humor in the seminary graduating class whose motto was: "Our boat is launched but where's the shore?" you will see no humor in Adrienne. If you see no unbearable pathos in that motto, or in Dulcy, neither in Adrienne will you see it.

And when life seizes her, shakes her, leaves her desolate and you have a new Adrienne, reorganized, kindled to realities, illumined, then not at all does she cease her platitudes. Here is the perfection of Miss Sedgwick's art, that on page 341 Adrienne talks just as she did in those first revelations. Now she says to Oldmeadow, by this time deeply in love with her and whom she is refusing to marry:

" . . . The war, that has torn us all. But when it's over, when you can go home again and take up your own big life-work, . . . happiness will come back; I'm sure of it. We are all unhappy sometimes, aren't we? We must be; with our minds and hearts. Our troubled minds, our lonely hearts—"

The drawing of the character of a beautiful performance, a promise of discernment in the fiction of tomorrow which has rarely been so exemplified in the fiction of today. One is reminded of the characters in Disraeli's novels ("Rise quickly, my love. Some one is approaching. It is a tramper!")—only Disraeli's characters were taken for granted in a mist, and Adrienne is under a microscope. A microscope which reveals molecules in arrangements which the novels of yesterday never even guessed at.

Richard Feverel and *Adrienne Toner*—two novels, each compact of all that novels are usually constituted of, human emotion, human relationship, human characteristics and choice and their outcomes—and yet so different in discovery and arrangement that they are virtually two distinct forms of art. Between Lucy and Adrienne is the difference between the worlds of Ptolemy and Copernicus. Lucy is two-dimensional, a flat surface of type. Adrienne is round and revolving and intent upon her individual orbit.

After Effie in *The Heart of Midlothian,* or after Hester Prynne, there is the same discovery and rearrangement to make before we come to Sheila Kaye-Smith's magnificent Joanna Godden. Joanna is the study of a woman whose dominating masculinity of temperament hides a nature exquisitely feminine, a combination which, as one of the reviewers notes, always "proves irresistibly fascinating to a certain type of highly organized and spiritualized man." This type of woman is perfectly well known, but she has seldom been used as a primary character in fiction save in such figures as Katherine, the shrew to be tamed, who is tamed, as a matter of course; or as some wild heart which inevitably came to grief if it didn't get tamed; or for episode, as O. Henry presented such women. But Sheila Kaye-Smith gives you Joanna, big, tousled, capable, self-centered, alive, so that you love her as much as you do Portia or Rosalind. And when, on market day, this great Joanna strides through the crowd to the son of a neighbor baronet and says: "You and I should ought to be better acquainted," the reader does not look at her with the eyes of the baronet's son, nor with the eyes of the tittering villagers, nor with the eye of detachment, but the reader not less than approaches the man with Joanna. And thereafter walks with her throughout the book. Yet judged by every known standard of the old fiction, save for what was once called a character part, Joanna is impossible.

As material in fiction is thus differently arranged, so style has necessarily followed after. Even with the humanity and poignancy of George Eliot, yet her long dissertations, her constant intrusions of authorship, are no longer tolerable. Even with the story-telling power of Scott we know now that when we used to skip his "fine writing," his "descriptive passages," we were fundamentally right, and that our sense of guilt was our literary taste, budding.

What is the significance of these new choices of character? It is not that the author's power tricks one into sentimental sympathy for Adrienne or Joanna. It is not only the infectious magic of the novelist's power of actual self-identification with "every kind of human life." It is not only that power transferred to the reader to identify himself with "the failure, the futility, the finiteness of all human beings"; with that which Dreiser calls their "somehow pitiable finiteness in the midst of infinity." It is not only because of our new enthusiasm for honesty, for disillusion, even for ugliness. No, it is more than these: it is the novelist's, the artist's, the creator's discovery that the old arrangements of human values actually have somehow been superseded, and that behind the ordinary aspect of quite ordinary things and ordinary folk, in ordinary reactions, there is visible a new pattern of the old spiritual treasure.

At intervals, in any art, this new arrangement takes place. The gnarled and knotted face in the monotype of a Provincetown art student today differs from portraiture of two decades ago, not primarily in method, but in that the artist of the monotype has made an arrangement of Man never before ventured upon, and has thus discerned an aspect of Man never before detected. We may not like the new reality or we may, but the point is that by this rearrangement of old materials, we have broken through to see more Man, more Woman, more Animal, more Thing—more Life. It was always there, but we have rearranged it, have caused it to leap out at us in a new guise—like a diamond in the coal-bin. These new valuations of the familiar come to every one in daily living. Edward Carpenter asks: "Who is there so unfortunate as not to have had the experience in ordinary daily life, of seeing some features, perhaps those of a well-known person, suddenly transformed, with the strangest possible sense of transcendent Presence?" It is from such moments that the artist, in plastic art, in fiction, and in music, is giving us new arrangements of old familiars, old familiars in new guises as different, surely, as the allotrope of water, whatever that allotrope prove to be, will be from water itself.

Those whose idea of art is a raft to rescue them from reality have not welcomed these revaluations. All that they now face in novels they have been accustomed to sense uncomfortably in newspapers and in life, but when they picked up "a good book" they wanted help in forgetting themselves. They had mistaken the sense of security for art. This is perfect as rest, but bad as a foundation of literary taste. Yet this type of reader has made this criticism again and again down the years, because the type has always been slow to recognize any extension of freedom.

It is an extension of freedom which the novel has entered upon, nothing more alarming than that; that which in art, as in the movement of peoples, and in the general mind and spirit of the race, has always been the goal. All that is happening to the novel, to poetry, to plastic art, to music, has happened over and over again to art, as to politics, to religion, to human relationship. But the search for freedom has a technique. When the technique is not regarded, the freedom discovered is formless or it altogether fails. And the chief article of this technique is not inclusion. It is selection. We did not advance from *Clarissa Harlowe* to *Ethan Frome* by including in novels everything which might be included.

The commonplace, the evil, the ugly are not necessarily suitable material for a novel, no matter how free the novel form finds itself. The novel has, of course, advanced partly by omissions—"refining by so much as he chiseled away," Pater says of his craftsman. The novel advances by extending its sources of material. But it arrives by selection.

The process of writing a novel involves: 1. The quickening within of something to be expressed. 2. The nourishing of that impulse. 3. The development of a technique of expression. All three processes involve both freedom and a selective use of that freedom.

Here we have a tentative outline of the process of any art expression: the quickening, the feeding, the technique. But this also is the process of education—the quickening, the feeding, the technique. And this is not less the story of the ideal of government—the quickening of the social impulse, the feeding of the social impulse, the technique of the expression of the social impulse in the "guardians." And religion, regarding it—as Mr. A. R. Orage has called it—as the process of the divinization of man, proceeds in the same fashion: the quickening, the feeding, the technique. Art is not more a process of creation than the true processes of education, of government, of divinization. All must proceed both by freedom and a selective use of that freedom.

Thus scholarship, government, religion, and art are all in the domain of the creative—all should be primarily powers of expression, of life more abundant.

Passing by government and divinization as improper subjects for social intercourse, consider the slow encroachments of everyday branches of the curricula upon realms of the creative. We have long been accustomed to this process in physics—in physics which used to be considered as pure scholarship, and in the Middle Ages was classed as an occult science, and then became the servant of man. Now we have yesterday's discovery of the new substance called fused quartz, which can send light and heat around a curve. There, in the laboratories of the Western Electric in Lynn, Massachusetts, they hold a rod of the fused quartz, heat one end of it, and while the rod itself remains cold the other end will shower heat. And it is said to permit the passage of the ultra violet rays, so that through its lamps we shall be independent of the sunlight and grow green plants which never see the sun. In geometry we have abandoned sobriety altogether and have entered joyfully upon fantasy under that stretched word relativity, and when expression fails us, we have always the two words *fourth dimensional*—they mean something too, even as Horace prophesied of words, that new meanings should creep in and possess them. And if there is a creative course in the universities, it is now psychology, though barely ten years ago the psychologists were saying that the human mind was charted, that *there* at any rate we should know nothing more.

It is true that all these adventures are but the uncovering of inner condition and relationships—but that is what the creative is. Even art does not invent. It reveals.

Here, for example, is architectural ornament as creative as Burbankism itself! For a most thrilling study of what is afoot in this domain, I commend to you a vast slim book lately issued by the American Institute of Architects—Louis Sullivan's *A System of Architectural Ornament, According with a Philosophy of Man's Powers* . . . with a prelude and interlude which are not less than poetry; its theory that the seat of power is the will to life in every creative worker; and its plates of geometrical figures so beautiful that you see them with the pang of a look at the ephemeral—and yet they are as eternal as the sky and as burgeoning as the Spring. And one will have such a caption as this: "Development of a blank block illustrating man's control over materials and their destiny"—a block growing from a dead cube to the quickened beauty of line and curve and star and trefoil—a child's block, evolving to an ornament of exquisite beauty.

Then simple leaf forms, the elm, the apple, the clover, rising to unimagined loveliness of form by springing line and whorl and tendril woven in gracious patterns about the central motif, "following," he says, "following nature's method of liberating energy." You can never again look at a leaf without seeing nature dreaming in maple and chestnut towards what Edgar Saltus called "excesses of grace." Perhaps the Sullivans dreaming new leaves and new adventures in line shall find their Burbanks to develop the potential and eternal energy of form. Then a page of pentagons, simple, expressionless, sleeping, then darting lines cutting their edges, crossing their surfaces, winging out from their angles, until there comes a page plate of something breathlessly lovely, something like crystals and ferns and lightning and the curve of rainbows and the rhythm of echoes—a beautiful entity. And the rigid original figure has vanished "in a mobile medium." He calls it plastic geometry, he calls it the awakening of the pentagon. We might call it—an allotrope of the pentagon. Plate after plate of beauty, and you wonder why our rugs and our wall-paper and our lamp-shades and children's play-rooms cannot be offered to us in these lovely guises.

One caption says, "There being no limit to the field of character expression, this design lies within the field of romance." You look and you know that halos of saints and crowns of kings represent actual structural beauty of line emanating from purity or from power in life, in human energy. You look—and you know that the outline of the Holy Grail itself grew out of some such conception of structural beauty momentarily uncovered to an eye of sufficient purity and power to perceive it. You understand the symbolism of the Host. You look—and you see in these figures approximations of the human form—and you realize with a thrill that our very bodies come under these laws of possible beauty and graciousness. That our bodies are walking the earth like figures of clay when they might be radiating loveliness, flashing atmospheres of beauty and graciousness —allotropes of the flesh. Yet once architecture was merely the raising of a shelter from the elements, the dry routine of draughtsmen earning a livelihood—no more of a creative art than that.

And then for all our adventures, see what remains untouched. The whole phenomenon of sound—what do we know of it? Acoustics is a mystery to modify which we use incantations of a stretched wire. Certain sounds produce madness in animals. From Alexander down, music has had the potency of witchcraft—yet what do we guess of the power of sound? If the walls of Jericho did fall down to trumpets, we shall not know it yet. For all the revelations concerning the subconscious, who shall be explicit about the reason that we can will to wake at a certain hour, and wake at that hour? Suggestion to the subconscious, yes—but *what happens?* Our explanations are as generic as that of the Yellowstone Park guide, seeking to account for the geysers. Said he: "I think this whole region was either let down or hove up." Yet thirty years ago Charles Godfrey Leland was saying that our drudgery of learning was already an anachronism, and that in time the whole routine of education, as we know it now, would be superseded by the auto-suggestive process; by *la volonté*. For that matter what, explicitly, is the process of rebuilding which goes forward during sleep? We sleep for five minutes and say that we wake incredibly refreshed, but what, categorically, has happened? And who shall say that the significance of this slow intaking and outgoing of the breath of the body, and of the spirit, is even remotely divined? Nothing in creation as we know it now is more mysterious than that rhythmic foundation of moment-to-moment life. Nothing unless it is our dying. But dying occasionally is given all the importance of art itself, as when in Paris there arises a society of which Madame Curie is one of the sponsors, organized "for the study of the phenomenon of death."—Unabashed by the mysteries of death and breath and sleep, we believe that we know all about our bodies. We will hardly listen when they tell us that they are permeated by a "new" substance, interpenetrating the physical body; and when they make known that this substance reveals different colors; and when it is suggested that behavior and mental attitude may condition those colors. When we deride such a new form of substance, we are asked in an article in *Harper's Magazine* to remember how lately it was that Benjamin Franklin appeared before the British Royal Society and announced to the members that there existed a new form of energy; and they solemnly ridiculed him. (We can forgive them though. Not one of the members of the British Royal Society of that day could have read *Ethan Frome* or *Joanna Godden* or *Adrienne Toner* or any of Joseph Conrad.)

By our derisions and our incredulities, we are irresistibly reminded of that Kentucky school board which once denied the use of its building for a discussion of the new invention of the locomotive engine; "for," said the document, "if God had intended man to go at any such speed as fifteen miles an hour, there would have been something about it in the Bible."

And we are reminded of Daniel Webster's Congressional speech opposing the building of the first transcontinental railroad. And when he had pictured the terrors of the Great American Desert, the impassability of the Rocky Mountains, the impracticability of settling that barren coast with its useless harbors, he concluded: "No, gentlemen! Not one dollar of United States money shall ever be spent, with my consent, to bring the Pacific Coast one mile nearer to Boston."

It is as if creative energy were constantly furthering a new rate of vibration in life, reflecting in some new and even outlandish response of man to his surroundings, the same old familiar miraculous surroundings and relationships, about which he is for ever discerning more. Sometimes these awakenings have come softly, in Italy, in Greece, in England, in Palestine, in Thibet—shy dawns on the hills or flaming suns across the miles. And now, in the confusion of the world, we are nevertheless in a period of intense response to this eternal outpouring of creative energy. When Professor George Santayana says that civilization may be approaching one of those long winters which overtake us from time to time; that a flood of barbarism may soon overwhelm all the work of our ancestors, as another flood two thousand years ago overwhelmed that of the ancients, it may be that his new flood is as mythical as the old one. For even so must geometrical figures in general react when they see an immobile pentagon awakening to plastic life. And picture the emotions of fused quartz when it feels heat and light pouring through its own cold length and escaping in glory! Even consider us, divining afar off, and occasionally, glimpses of allotropes of ourselves.

The allotropes of ourselves. Why not? What if man's persistent belief in his own spirit is his divination of his own allotrope waiting in his flesh to be at last released from that ambiguous laboratory? What if every one of his faculties, with which he muddles along, has in reality this other potential functioning, according to some deeper law, by which it could contact and express more beauty, as an awakened pentagon can express more beauty than a blind block. Have not the creators in plastic and pictorial art long since seen a lovelier and a stranger world than you and I see—a world which is actually here, only we have coal sight and cannot contact it, cannot vision that light and line and distance?

There may have been a fourteenth-century monk, bending over his manuscript, copying it by hand. And Mercury may have come to him and said: "It shall soon go, that manuscript, under the sea and through the air, to a land of which you have never heard, and there by a process which you do not now know, it shall be multiplied by the million and shot forth over miles of fine wire and length of steel, and be read by thousands of eyes, it may be at one time." And without even raising his eyes to Mercury, the monk would have said: "What you say is impossible. Do you not see that I have here the only copy of the manuscript in existence? You speak of an illusion."

When allotropes of tomorrow try to get themselves discovered, in perception or in opinion, allotropes which seem to deny the scholarship of today, or to transcend its art, we need not believe—belief is too much to ask. But we need not be fourteenth-century monks.

For not all of us is incarnate. Some of us is spirit. And it is required of us that we see ourselves both in flesh and in spirit all the time.

ARTHUR SYMONS, SURVIVOR OF THE YELLOW DECADE [1]

By HERBERT S. GORMAN

ARTHUR SYMONS: A CRITICAL STUDY. *By T. Earl Welby. The Adelphi Company, New York.*

STUDIES OF MODERN PAINTERS. *By Arthur Symons. William Edwin Rudge, New York.*

THE MERE mention of Arthur Symons's name evokes a delicate procession of shadowy and exotic shapes. The Yellow Nineties stream back into consciousness, and, led by the bulky, archaic-lipped Oscar Wilde, a host of troubled figures pass to a music that is a queer mingling of Pan's pipes and "Daisy Bell." There is Ernest Dowson and Aubrey Beardsley and Henry Harland and John Davidson and Hubert Crackanthorpe and Lionel Johnson. The Yellow Book and The Savoy and The Hobby Horse flutter in the air. The atmosphere is scented with patchouli. Glittering ballets sweep toward the footlights and the hansoms slur through the London mud. It is an era of flung roses and borrowed French decadence and sighing lutes and bicycle bloomers and "Ta-ra-ra-boom-de-ay." All this is no more than vaguely hinted at in Mr. Welby's study of Arthur Symons, who alone of the 1890 figures—if we except Max Beerbohm (who

[1] From *The New York Times Book Review,* January 31, 1926.

was never quite of the group) and Richard Le Gallienne (who transplanted himself to America shortly after the finish of the Beardsley era)—lives to represent a movement that is now a part of the romance of literary history. Mr. Welby ignores what is now popularly termed the *fin de siècle* group with an avowed purpose, and that is to separate Mr. Symons from it to a great degree and to portray him as a poet and critic whose best work is not an integral part of it. He will have hard work convincing readers, for the most novel portion of Mr. Symons's contribution to English letters is to be found in the poems of *London Nights*. He is associated in the popular mind with this work, even though, as Mr. Welby justifiedly points out, he has continued to write better poetry since then and has delivered himself of a body of critical and revelatory prose that is unique.

Although Mr. Symons has been treated at length in various books—Holbrook Jackson's *The Eighteen-Nineties* and Osbert Burbett's *The Beardsley Period,* to cite two examples—this is the first volume to be devoted wholly to his work and to consider it as a coherent and rounded whole. Heretofore there have been essays on Symons the poet and Symons the critic, but Mr. Welby's thesis is based on the premise that the poet and critic must be considered together if the whole man is to be revealed. Of course, this is superficially true of any writer. The personality of the individual writer is upon everything he does. Mr. Welby, however, is anxious to show that the poetry of Mr. Symons is but one side of his nature and one that dovetails with that other side that continues the self-expression in prose. If, for instance, you read Rossetti's poetry you get the whole of Rossetti, for his complete nature is fused in his writings. The same is true of his paintings. You get the whole of Rossetti, for, again, his complete nature is fused in the pictorial conceptions. This is not true of Mr. Symons, who expresses one part of him in his poetry and the other part in his prose.

" . . . Mr. Symons [notes Mr. Welby] partly, we may assume, through natural limitations, partly through concentration on the task of dissecting his own moods, has found in writing his poetry something less than the complete satisfaction of his creative impulses. As a critic, therefore, he has on occasion been tempted, very likely without being aware of it, to write a not quite legitimately creative criticism."

This has never been the case in any considerations of literature, however, the commentator is quick to point out. But literature, again, is but a facet (an extremely large one, it is true) of Mr. Symons's prose. The whole field of the seven arts is traveled by him. He will write about paintings or music or the spell of cities with the same creative intensity with which he will create a lyric. Part of the man goes into this work. All this, of course, is quite in accordance with the peculiar temperament of Mr. Symons, who is, first of all, a vibrating chord touched constantly to music by the sensuous and visual aspects of living. He, more than any living writer today, can reach most sensitively to the multitudinous surfaces of the fine art of living. He is essentially civilized, almost artificially so. He senses the soul of a city as acutely as he does the soul of a flower or the soul of a fleeting beat of melody.

When we first think of Mr. Symons's work we think of that sensuous sensitivity that responds so poignantly to the odor of perfume, the soft feel of silk and flesh, the delicate artificiality of rouge, the blaze of the footlights and the petaled skirts flaring behind them, jewels and rings and hansoms—indeed, all those fair fleeting things that time so cruelly snatches up and demolishes. We are apt to forget that the poet's province is wider, that he finds eternities in ancient cities and country twilights, in the gray wastes of the sea, in the ancient passions of Helen of Troy and Iseult and Cleopatra, even in the spirits of energy and air and earth. The "London after dark" proclivities, with their occasionally delicately perverse implications, are concentered in a brief span of Mr. Symons's development. But the novelty of this span and the completeness with which Mr. Symons gave himself up to it have served to hallmark the poet as the representative of this orchid-like existence. Mr. Welby makes it plain that the poet transcends these moods and that he is moved by a higher philosophy of things. He points out, and quite justly, that Mr. Symons reaches a Donne-like eminence in his meditations upon modern love and passion. He also points out that the poet is pretty much of a solitary, an individual going his own way, and not part of a movement that can be dismissed with a brief paragraph of description. All these things readers who have followed Mr. Symons's work know well, but it is pleasing to have them set forth with coherence. Another thing that Mr. Welby does is to point out the high degree of achievement in Mr. Symons's tragic play, *The Harvesters.* It was George Meredith who prophesied that Mr. Symons would do important things in drama, but somehow the urge did not seem to come upon the poet until his career had been well defined.

The various comments that Mr. Welby has to make on the prose of Mr. Symons are keen and well justified. In the various volumes that have succeeded each other since "An Introduction to the Study of Browning" appeared in 1886 (and how far away that date seems!) a tremendous breadth of vision and catholicity of taste have made themselves evident. Whether it be Charles Lamb or Baudelaire, William Blake or Stéphane Mallarmé, St. Augustine or Paul Verlaine, Robert Browning or Ernest Dowson, Mr. Symons manages to get emphatically beneath the surface and discover the real urge that animates these figures so discordant in juxtaposition. He is a born critic, a sensitized plate that reflects clearly the image thrown upon it. And besides this, he nearly always finds these figures notable pegs upon which to hang his own convictions regarding esthetics. It is not that he arbitrarily uses these writers for such purposes, that he perverts them into his own scheme of things, but that, while he reveals them, he also reveals himself. It is their impingement upon his own consciousness that is so feelingly set forth in lucid sentences beneath which the reader may vaguely glimpse a poetic ardor and a gentle wit. And it is not alone in literary figures that he so finds a way of expressing himself. It is true in his observations on paintings, in his critical notations of music, in his violent or subdued reactions to the essential essence of the variegated cities of the world, in his comprehension of architecture, in his clear delight in dancers and plays. He touches the esthetic world at all points and he finds himself through it. Such a catholicity would seem to predicate an equalization of the arts, a running together of the esthetic impetuses, but this is hardly ever the case with Mr. Symons. Literature, admittedly, is the art to which he is certainly born and in which he actually achieves, but he strives to view the sister-arts from their own perspectives. "He looks at pictures," writes Mr. Welby, "and at architecture, he hears music, he watches acting and dancing as nearly as may be from the position of the painter, the architect, the musician, the actor, the dancer. He avoids —and how rare is such avoidance!—the confusion of the arts." It is because of this clarity, this feeling for the virtues of each art within its logical confine, that his criticism is so good. He may not be the finest literary critic living, although some would maintain so, nor the finest picture critic nor the finest music critic, but what writer has achieved so talented and distinguished a versatility in these days? One must go back to Pater to find a comparison, and even there the reader will find a man more limited in receptivity albeit deeper in esthetic apprehension. Mr. Symons is directly comparable to Pater when he writes about painting, perhaps, but such a comparison can mean nothing. We read the contemporary man for the pleasure he gives in so revealing to us the artistic urges of our time. In *Studies of Modern Painters,* for instance, a book beautifully fashioned from a typographical point of view (it is a Bruce Rogers creation, and that should explain everything to the knowing bibliophile), we find a series of comments on London exhibitions and gallery shows. Most of this matter is dated and one could wish that Mr. Symons had revised it accordingly when he decided to make it permanent between covers. But even as it is, there are rich nuggets here for the lover of Mr. Symons's lucid approach to the art of painting. When he writes about Augustus John's work and states: "In a few scrawls of the pen, indicating an attitude rather than a person, John brings life into a gesture, and sets a gesture talking with a singular vivacity. He amuses himself by taking nature always at a disadvantage; he waits on a woman's beauty until it sharpens or thickens into character; he waits on an abrupt gesture as other artists wait on a gesture which falls into some continuing curve." It is true that the reader will not find Arthur Symons at his best in this book, for the greater portion of it is certainly fashioned or recovered from journalistic pages, but still it is Arthur Symons, and that is saying much. His peculiar sensitive approach to the arts is evident even in his most occasional ventures. He cannot but react strongly to the esthetic implications of any work that is set before him. Indeed, this is true of life in general so far as he is concerned, and if we want an authentic picture in our minds of Arthur Symons, we will visualize a man to whom the aesthetic in everything, painting, literature, music, dancing, cities, women, jewels, rouge, and even hansom cabs, finds a distinguished and entirely individual reaction.

A SUPERB BRIEF[1]

By Alyse Gregory

The Pilgrimage of Henry James. *By Van Wyck Brooks. E. P. Dutton and Company, New York.*

Mr. Van Wyck Brooks is always driving the same jaunty, brightly polished trap up to our door; and—like some trim, punctual, somewhat sly guardian of an aged relative who is both a disgrace and an honor to his family—he helps to descend the latest victim of his penetrating concern. Our emotions felt no stirring of protest when Mark Twain, downcast, but still able to jest, lean and jocular, appeared before us, but when Henry James, a little ponderous, yet so very, very soft of foot, is produced in order to be closed away in some obscure niche of partial failures, we are decidedly put out. For do we not recall our old boundless gratitude in those early days when his pen created for us a sophistication of intercourse we had never dreamed could exist; when the haunting miasma of provincialism in which we unresistingly moved was for once inconceivably dispersed and the pulse of our thought beat with an odd new tension and insight, the effects of which could never again be lost or forgotten, as also the inadequacy of our environment could never again quite blot out for us

[1] From *The Dial,* September, 1925.

the compensating perception of our predicament, with its most subtle implications mirrored back to us in artistic utterance? So we recall with fresh assurance the unique debt we owe our favorite American author, and we regard Mr. Brooks with intrepid skepticism. Yet we listen, and as we listen we become involved in his argument, then we become amused, and finally we smile a light, somewhat ironical, yet wholly admiring smile; for Mr. Brooks, besides being nimble, is persuasive, and all the little bits of evidence he so ingeniously gathers, so sedulously and absorbedly picks out from the writings of the great man himself, with the sharp, nipping, unwearied eagerness of a woodpecker, a woodpecker whose red cap flashes in the sun as it draws reluctant booty from under the crinkled bark of some solid, delicately blossoming locust tree, are made in the end to form a pattern which, if dubious in intention, is at least brilliant in design.

The predicament of Henry James, as seen by Mr. Brooks, is as follows. Nourished by his parents on stories about the graces of the old world, James absorbed even as a small boy a distrust of the barbaric crudity of his own native land, and together with this distrust, a desire to ally himself securely with the ancient, more exclusive, more engaging traditions of European culture, a desire sustained and fortified, given his first opportunity of testing the response of his senses in the European scene; a desire which, indeed, hardening finally into a somewhat affrighted purpose as the years progressed, led finally to his becoming a stranger stranded in a society in which he could never feel wholly at home and alienated for ever from the only environment which might, since it was his native air, have helped to sustain his intensity and to fructify his genius. Thus Mr. Brooks traces in James's writings the rise and decay of his inspiration, marking it as at its highest expression during that period of his life when his knowledge of his country was most emphatic and as at its lowest in those later years when his memories of it had become dimmer and dimmer in permanent expatriation.

And it is just here that one feels a weakness in Mr. Brooks's argument. For in the interests of his thesis he shifts and classifies James's disparate works with the unsleeping, unillumined eye of the social scientist rather than with the nervous, conjuring fingers of the artist to whose gentlest pressure innumerable doors swing soundlessly back to reveal incomparable treasures within. For how can Mr. Brooks see as unreal or sterile that later novel of Henry James in which his matured technical skill was rendered so willing a handmaiden to his harvested and mellowed intensity? And though the present writer admired so much Mr. Edmund Wilson's admirable essay in *The New Republic* on Mr. Brooks's work, yet she must beg to disagree with both Mr. Brooks and Mr. Wilson in this matter of *The Wings of the Dove*. For surely the dramatic motif which actuates the story is just that malevolent cynicism and base duplicity which Mr. Wilson denies; and yet at the same time Merton Densher does remain throughout the "gentleman" which James has established him at the outset of the novel, more conspired against than conspiring, and explained with so lucid an adequacy that one shares with him at every step the embarrassment of his plight; while Milly, the innocent "cat's-paw," though dead, wins a lasting victory over the crafty Kate, who must view her lover initiated into some deep and tender secret, the soft energy of which will separate them for ever. Thus evil is irretrievably overcome by good, and Mr. Brooks's estimate of this book is shown as biased in the interests of his theory.

But one feels throughout this study that Mr. Brooks in some subtle way is allying himself with the Philistines, and one experiences a curious kind of gratitude that Henry James was after all able to escape out of that deadening Cambridge society set in its "box of sky lavender," from the center of which his brother once complained that the name of Bernard Shaw was banned. And is there not something peculiarly irritating in the attitude of this same brother who, after visiting Henry James in his English home, refers to him thus in a letter to Mrs. James: ". . . the same dear, old, good, innocent and at bottom very powerless-feeling Harry . . . caring for little but his writing, and full of dutifulness and affection for all gentle things"? "Powerless-feeling Harry" and "dutifulness and affection"; are these not the very phrases that Cambridge would most applaud and that Mr. Brooks seems not to disapprove? And again he writes, this time directly to his brother: "For gleams and innuendoes and felicitous verbal insinuations you are unapproachable, but the rare perfume of things will not support existence, and the effect of solidity you reach is but perfume and simulacrum." Pray, one feels like asking, what else, if not the bare perfume of things, will support existence? How often this kind of observation is made with a sort of patronizing finality by the moralist to the poet, the social reformer to the artist; and what a wealth of provincialism it denotes in the present instance, of lack of understanding of the peculiar genius of Henry James. Indeed, one begins at last to feel glad that this wary and sensitive American should have been made to spend so many painful hours, finicky and attentive, knocking vainly at the stupid, impregnable portals of English society or assuaging his confusion in his dim, well-regulated, solitary habitation. One begins to surmise that these ignominious postures were important contributing factors toward those artful insights of his which are our especial delight; and surely if one is to judge him by most of the Americans who have stayed at home, one's gratitude increases that this velvet-footed thief of perfect phrases should have made so felicitous an escape. One permits one's fancy even further scope, and wonders whether the genius of William James would not too have flowered more nobly and with more delicate an imagination had he likewise turned his back squarely and for ever on his native shores.

It is true that one is conscious at times of a certain confined sterility in Henry James's writings, but one can imagine the kind of exhaustive and convincing treatise Freud might devote to an explanation of his weakness, tracing its cause ultimately to some deep fissure in the sex life of his subject, or one could quite simply say that some insufficiency of passion was native to his temperament and that with the vanishing excitation of his youth and early manhood his writing did become more and more mechanical. Yet to the present writer James's later period, with certain few exceptions, remains the period which has given her the greatest pleasure.

If one can bring to the reading of Mr. Brooks's study, however, a mind purged of preconceptions, washed quite clean indeed of any previous knowledge of the subject, one's admiration will remain unshaken to the end. How well one can visualize this neat attorney of letters in a crowded court room, unflustered and precise, the patriot of American culture, amid his dry, infestive enemies, unrolling his immaculate brief and with pungent directness and a limpid grace of style presenting his case to the judge in such a manner as to bewilder and to charm him into immediate acquiescence. And with the judge we too must needs bow low to this eloquent sentry of our inclement shores, grateful that those of us who are inclined to succumb perhaps a little too easily to Europe's perilous appeal can be sure of leaving at home so constant and honorable a custodian of our intellectual heritage.

THE CONSISTENCY OF ANATOLE FRANCE[1]

By ALBERT GUERARD

AT THE close of a banquet given in his honor by the British intelligentsia, Anatole France opened his arms and, in true Gallic fashion, kissed G. B. Shaw; and Shaw, possibly abashed for the first time in his life, gallantly returned the compliment. A wonderful symbolical scene! It comes to my mind whenever the flippancy of Shaw or the skepticism of France is mentioned. I would rather have witnessed the osculation of these two gray-beards than the most expert vamping of Antony by Cleopatra.

In the fullness of time Anatole France grew weary of his fame, of his bric-a-brac, and even of the nymph of the Boulogne grove (*vide* J. J. Brousson); and he consented to die. His funeral was a grand civic pageant—a more restrained replica of Victor Hugo's democratic apotheosis in 1885; and while literati all over the world were attempting to season their reverence with the proper dose of Anatolian irony, the people of Paris, in all simplicity, mourned for a man of the people and a faithful servant of social justice.

[1] From *The New York Herald Tribune* "Books," September 27, 1925.

159622

Which were right—the knights of the quill or those of the hammer? I know one man, at least, brought up on Anatole France as the Scotch are brought up on the doctrine of "total depravity," who feels like repeating the words of La Bruyère: "The people have no wit, and the great have no soul. If it comes to a choice, I want to be with the people." The Parisian workman is nearer to France in spirit than all the Menckens that ever menckenized. He understands that with France, as with Voltaire and Renan, irony was a weapon, not a goal. A soldier may love his weapon, an artisan his tool, and so a great man may be a virtuoso, but no mere virtuoso is genuinely great.

Anatole France left no doubt as to the "fundamentals" of his faith. Irony he wanted by his side, as he watched the witless revue we call Life; but he invoked also her greater sister, Pity. Now Irony and Pity are both condemned under the Golden Rule; for if we love to practice them upon others, we hate to have them practiced upon us. Call them Humor and Pathos, and they sound a trifle more Nordic and respectable. Call Irony the hatred of all Pharisaic pretense; give Pity her Pauline name, Charity; and you will have turned the old satyr, not into a Christian, but into a disciple of Christ.

Anatole France's Dreyfusism, his Socialism, his Pacifism, his Bolshevism, are blocks of stumbling for those dilettanti of mocking Nihilism who deem themselves his spiritual heirs. And yet his sincerity could not be impugned; the faith he adopted was too naïve, too commonplace, to be a pose. Hugo, Zola, might be accused of plebeian ambition; Barrès, d'Annunzio, after they had wearied of perverse eroticism, found in nationalistic activity a purple cloak for their worshiped Ego. Not so with Anatole France: his socialistic ventures were perfectly disinterested. They hurt him with the classes best qualified to appreciate his art; so that it became the fashion with the younger bourgeoisie to dismiss him with a shrug.

We must admit there were at least two Anatole Frances—the pure hedonist—*animal triste post coitum*—and the humanitarian. To reconcile them into a single "true Anatole France" is not my purpose. France, like each of us, like Mr. Bryan or President Coolidge, was at least seven men under one skin—man and beast, angel and devil, all playing tricks upon one another and upon the world. But I claim that he was fully as consistent as the common run of mankind. The apparent antinomies in him were the result of an inner contradiction in his upbringing. I have had the opportunity of watching an education somewhat similar to his; and a few chance words in *Contemporary History* and in J. J. Brousson led me to a hypothesis which might explain his bewildering evolution.

Anatole France was educated at Stanislas, a Catholic school. To those alleged "Free Thinkers" who assert that Romanism stifles the independence of the mind, the priests can reply that it was they who gave to the world Rabelais, Molière, Voltaire, Renan, and

Anatole France—a very creditable record. Stanislas was an aristocratic institution. Not that the teachers could be accused of deliberate snobbishness: but their *clientèle* was drawn from the Faubourg Saint Germain, and they were, on principle, scrupulously respectful of the established social order. This conservatism was naturally much more unquestioning in the early years of the Second Empire than it is today. Anatole's family, well educated and perfectly respectable, belonged to the lower middle class. Young Thibaut was not a pariah, as a Jew or a Negro might be in this republic of ours, so happily made safe for democracy. But his little soul was, at every turn, conscious of social lines, invisible and yet cruelly sharp. It is the cardinal fact in Anatole France's development that he was taught a fashionable piety of a rather sweetish and inane type, which he could not forever respect; and a code of social values which hurt him in secret.

Yet, for many years, Anatole did not rebel. He was not a born iconoclast, or even a skeptic. He was a conformist, a lover of tradition. His masters were genuinely kind; the atmosphere of his home was conservative. And in the days of his young manhood the alternative to conservatism was abhorrent to a man of culture. The Commune had made democracy a hideous farce. Renan for a time, Taine to his dying day, were estranged from "progressive" ideas. Victor Hugo had been deified by all third-rate "Liberals" supported by the Great Unwashed. The fetid notoriety of Zola enhanced the same impression: democracy, free thought, anticlericalism, were in damnable taste. A gentleman of delicate habits could not bear the stench of that pothouse. And France, whom nature, habitat, home, education, had refined to the point of squeamishness, remained far into middle life a professed conservative.

But a conservative for purely negative reasons. The authorities he had been taught to worship had left in him a secret resentment. Anatole France was an anticlerical at heart long before he confessed it to himself. Partly through the influence of Renan, then the sovereign of French thought, chiefly because with growing years and success he dared to be himself at last, he renounced all the authorities that, so far, had—nominally—guided his course. It was, not an orgy, but a Lucullan feast of negation, the glorious anarchism of his middle period—*Thaïs, The Red Lily, Queen Pedauque.* He used the artistic weapon that tradition had given him for the utter destruction of traditional authority and Paris, the conservative circles in Paris, applauded, not merely because the books were marvelous, but because nihilism was in fashion.

Yet Anatole France was not a skeptic even then, any more than Julian was an apostate. He was discarding ideas which had been imposed upon him, and which were at odds with the self-respect of his class and of his intellect. No one could expect Anatole

France, at forty, to revere a society of which M. de Charlus was the apex, or a theology expounded by Father Didon.

It was a period of anarchism, not of conversion, because his old-established distaste for vulgarian democracy could not be overcome. But with the Dreyfus case came the challenge prophesied by La Bruyère: "The people have no wit, and the great have no soul: Choose!" And Lucien Bergeret chose.

There entered into his socialism not merely his intellectual integrity and his genuine power of sympathy ("he was sensual, therefore human") but a forty-year-old impatience of false superiorities: the innumerable little snubs he had suffered at Stanislas were to be paid for, a hundredfold. The smooth frivolity, the banal elegance, the imbecile cleverness of the social élite, had long jarred on his taste. The society that had lionized him had wounded him in many subtle ways: for to lionize is to patronize. He, a son of the people, "unclassed and free," could at least express his opinion af aristocracy without fear of a warning voice within: "Sour grapes!" Yes, the grapes were sour; but he had tasted them.

There is nothing mysterious in his career from the time of his conversion until his death. This swaying to and fro was determined by the vast swing of history, by which only a few Olympians and the hopelessly frivolous fail to be affected. Along with the majority of earnest Dreyfusists, he grew disgusted with the radical gang which grabbed power in the name of Truth and Justice; hence the savage pessimism of *The Gods Are Athirst* and *Penguin Island*— the wrath of a frustrated idealist. In 1914 he was willing to believe, with the simplicity of a man of the people, that the war was a crusade for democracy: and he found out that the prophets of the time were not Jaurés, not Wilson, not even Clemenceau, but Maurras—and Loucheur. No wonder that he grew weary; and we must not forget he had loved pleasure too ardently, that pleasure which, when the grasshopper has become a burden, is such bitter mockery.

So he was blandly ironical to a world which was ironically reverent before him; and he was as corrosive as Swift among trusted friends who proved untrustworthy. But even that he must have foreseen, and chuckled at the exposure that a few smartish young men would make of themselves.

Those who see in him the prince of sophistication among the sophisticated tribe of quill-drivers are abundantly right. Justified also those who remember him as the aged amorist sporting with red-skirted Amaryllis in the shaded Boulogne; or those for whom he is an exquisite trifler, engrossed with chiseled cup and jeweled word. They have their Anatole France, a delightful lay figure, with the skull cap, the gorgeous dressing gown, and, on the Brousson level, the slippers. Their Anatole France shall not be taken away from them. But Pied d'Alouette Crainquebille, Roupart the cabinet-maker, have chosen the better part.

VAGABONDS[1]

By Joseph Wood Krutch

Dark Laughter. *By Sherwood Anderson. Boni and Liveright, New York.*

When one thinks of the contemporary commentators upon the American scene the names of Messrs. Sinclair Lewis and Sherwood Anderson come naturally to mind, and yet it is a curious fact that, though these names are so frequently linked, the men themselves belong to the two different classes into which all societies are divided. The mass of any population is composed of those whose nature it is to play, as it were, the game. They clear the forests when forests are to be cleared, they build the industries when industries are to be built, they catch the rhythm of the step when their comrades march away to war; and in whatever world they happen to be they definitely, in the words of the Hairy Ape, "belong." Mr. Lewis, by virtue of his peculiarly American vigor, of his zeal, and of his positive, confident determination, is a member, in so far as any artist can be, of this group; for satirist though he be, his participation in the life of his time is active and enthusiastic. But there is another class, composed, like every class of

[1] From *The Nation,* December 2, 1925.

big men and little men alike, of those who are the vagabonds of body or of mind. The spirit of their own or of any age seems never to grip them; they do not understand the value set by their fellows upon the prizes for which the races are run; and in the midst of the bustle they stand wondering by. When one of them charms us we call him a dreamer and when one, vaguely ineffectual in the performance of some task we have set him, moves our anger we call him shiftless; but we know the class to which they all belong—they are the moonstruck ones who seem never able to share the unquestioning faith in the worth of this or that which keeps the others so intent on their pursuit of wealth, of fame, of respectability, and of comfort. The most articulate and the most self-conscious of the class write the dreamy poems, essays, and novels which fascinate without ever deeply entering into readers in whom the will is more dominant; but even in the midst of the busy American civilization one may see the lower ranks of the order who have calmly detached themselves from the hurly-burly and are sitting, perhaps, by the banks of some stream into whose waters they are contentedly dangling lines never yet bitten by fish.

That Mr. Anderson's father was such a one Mr. Anderson revealed by the delightful picture which he drew in *A Story Teller's Story,* and that he is himself his father's son grown sophisticated and self-conscious his own novels confess. The old man who could always find some excuse to leave his family behind and wander about the country, fascinating the inhabitants of lonely farms by the resplendent and lying tales which he could so readily imagine, is the true begetter of the novelist Anderson, for he too, when he lets his fancy wander, can form the most delightful of day-dreams. But partly because he happens to have been born in an age but little inclined to yield to the charm of fancy, and partly because he has become too sophisticated naïvely to indulge the day-dreaming faculty, he holds himself in check and describes rather the deeds and the souls of those who, like himself, belong to that moonstruck class whose members find themselves temperamentally alien to the orderly and busy world in which they happen to have been born. The hero of *Dark Laughter* is such a one, and though he has a story—the story of how he escaped from the routine life into which he did not fit, how he wandered dreaming here and there in search of he knew not what, and how finally, with fitting irony, he stole the wife of a respectable though unexciting manufacturer while the latter was taking part in an Armistice Day parade—this story has actually neither beginning nor end, and the charm of the book lies in the author's evocation of the vagabond mood.

Anderson is not a deep thinker, and it is one of the absurd results of the conventional thought-pattern of our age that he is taken seriously as a critic of society; but he is, nevertheless, a poet who feels things deeply in his own particular way. His characters live chiefly by virtue of that part of them which is himself; certainly his two most vivid personages in the present book—the hero himself and that middle-aged fellow-workman of his who is accustomed from time to time to slip away for a night with his wife and a bottle of whisky, ostensibly to fish, but really to lie in the moonlight by the river and feel himself as free as an animal from the thoughts and responsibilities of man—are vivid because of the extent to which their mood is his own; and he is best of all when he is communicating to the reader by delicate exposition, by vivid picture, or in Whitmanesque prose-poems, that soft, vague reverie, too little definite to be called thought, which all have known in some moment of summer idleness but which is the natural mood of those who are born like himself to drift gently through life. In many a passage of *Dark Laughter,* especially in those which describe the life along the river, he has caught it with a nearly flawless art, and realizing that it is an attitude to be felt rather than a philosophy to be intellectually defended or understood, he has wisely refrained from argument and left it to be symbolized by that mellow, careless laughter with which the Negroes, the perfect vagabonds, greet the situations over which those of another race puzzle their heads and search their hearts. There are some who choose to breast a current, but there are others who find it sweeter to drift dreaming downstream.

SELF-CONSCIOUS AMERICA [1]

By Sinclair Lewis

I

Théophile Gautier in his red waistcoat, parading proudly as the child who waves a wooden sword and without mercy for grown-ups, pipes, "Notice me—notice me!" François Villon and d'Annunzio and, to descend many leagues, Frank Harris, each shouting that he is so very ba-a-ad, the baddest boy in the whole neighborhood. Lord Byron, weary with the self-imposed duties of making love and of liberating those Greeks whose suavity as waiters and integrity as fruit-vendors we all admire. Victor Hugo and Lord Tennyson, presiding without one hidden grin over courts of soapy admirers.

Always, everywhere, writers and painters and their kindred have been self-conscious—and by self-conscious I wish to denote an undue perception of one's own importance and interest. That self-consciousness is displayed in England today by the renowned dramatist who on all occasions gives final opinions, particularly on the purposes and customs of America and Soviet Russia, two countries which

[1] From *The American Mercury,* October, 1925.

he has not troubled to visit; it is displayed by the corpulent and agreeable essayist who has just pantingly discovered Roman Catholicism and the Jews. In the patience with which French men of letters acquire a name for peculiarity by making themselves enjoy the horrors of impressionism, tolerating the most distressing paintings on their walls, in the wistful courage with which certain German authors work away at trying to become perverted, in the earnestness with which authors of all lands, from China to Peru, maintain their superiority to ordinary idiots and thus bar themselves out from the delights of inconspicuousness and vulgarity—in all these phases of megalomania is betrayed a self-consciousness universal and dreary. But nowhere save in America would it occur to the most pompous author or painter or musician that he must be self-conscious as a civic duty.

With us, any proper artist knows that he must yield to the criticisms of all fishmongers and blotter salesmen and wives of non-conformist pastors as though he were a public official. He begs them to vote upon what literary themes, whiskers, income, and golf-trousers they may desire him to adopt. In Europe, save perhaps in Moscow, the most childish literary exhibitionist performs his little self-conscious tricks entirely to amuse himself and to irritate his wife. It does not enter his mind that the local Purity League or his unknown correspondents in the backwoods must be consulted as to which eccentricities he may choose; and what is more important, not the boldest Purity Leaguer nor the most itchingly epistolary customer in those cynical countries would assume that any artist is waiting to hear their demands.

In America alone does the fiction-writer or the sculptor or any one else have a duty—a Duty—of being naughty or austere, documentary or frivolous. One may not decently be a Prohibitionist or a booze-h'ister or both, a tennis fanatic or a loafer, a prosy fellow writing free verse or a frenzied poet writing radio advertisements because one happens to like it, but only because one is thus Doing Something Worth While. No conscientious American trolls out bawdy ditties because he relishes them, but always he does so for the purpose of cheering the bed-ridden victims of paresis in his neighborhood. He may not write a flippant chronicle of a village, a church, or the diabetic institution of matrimony because it interests him to write thus, but only because he is Revealing Conditions and Making People Stop and Think. He must never, if he be a composer, emit a blast of jazz for any less pious reason than the Creation of Native American Art. Whatever he does, he must be original, forceful, and defiant of criticism, and with these bold virtues he must combine a willingness to heed every warning from each of the 110,000,000 persons who by their residence in the United States are automatically constituted the equals not only of kings but of William Lyon Phelps.

(I had a letter once from a Chicago lawyer whom I have never met. Addressing me by my first name, he admonished, "I've considered your stuff pretty average rotten till now, and thought of taking the time off and telling you to quit till you learn to write, but this last story of yours is fairly good. Go ahead. Drop in and see me here at my office and we'll talk your junk over.")

But the amateur critic who spends Sunday afternoon in coaching his favorite writers has caused less lamentation and salt weeping among judicious persons than certain of the highbrows guaranteed by the *Dial,* the late *Freeman,* the *Little Review,* and the more esoteric pages of *Vanity Fair.* Out of 1,857 critics holding the Authors' League of America diploma certifying that they really like Picasso, that they have read most of Proust, and that they can tell Mouton Rothschild from Nuits St. George, there are not more than sixteen who consider a writer as a person doing something because he enjoys it or because he has been lured into it by the fashion, and doing it well or badly. The others dolorously analyze him as an employee of the Federal Department of Uplift, and consider whether he has Advanced American Culture, Been True to His Higher Vision or—most dread and lofty Duty of them all—Shown Himself Aware of the New Tendencies in French Literature.

II

Nowhere in America itself is this duty-ridden earnestness of the artist and his disciples so well shown as at that Brevoort and cathedral of American sophistication, the Café Dôme in Paris.

Among the other advantages of the Dôme, it is on a corner charmingly resembling Sixth Avenue at Eighth Street, and all the waiters understand Americanese, so that it is possible for the patrons to be highly expatriate without benefit of Berlitz. It is, in fact, the perfectly standardized place to which standardized rebels flee from the crushing standardization of America.

On view at the Dôme is the great though surprisingly young author who, by his description of vomiting and the progress of cancer, in a volume of sixty-seven pages issued in a limited edition of three hundred copies, has entirely transformed American fiction. There is the lady who has demolished Thomas Hardy, Arnold Bennett, and Goethe. And king of kings, Osimandias of Osimandiases, supremest of Yankee critics, *ex cathedrâ* authority on literature, painting, music, economics, and living without laboring, very father and seer of the Dôme, is that Young Intellectual who, if he ever finishes the assassinatory book of which we have heard these last three years, will tear the world up by the roots. He is going to deliver unto scorn all the false idols of the intelligentsia, particularly such false idols as have become tired of lending him—as the phrase is—money.

These geniuses are never offensive—well, not too offensive—that is, no worse than an American banker holding forth in Luigi's bar about the gas-mileage of his Packard, a German *Schieber* at San Remo with binoculars on his manly breast, or the small, neat Frenchman with gray silk gloves who in every railway compartment demands that you close the window. The geniuses do stride to their appointed tables with the quiet and amused modesty of the *maestro,* so like the forgiving smirk of a Christian Science lady, and for persons who have never heard of them and of their talented friends they are icily sorry, yet something must be said for them. Almost all the authors have written two or three devastating stories for the magazines which are printed on lovely, thick, creamy paper and which last, often, for five months, and one of them once bought a drink for a woman from his home town, and paid for it.

No, it is not the geniuses who invite homicide but their disciples, and for every genius at the Dôme there are seventeen disciples, mostly female. They are the amateur press-agents of the amateur arts. They are the military police of radicalism, the Sumners of obscenity, and the house-to-house canvassers of culture.

There is the widow of the Milwaukee coal magnate. When a simple layman—a stock-broker or doctor or writer for the magazines—is delivered into her voice, she attacks without a declaration of war. Really? He hasn't read Thaddeus Boniface's volume of symmetric verse, "Pi R Square"? He hasn't subscribed to *Complex: A Magazine of Sublimation?* He hasn't seen Savinien Skjalgsson dance? He hasn't even heard of Bill Benner's new school of Intimate Painting, with Bill's portrait of Advanced Cirrhosis as the Sistine Madonna of the movement? Then the man's a fool, and the coal magnate's relict feels a divine compulsion to tell him so.

There is the bobbed-haired Jewish girl who announces nightly that she is proud to be the lady-love of Stephen Kriechfisch, the symbolistic novelist, and that any one who has ever written an intelligible sentence is a worm. There is the young old man who wears a thumb ring and whose subtle pleasure it is to trap sightseers from Minneapolis into a confession that they rather like Minneapolis, golf, and Dickens. "Really, my dear, they were too pricelessly precious!" There is the skinny lady who has gone out for vice with the same relentless grimness with which her sister back home exploits virtue. She smokes cigarettes till her head aches, she has devoted seven laborious years to getting herself seduced, she hates brandy and becomes frigidly drunk on it nightly, and to any layman so bourgeois as to go home before two A. M. she remarks, "Yes, that's the sort of thing you *would* do."

I listened to this Salvation Army of compulsory sin. I first learned from them that it was imperative to adore—though not necessarily to read—Mr. James Joyce's *Ulysses*. Then the guiding geniuses and their disciples had a change of heart, whether because they tardily perceived that by printing all six of the unprintable Anglo-Saxon monosyllables Mr. Joyce had ruined their own chances to be shocking, or for the less metaphysical reason that the fellow had come to a measure of popularity and sales. Today, Joyce is more passé than James Russell Lowell. The disciples snap that here in the Dôme at this moment are at least seven fictionists who can excrete prose more turgid, more illegible, and generally more distinguished than his. To admire him is to be a provincial and even—most withering of condemnations at the Dôme—to be a person who does not live on the Left Bank but in the Philistine sunshine and air of the Champs-Élysées.

From the disciples I had a bacchic glint of the new beauty which was to be bootlegged into America and save it from radios and the *Saturday Evening Post*. As an Iowa newspaperman I had learned that a "penman"—so we yearningly called them there, in a literary society unbibulous but otherwise astoundingly like the Dôme—a penman must be patriotic, pure, and reverent toward the Hebrew God, but nasty toward the Hebrews. Now, at the Dôme, I acquired a whole new code of Duties:

(1): Literature must be absolutely untrammeled, uncensored, and unimitative.

(2): All literature must be imitative of (a) Joyce; (b) Gertrude Stein; (c) Ezra Pound; (d) André Gide; (e) Jean Cocteau; (f) Sherwood Anderson; (g) Waldo Frank; (h) Marcel Proust. You are permitted, by the ruling of the International Convention of 1925, to choose any one of these models or to mix all of them, but any writing which does not obviously proceed from these Eternal Prototypes is to be censored.

(3) : is the same as 2, except that the eight Prototypes are sharply condemned as old-fashioned, and their names are replaced by those of any eight acquaintances of the person intoning the code.

(4) : You must write about a thing called "the American Scene."

(5) : You must never, since all Americans are dubs, write about the American Scene, but only about the Left Bank of the Seine.

(6) : You must not write about any scene whatever, since that is Merely Pictorial. Your characters must wriggle through a void, to the sound of Wagnerian overtures played on tin whistles and jews'-harps.

(7) : The judges in this match shall be Ernest Boyd, Gilbert Seldes, Ezra Pound, Albert Nock, Paul Rosenfeld, Cuthbert Wright, Harold Stearns, and Djuna Barnes. No person shall be considered a competent writer unless this committee agree upon him, unanimously, and as that has never happened and by no miracle could happen, a great deal of liveliness is added to the sport of literary competition.

III

I had listened—I had learned—I had striven to keep myself from writing with cheerfulness; but came a night, as Mr. Wells is fond of saying, when a native cussedness stirred in me. I fell from grace, I left the Dôme, and as I wandered in such unsanctioned portions of Paris as the Rue Royale and the Grand Boulevards, I was sore-laden with a notion that the patronizing observations about other writers made by the geniuses at the Dôme weren't papal bulls, but merely damned impertinence on the part of young literary bounders. At that moment I craved the company of the most lowbrow magazine star who booms that he is a "real he-guy and not one of these knitting champions," who volunteers that he merely scribbles enough to make a living, in between his real duties as a man and a citizen—fishing, poker, addressing hard-boiled press clubs, teaching his seven sons to play golf, and mixing cocktails on the Italian terrace of his new $200,000 country residence—all the domestic delights whereby he proves that a Stout Fellow who has been properly trained in "the newspaper game" can produce literature and yet remain as sane and strong and pure as a Y.M.C.A. secretary or a prize-fighter.

I contemplated the valiance of these Stout Fellows as I sat melancholy and alone before a lemon soda at the Café Napolitain. I remembered one of them who used to warn me against reading the contemporary English writers because they were, by "taking all these dirty cracks at decency," contaminating an erstwhile innocent world; and who revealed to me that it was all bunk to say that this guy Conrad was a high-grade author, because he knew absolutely that Mary Roberts Rinehart and Irv Cobb and Pete Kyne got more per story than this Conrad bird ever heard of. Himself, he had a pretty foresight for market values, and while his rivals were blindly sticking to the Prizefight Story (how the Yale Junior defeats the world's champion, but only in the sixteenth round), he would perceive a public tend toward inner nobility, and switch overnight to the Domestic Story (how grandmother saves the flapper from gin).

I recalled a dinner of the more opulent literary gentlemen, ample and pleasant gentlemen whose names are forever on the magazine covers, and not one of whom, save myself, weighed less than two hundred and ten pounds or had a literary distinction of less than fifteen hundred dollars a story. I remembered their easy talk—free from all the precosities of the Dôme—about their motors, their investments, and their annual pilgrimages to Europe, consisting of a week of seeing the smuttier Parisian reviews and helping their daughters buy frocks, a motor trip along the Riviera, and a fortnight in such Italian hotels as were guaranteed free of all Wops, Frogs, Huns, Hunkies, and Yids. I remembered how their large blandness of world-survey, unprejudiced as the politics of a banker, untrammeled as the biology of a Baptist, gracious as a motorcycle cop, flowed over me and engulfed me and left me desirous of becoming a chiropractor and having done with it.

The diners referred with nausea to the "little

literary lice," whereby they indicated the very cross-word-puzzle geniuses of the Dôme who that night seemed too much with me, late and soon. But meditating thus over my root beer at the Napolitain, I perceived that these Stout Fellows, the major generals and heavyweights of story-manufacturing, best-sellers and saviors of morality and lovers of the perilous sport of watching baseball, were not less but considerably more self-conscious and egocentric than the children at the Dôme.

Certainly men and women who have done fine and distinguished things do appear at the Dôme and its allied colleges, on the Left Bank, in Chelsea, in Greenwich Village. All the chattering lads in those retreats, however competently they may lie to themselves about the actual amount of work they do, however superciliously they look down on Thackeray and Hawthorne, are yet authentically alive to a revolt against the Mark Twain-O. Henry-*Saturday Evening Post*-Hearst-Munsey tradition that, to avoid pedantry and effeminacy, a writer must have the oral vocabulary of a truck-driver and the inescapable joviality of a pool-room; and that however he may hate sitting in puddles, he must go fishing.

Even the scorn for all places outside the grubbier alleys of the Latin Quarter (or Greenwich Village) which one finds so irritating in these new self-conscious Bohemians is generally to be explained by a proud recent arrival from the silo belt, or by poverty. The lads who cannot afford sunshine and privacy make up for them on the principle of the fox who very properly jeered at the grapes he could not reach.

But of such self-defensive sneering one becomes as weary as one does of that incessant excuse for people with atrocious manners, that whelp of psychoanalysis, which the friends of bad-tempered geniuses produce daily: "You mustn't mind his rudeness—he's really awfully shy." Neither shyness nor poverty nor the ravages of disease need be paraded outside the home. Poverty is no more than riches an excuse for superciliousness. And to have to choose between literary baseball fans and the Boy Scouts of Dadaism is a hell of a choice . . . and one that is necessary only among that zealous and proselytizing folk, the Americans.

IV

In casting a leering eye upon the American theory that it is a Duty to be deliberately high- or low-brow, that it is a Duty to be or do anything in the matter of literature, the question is, naturally, not so simple as the elementary inquiry: "Is it permissible for an author to mix propaganda with fiction or poetry?" This controversy, like most critical discussions, is very ancient, always appearing as new and important to some delighted commentator, and in all ages equally meaningless. Is it permissible for a narrative to express its author's theories about the structure of the state or the criminality of Sunday theaters? Certainly. Is it permissible for an author to avoid, so far as he can, all propaganda? Certainly. Despite the existence of the American Academy of Arts and Letters, Mr. E. J. O'Brien, and the O. Henry Prize Committee, there is as yet no authority other than the author's own desires which shall decide what he may or may not write. Even economic duress does not dictate, for a brisk fellow can make his honest fifty thousand a year equally by doing naughty stories or by upholding virginity, so gratifyingly broad is the present scope of our more vacuous magazines.

As a matter of fact, Mr. Upton Sinclair, in *Mammonart,* has come near to proving that no one can write without propaganda, will it or no. He shows how ardently Conrad, usually instanced as the pure artist free of all controversy, does press-agentry against the vile walking delegates who would annoy ship-owners in their right to overload steamers and send unsafe hulks out into storms. He might have shown that Hergesheimer and Cabell are propagandists in their hatred of propaganda.

Mr. Sinclair himself is one of the worst of the evangelists; he insists that social justice is the one fit topic for any writer. He is unable to find anything save viciousness in the French minor poets, futility in much of Swinburne, and patent medicine in Coleridge; and with the zeal of a William Jennings Bryan he would lure away from them all the rare and solitary youngsters who in them have discovered a solace and exaltation incomprehensible to crusaders. He praises "The Psalm of Life" as excellent poetry because it is "an incitement toward diligence and sobriety," though for reasons unknown he fails to recommend the Methodist Hymnal on the same grounds. He does worship Shelley, but chiefly as a rebel, and "magic" in poetry he ridicules. A debate with such a man regarding poetry would be as sensible as an argument between a Paulist Father and a Christian Science healer.

Yet Mr. Sinclair is high-spirited, suggestive, original. He is wholesomely unafraid to tear down the taboos about even Shakespeare; he is unabashed in the senile presence of the high priests. And as a psychological study the book is valuable in its indication of how twisted an intelligent person may be when he insists that people write (or swim or vote or make love or do anything else) in any one particular way.

Throughout, Mr. Sinclair assumes that if Shakespeare, Goethe, and the other Tories had seen the cause of the people, it would have made a difference in erecting a reasonable world. I wish he would ask the author of *The Jungle* whether that vivid book has made any lasting difference in hygiene or labor conditions in the Chicago stock yards; and ask the author of *Main Street* whether that diagnosis of village dullness has rendered conversation at the afternoon bridge-parties on Willow Avenue much more amusing. I suspect that the authors of both these books wrote them—whatever reasons they may have given to their earnest surface selves—

essentially because it tickled their sense of mischief to write thus, and that later, when they found their fulminations perfectly ineffective, they have gone on to other manners and themes with no vast grieving. I suspect that though they are probably both of them good enough Socialists, as is Bernard Shaw, to look with relish upon the immediate hanging of all insurance-hunting ship-owners, all sellers of bad meat, and all persons who make Main Street life a horror by droning "Hot 'nough for you t'day?" yet secretly they see that in the long run it is not the machinations of these tyrants but the mass of smug human stupidity which keeps the world uncivilized.

Despite the protestations of Mr. Sinclair that one must write tracts, despite the sniffs of critics to the effect that Mr. Sinclair has no license to write tracts, is there any sort of high literature or of low scribbling which it is really despicable to produce? May one exude the cryptic, elliptic, symbolistic-impressionistic-esoteric sort of fiction in which every word means something besides the one thing it can mean, in which by the omission of verbs and transitions it is guaranteed that no lowbrow trespasser will get beyond the first paragraph, and in which the brightest moments of the indistinguishable characters are concerned with neo-Freudianism or neo-salvarsan? Certainly. Why not—if the author enjoys it? There are enough handy men producing obvious Wild West stories, Riviera decamerons, and exposés of college presidents. But contrariwise, may one write pink romances? Certainly. Why not?

What critic yet born has enough divinity in him to dictate to melancholy married spinsters on side streets that they must, in decency, be bored by Dorothy Richardson instead of enjoying Berta Ruck?

Write shameless adventure—the roll of the sea, the shine of the jungle, and all the rest of that puerile stuff of escape, which neither corrects prison conditions nor illuminates the Œdipus complex? Write adventure? Why not? Homer and Cervantes, Vergil and Dean Swift and Mark Twain, Melville and Kipling and Stevenson wrote as gleefully and coarsely of blood-and-thunder as any Harlem hack; and whenever he will permit himself, Hardy slips from gloom into a melodrama as adventurous as the print-paper magazines. Hergesheimer's *Wild Oranges* is hectic adventure, and it is in no way inferior to the most spacious of his later novels. Nothing in Frank Norris is better than the latter, *i.e.,* the galloping adventurous portion of *McTeague;* nothing better in Wells, not even the soul of Mr. Polly, than *The Island of Dr. Moreau* and the swashbuckling quest for quap in *Tono-Bungay;* and so far as Jack London lives, it is for his sheer adventure and not for his sociology. Out of adventure and melodrama Joseph Conrad makes a new world of unassailable beauty. Yet now and then arises some lady sage who protests that vulgar adventure, or any other definite form of doing, is necessarily inferior art, and that the ticking of little gray souls in little gray rooms is the only noble matter of the novel.

May one write laborious accounts of provincial customs? Why not? The pained esthetes who would abolish them, who would license only the delicate quiver of obvious beauty-hunting, have also to abolish Balzac, Zola, Fielding, Bennett, Wells. On the other hand, may one descend so muddily as to turn out detective stories? Why not? It is unproven that the dialectic of this metaphysical art of plot-guessing is inferior to laboratory research, or the picking out of themes in music, and certainly it has satisfied many curious persons who otherwise might have sickened themselves with theology. It is doubtful whether any character in the last hundred years of fiction, even Pickwick or Mulvaney or Anna Karenina, is more living than Sherlock Holmes.

Solemnly to counsel authors that they may write as they wish seems as puerile and platitudinous and absurd as to quote "Honesty is the best policy." Anywhere in Europe it *would* be absurd. But in a country where every one, from the newest reporter on the Kalamazoo newspapers to the most venerable professors at Harvard, from the Oklahoma clergy to the more scholarly movie actors, is replete with holy alarms for all contemporary authors, there is no gospel more novel—or more repulsive—to Americans, the most self-conscious and exaggerated people in the world.

V

The general opinion here is that Jews, Italians, and Frenchmen are neurotic, full of hysterical excesses, becoming either Bolsheviks or flinty aristocrats, degenerates or ape-like peasants; while Americans, Englishmen, and most Germans and Scotsmen, are in general judicious and unprejudiced, flushed with common-sense, and despising the manners of dancing-masters. The opposite is the case. Americans are the most self-conscious, the most neurotic, the most esthetic, the most stubbornly unesthetic, and incomparably the most interesting tribe living, and next to them come the Britishers and Germans.

Our self-consciousness proceeds from the most important of all American traits: the tendency to exaggeration in every department of thought and conduct, which in turn comes partly from our hothouse growth, our lack of slowly matured traditions, partly from our hybrid and contradictory stocks, and partly from the sentimentality which afflicts all Northern peoples as weather drives them from the reality of out-doors to the brooding unrealities of the hearth and candle-light.

This winter-bound sentimentality governs the English, the Scotch, the Germans, the Scandinavians, the Russians, nor are any of them so aged and traditional as they first seem to a tourist American who has never beheld a building erected before 1820. The Englishman considers himself instructed by immemorial tradition, but Rome was hoary and the Riviera had been the battleground of articulate clans for forty thousand years when London was still a litter of reed huts, and Oxfordshire a wolf-haunted wild. No, it is a newish race, the British, and hectic by comparison with the cynical French, the mature and compromising Italians.

The difference is seen in a comparison of French and English poetry. The theory of Cook trippers and of English pro-consuls is that the French are hysterical little people, clever but unsound, given to gesticulations, silly food, and the practice of weeping on all occasions, whereas Englishmen are hard, practical, beefy fellows who would rather die than be caught expressing emotion. But French poetry and fiction, the real expressions of the national soul, are, except for Victor Hugo and a few females and one or two novelists popular among the wives of respectable tradesmen, as heartless and practical and deft as a diamond glass-cutter, while English literature, especially the greatest, is dripping with sobs and Utopianism.

The British are just as likely to produce a Shelley, a Keats, a Byron, a Coleridge, an Aubrey Beardsley, an Ernest Dowson, a Dickens, a Wyndham Lewis (the *Blast* man), a right believer in the angels of Mons, a Jack Jones shrieking in the House of Commons, an exhorter praying by the hour in a moldy chapel of the Peculiar People, a Kipling bawling that all Hindu Nationalists are fiends, a suffragist burning mail with acid, a Lord Banbury justifying them by his sneers at suffrage, or any other passionate and slightly hysterical type, as to produce the stolid red-faced squire of their ideal. If once in Mrs. Humphry Ward they admired the mirroring of their own honest whiskers and square-toed boots and square-headed statesmanship, today the young generation flocks to Margaret Kennedy, Rebecca West, May Sinclair, and E. M. Forster, four authentically brilliant novelists who, writing with the gay delicacy which is so British and is supposed to be so French, stuff all the squires and Anglo-Indian colonels and solid bishops into the waste-basket, and reveal a world of young Britishers as eager and unstable as the dancers of Henri Murger.

Exaggerative, these British, yet withal it is in but a few realms—their belief in the sanctity of games for their own sake, the universal opinion that all persons save stay-at-home Britishers are colonials, and their reverence for the most distant sprig of the royal family. In politics the British are exaggerative enough. The county family piously believes that all labor-union officials are in the pay of Red Russia and should be hanged at once. The Clydeside Socialist believes that the country can be preserved only by shooting the aristocracy, most of the Oxford professors, and all the journalists. But this exaggeration is not significant, because politics is paranoiac universally. The debates in the Chambre des Députés are of the madhouse; Bolsheviks and Mensheviks murder one another and join to murder the anarchists; Fascisti and Communisti express with machine guns and castor oil a certain lack of political blandness; and on election day in Berlin, 1925, the Hindenburgites and Marxites voted with clubs. Indeed, Britain is more decorous and balanced than other lands. Ramsay MacDonald, as labor prime minister, was able to spend a week-end with the King, to go to the garden-parties of dukes, without much anguish on the part of either the Conservatives or the Socialists. I have seen that most oligarchic peer, the late Marquess of Curzon, applaud the Labor air-minister, Lord Thomson, for the gallantry of his attack on Curzon's ally, the Duke of Sutherland.

In America, a Ramsay MacDonald would have been kicked out by the butler and assassinated by his own followers, had he appeared at a smart garden-party; and in any case he would never have secured office, but would have been ousted as illegally as was Victor Berger from the House of Representatives and the Socialist assemblymen from the pious legislature at Albany.

However dismaying their exaggerations about Americans, Hindus, and the importance of dressing for dinner, the British are painfully well balanced compared with us—all of us. There is nothing we do not overdo. To Europe we are still the dollar-chasers, and it is true that when a Yank finds it interesting to amass wealth, he pursues the dollar with all horns tootling, taking six-barred fences and water gates and tearing off his scarlet coat in the amorous fury of the hunt, while the French peasant merely pinches every centime and the English merchant regards every shilling in the till as his by sacred right. But if the American exaggerate in money-chasing, he flings the same money away with a passionate glee unknown elsewhere in history. He hurls ten millions at universities he has never seen; he wants to buy all the Rembrandts in Europe, and to feed the Letts, the Syrians, and all the secretaries of all the reform leagues in Washington, D. C.

The only human being more exaggerative than the American Prohibitionist, with his unshaken belief that hardy pots can be made to like strawberry ice-cream soda, was the old-time American drinking-man. He never was content with *Bierhallen* or placid sidewalk cafés. He had to stand up at the bar, shoot his whiskies straight, go home drunk and penniless, and justify the insanities of Prohibition. And thus when an American is lowbrow (and he may be a lumberjack or a chemist, an insurance clerk or a newspaper editor), he is monstrously lowbrow. He views any male person who plays the piano, reads Sir Thomas Browne, or speaks in an agreeable voice, as a sheer degenerate. The American highbrow regards any person who has a liking for chewing tobacco, fire-engines, or the long, delicious, drawling anecdotes of backwoods general-stores as a blatant moron. And this highbrow, this precious laddie speaking an English more Oxonian than Oxford, is not the product of a slow autumnal coloring by rot, but springs in one generation from the hardiest roughneck. The son of the morose, bacon-chawing Indian fighter is heard whinnying that he simply cannot endure these terrible Americans one encounters in Paris: only in Capri, in the more select villas, does he find delicate companionship and a serenity in which to contemplate the art he is too feeble to pursue.

The American Tory is so complete and humorless that merely to speak of the I. W. W. or of Debs is to become suspect by him and his satinwood-paneled wife. Side by side with his intransigence is American democracy, that faith whereby any waiter, elevator runner, trolley conductor, clothing salesman, or taxi chauffeur who likes his job or who enjoys being courteous to his patrons, is suspect as a coward, a weakling, and a traitor to that free-born American independence which is particularly to be noted in recently arrived Greeks, Sicilians, and Finns. These innocent and unprejudiced arrivals see with a glad new light that independence is not, as they had thought, self-respect, but rudeness, and the lesson in Americanization they learn with alacrity.

Exaggerative American youth—it feels itself persecuted if the family fail to have a radio, a closed car, and the movies four times a week. The American motorist—if his car has a potential speed of less than seventy miles an hour, he is ashamed and miserable, though in no state of liquor would he dare to drive more than fifty. The American poker-fanatic—to him a game which ends before five in the morning, before the players are sick with nicotine and alcohol and the boredom of shuffling and dealing, is a pastime fit only for missionary societies.

And American philosophy—not since the orgies of Savonarola have the gods witnessed so obscene a spectacle as a country seriously accepting and discussing Frank Crane, the Fundamentalists, John Roach Straton, Dr. Albert Abrams, osteopathy, Bernarr MacFadden, *Abie's Irish Rose,* Shriners' conventions, Mayor Hylan, and the advertisements in the *World Almanac* of mail-order home-training courses whereby, without deserting the soda-fountain, young men may become finger-print experts, dancers, mail-carriers, orators, railway-station superintendents, violinists, evangelists, authors, aviators, and managers of tea-rooms.

VI

One of the most instructive examples of the American ethic is the solemnity with which the populace consider whether or not their loyal countrymen, especially writers and painters, may stay abroad.

Recently the Paris editions of both the *New York Herald* and the *Chicago Tribune* have maintained earnest symposia on the reasons why so many American writers live in France for considerable periods. In Paris or at the dock in New York the first question of the reporters, unless they are wise ship-news men who have learned that liners are not ships but ferries, is "Should writers go abroad? Do you feel that you understand America better that way?"

I had supposed that any one—even a writer, with his burden of moral duties toward his congregation—went to Paris because he liked to; because the wine is cheap, the girls pretty, the crêpe Suzette exalted, the Place de la Concorde beautiful, and the theater so bad that one can, without the inconvenience of remaining in New York, still acquire vanity in being a New Yorker. But such reasons are frivolous. One goes to Paris, one has a Duty in going to Paris, because there one receives inspiration and stimulation at the tombs of the great, before the Mona Lisa, amid the collections of lace, and in the high-soaring conversations at studios belonging to music students from Nashville. One acquires Culture and a Broad View through meeting the French poets and historians whom one never meets. One adds piquancy to one's literary manner by learning the names of seven French wines, the appellation Boul' Mich', and such jaunty phrases as "nom d'une pipe," a phrase used as frequently in Paris as is "begorra" in Dublin. Whatever spiritual replenishment one gains, one unquestionably Gets a Better Perspective on America, and year by year in damp corners of cafés one sits talking of that Better Perspective which one acquired while forgetting what America is like. I know an American novelist who has been Getting that Better Perspective for sixteen years, and who has so much Perspective now that the American characters in his book are as accurate and well-rounded and bucolic and nasal and generally profound as the American characters of *Punch* or Mr. Michael Arlen.

The opposing school holds as firmly that the American writer has a Duty *not* to remain in Paris. They permit the refreshment of six weeks in Europe every two years, providing that the only purpose of such a sojourn shall be a perception of how much better and sweeter and less expensive America is than these dying and neurotic countries. This grim school, no more than the Perspectivers, allows the belief that any decent Yankee may visit Europe merely to save money, get a drink, and admire Gothic doorways, and it insists that after the six weeks the literary explorer, laden with Dunhill pipes and little leather boxes from Florence and Tauchnitz editions of the more antiquated American novels, shall return to the Greenwich Village flat from which he or she so intensively studies Alaskan folklore and the agrarian movement in Montana. Not only do our writers themselves thus moralize about being abroad, but any clubwoman from Fort Worth, any professor in a one-building university, has a right—indeed a Duty—to instruct them; and the daring leaders of thought listen reverently.

No part of the Continent and Britain is free from smugness about itself. Oslo and the Oslonians believe as prayerfully as Chicago that any reason for staying in, or staying away from, Oslo is somehow a compliment to Oslo; and Tokio and Antofagasta and Wiggan as well as Los Angeles esteem themselves each the center of the universe and the wellspring of all the arts. The Englishman believes that his street of damp brick villas is the flowering of civilization; and to all right-thinking persons India is not a land which has more or less to do with the Hindus but chiefly an interesting background against which Englishmen may display anew the changeless virtues of Tootlebury.

Yet always, since the days when scholars went inevitably to study at Padua or Pisa, the British writer has gone abroad without thinking it necessary to excuse himself. Browning, Shelley, Borrow, or, today, Bennett, Maugham, Walpole—such men have always wandered; and for any pressman to demand their reasons would have been considered by everybody, including the uncomfortable pressman, as impertinence. It is nearly inconceivable, even with the present rapid Americanization of the British press, that a London daily should hold a debate on "Is it wholesome for British writers to live in Italy?" It is impossible that the standard sister of the standard Dorset vicar should on the high moment of meeting her favorite author, say Hichens or Locke or Oppenheim, inform him that his Duty toward her was to spend less time in Cannes.

Such magnificence of self-consciousness and duty-mongering and hysterical bounding to extremes may in all its richness be found only in our sturdy land. To the question beloved of all Sunday newspapers and teachers' associations, "What is the Matter with America and How Shall We Do Something About It?" there is one final answer: There are too many people who ask "What is the Matter with America?" and then dash out and try to Do Something About It.

And there are idiots who will consider this philosophical inquiry an attack on our fair land! Actually, to say that we are the most neurotic, most self-conscious folk in the world is to say that our provincial days of sockless statesmen, merchant princes pompous in broadcloth, and oratorical second-rate lawyers are over; that we are feverish with the pursuit of every wisdom and every agreeable silliness; and that overnight, without even ourselves perceiving it, we are changing from the world's dusty wheatfield to the world's hectic but incomparably fascinating capital.

SANTAYANA, THE POET[1]

By Archibald MacLeish

George santayana, the poet, disappeared from the world of polite letters a great many years ago, leaving as the principal reminder of his existence a thin volume of sonnets. It was not understood at the time that his disappearance was to be permanent and the usual appreciations were omitted. There is a certain danger in appreciating poets who may return to outsell the appraiser. But the passage of time and certain intimations from what the *Times* would call "reliable sources" make the matter reasonably clear. Santayana is not to reappear. And it is a fair inference from the evidence that he was never expected to reappear; that his heir and executor, the philosopher, had dealt with him privily but effectively and acquired a very certain hold upon the inheritance. Not banishment from the Republic as became a poet, but death and determination were adjudged upon him. "Youth and aspiration," wrote the philosopher, "indulge in poetry; a mature and masterful mind will often despise it and prefer to express itself laconically in prose." And so that drug where-

[1] From *The Bookman,* October, 1925.

with philosophers have a poisonous familiarity was administered, and the poet dreamed the forbidden dream and died.

It would be interesting to consider the motives of the deed in all their considerations of reason and intent. But failing an actual knowledge of the facts, presumptions are a necessity, and the fairest of presumptions puts the crime upon a generous ground, a basis of principle. George Santayana was removed because he was not a proper poet within the meaning of the philosophies. He had not, it would appear, grasped the poetic function. He did not understand that it was his, retaining an "innocence of the eye" to "repair to the material of experience, seizing hold of the reality of sensation and fancy beneath the surface of conventional ideas," quarrying from the sensuous world pictures and emotions wherewith the philosopher should construct the temple of divinity. On the contrary, he desired not only to hew stone but to build towers. He was no poet royal to the philosophical household, but his own king and philosopher. He did not propose to serve the religious sense by gesturing in inarticulate images toward the Almighty, but rather to find God out in his dark and difficult universe and close with his divinity. And if he had eyes, they were not the eyes of innocence. He saw nature with no embarrassed and Wordsworthian surprise, but mirrored at two or three reflections from herself in the unbreathed metal of his mind. He was not to be startled by daffodils but

To the fair reason of the Spring inclined
And to the Summer's tender argument.

And when he did capture in immediate words the taste and smell and feel of the natural world it was never for remembrance' sake, but to throw open windows of sense upon the brain's far faint discoveries—

Out of the dust the queen of roses springs;
The brackish depths of the blown water bear
Blossoms of foam: the common mist and air
Weave Vesper's holy, pity-laden wings.

We may say that if this is not within the philosopher's conception of poetry, then the worse for philosophy. But we may not doubt that within the *Interpretations of Poetry and Religion* George Santayana was an altogether improper poet.

There are, however, various conceptions of the poetic method and the poetic function. There have been philosophies in rhyme since the *De Rerum,* and there had been poems of religious experience before the *Sonnets* of Santayana. And it is not the least of Santayana's triumphs that he was later justified out of the mouth of his traducer in the *Three Philosophical Poets.* Of the imagined most high poet the philosopher says: "He should live in the continual presence of all experience and respect it; he should at the same time understand nature, the ground of that experience; and he should also have a delicate sense for the ideal echoes of his own passions, and for all the colors of his possible happiness." And it is given him for task "to reconstitute the shattered picture of the world." He is permitted the kingdom of the brain at last and every avenue of realization is thrown open to him.

George Santayana was very clearly not the most high poet, nor was he within measurable reach of such greatness. But the air he inhabited was the air the expected genius must climb and his defects were the defects of supreme qualities. He stood upon experience, but his experience was esthetic altogether. He painted the colors of a possible happiness, but indirectly and in fitful relief against a dark and brooding present. He relimned fragments and glimpses of the shattered picture of the world, but it was a world in which he lived alone. There is nothing universal, nothing drawn from common experience, in his verse. He stands altogether aside from that great tradition of English poetry which has laid hold upon earth and the flavor and saltiness of earth, imaging man as a figure in the pageant of the world who may rebel against the blind mischance of life but who will never challenge its reality nor deny his blood kinship to beasts and trees and all things that die upon the grass. Santayana is too perfect an artist to reach perfection in poetry. His sense is too delicate to give him apprehension of the deep tones and slow vibrations of the seasonal earth; it is only the overtone of human passion that he hears, and faintly and silverly and far away.

And yet the joy of his verse is not so much its

delicacy as its brilliance and the temper of its strength. His manner is the manner of swordsmanship, and the blade, though daintily raised, bites in. He is an exquisite in thrust and parry and a master of the subtle feints of fence, but there is more than swordplay in his skill. There is sometimes a desperate courage in the stab of a phrase, as though he drove against a shadowy antagonist always at point to strike and overwhelm. Against the mockery of nothingness he turns the deftness of that line which has for hope

> To trust the soul's invincible surmise—

and against an inexplicable fate the words:

> So in this great disaster of our birth
> We can be happy and forget our doom.

It is disaster that is sure and hope that is adventurous.

> Wait for the Spring, brave heart, there is no knowing.

And man's victory over earth is at once the realization and the destruction of the brain's hope for an eternal victory:

> Sing softly, choristers; ye sing
>   Not faith alone, but doubt and dread.
> Ring wildly, Easter bells; ye ring
>   For Christ arisen, and hope dead.

But for all its intensity the poetry of George Santayana never fails of a fine restraint and an unobtrusive mastery of form. His glimpses of reality are labored into closely articulated epigrams, and his phrases of wonder or of doubt or grief are inevitable unities, perfect to the uses of his will. His use of rhyme and rhythm is beyond praise. Under his hand the reiterated iambic insistence of the line is so softened that the stubborn sonnet becomes at once flexible and a thing of change. And even the rigors of the strict Italian form never drive him to forced, or flat, or uncertain rhymes. Whatever may be the relative merits of prose or verse as a vehicle for the philosophies, this much is sure—Santayana's was an art in poetry that should not have heaped the sacrifice to any god.

THE AMERICAN BACKGROUND[1]

By Edgar Lee Masters

To show that artists have lived in America, and that they live here now, disposes of the question in its categorical form. Poe lived in New York when it had a population of about 200,000 people, and when the literary market was about what it is in Omaha today, or worse; because modern communication brings Omaha within fifteen hours of New York, and so puts it not greatly farther from the magazine counters than Fordham was in 1840. Whitman lived in America contemporaneously with Poe, and many years after Poe's death; and he managed to sing his songs in spite of hostile publishers who aggravated the poverty which more or less crippled him, and in spite of the onslaughts of the reigning New England school, chiefly Lowell—James Russell, I mean. Emerson lived in America and fared famously while using rebellion against Puritanism and orthodoxy as his material. His nature took to plain living and high thinking, and that is a course well adapted to the generally frugal circumstances of the artist's life. Longfellow lived in America and wrote of America, not deeply, but by name and place and token. Haw-

[1] From *The Nation,* August 26, 1925.

thorne lived in America and wrote of the part of America where he was born and where he grew to maturity. So the list might be amplified with the names of Cooper, Mark Twain, and many others; and artists are living in America today who have done their work in America and of America, and who will do as good or better things in days to come. We have had musicians like MacDowell, and sculptors like Saint-Gaudens, who lived and wrought in this land of corn and beef.

Is it asked, then, whether the names of these men are as great as certain names of England? Granting that these men accomplished their course here, might they not have done so better in England, France, Germany, or Italy? Is it not true that some of these countries, by virtue of their more settled life, their greater respect for the artist and his work, and their greater exemption from noise and strife and materialism, are better places to work? To answer these questions requires the careful consideration of many things. But merely by way of suggestion, it may be said that if an artist is American to the core, and sticks to the thing he knows and learned with the milk that nourished him, he will lose himself or his material or both in a foreign environment; and next, which is part of the same matter, he will be deprived there of the native irritants which make him not English or French but American. When I hear American novels and poetry compared to English novels and poetry and disparaged in the comparison, as if there were one standard and we had to conform to it or fall below grade, I am inclined to lose patience. We can be receptive to whatever comes from abroad, and at the same time stand by our own. An audience which keeps its face turned eastward may to some extent influence American writers to look eastward too, and it is perhaps remarkable that the American author has not taken his cue from foreign countries more than he has. I should like to see the game reversed a little. For example, it remains for some American dramatist to put Cromwell in a play and in doing so to twist the history, sentimentalize the material, and capture London. I mention these things because the life of the American artist is conditioned by a multitude of factors like this, which bear upon his creative life fully as much as the general problem of financing himself—of which they are, indeed, a part—and fully as much as the turbulence and materialism of the country.

The handicaps upon creative life in America are the sources of our peculiar note, of our individuality, and of our success. This country is our fate, and we cannot escape it. For myself, I think it probable that America will yet produce one of the most powerful and distinctive literatures of the world; I share the enthusiasm of Walt Whitman upon this subject and have done so since I began to think and write. When that great apostle of the American epic shout passed from the world, I wrote and published an ode which reflected this very conviction; and I retain it still, in spite of the fact that I see many ways in which our civilization may succumb to the despotism of lard. If we can better our work only by getting away from what we know and are, I see no possibilities of originality or greatness. Just as soon as the Greeks wandered to Alexandria and Italy, and there planted their Athenian culture and began to write, they passed into pale imitations of Plato and into the lesser strains of poetry. An exodus with us might have a better fate, leading to something unique in the combination of Americanism with more cultured growths; but it would not be American. I repeat: for good or evil we are fixed in this place and in this time, and we must make the best of it.

At the time that the *Spoon River Anthology* was published, and up to the time that I published *Domesday Book,* I was maintaining a law office in Chicago, in the district called the Loop, amid sounds and sights and smoky air which to visitors seemed horrible but which to me did not seem so. On the contrary, I was habitually thrilled by the psychical cyclone of that place, constantly teased to record in verse the stories of the men who had built the city, the careers of the colorful and unique characters who furnished material day by day for the newspaper paragraphers. I wrote the *Spoon River Anthology* in my law office on slack Saturday afternoons, between telephone calls and the interruptions of calling clients. And when I came to the composition of *Domesday Book* I rented a small room in a tower overlooking the waterfront and

Michigan Avenue, from which I could see the boats and the gulls and hear the whir of the thousands passing on the pavement a hundred feet below me; and these surroundings stirred my thinking and imagining. They were my background and my material, and my irritants, and so my creative life. I was often asked by visitors from the East, from England and elsewhere, how I could work in such a city of noise, confusion, hate, strife, quarrels, violence; and I habitually answered that I thrived upon all this. I was falsely quoted and requoted as having said that I hated Chicago; I never said it. I did hate these things at times, when they wearied me—as whom would they not? But at the same time I said that they stirred me into expression. Well, surely not the expression of the "Ode to the Skylark," or of the "Grecian Urn"—but what of it? Here is the point: it is in no sense necessary that we shall write what has been written before, or express new phases of the conditions out of which the work of Shelley and Keats came. It is only important that we shall portray in our own way what is our own, and to do this the American writer can live here and must live here.

There are parts of America in the great cities, as well as in the illiterate belts, that are repressive and dull to the last degree. The Baptists, the anti-evolutionists, the Protestant reformers and revivalists, the prohibitionists, in so far as they are articulate, which is far enough, make America peculiarly ridiculous and intolerable. And I can sympathize with any creative mind which does not want to live among them; but at the same time it is possible for a writer to arise among them and celebrate them in sarcastic song, for the delight of the world and for his own immortality. In thinking of other times and other places it is well to rid oneself of the hallucinations incident to the disease called nextplaceitis, and really to visualize the conditions under which such men, for example, as Burns and Voltaire lived. One reads the life of Burns with uncomprehending mind who does not fully realize the tortures and difficulties with which he was beset in that Presbyterian community—a poet to be sure, but so much the worse for him, since he was an unsuccessful farmer and a man too fond of Sowter Johnnie and the wine cup. And the greatness of Voltaire consisted as much in the humor with which he could escape arrest by placing his house between the boundaries of France and Switzerland, so that he could dodge out of the back door into Switzerland or out of the front door into France, as it did in the genius with which he pickled in saltpeter the prohibitionists and the clergymen of his day. Of course, this was not the calm art of Goethe; but Voltaire was working out his own material; and being a man of courage and originality, he could do nothing else. Even so with us, whatever be the place or the task.

There are all sorts of ways of remaining an American and drawing upon its material and at the same time avoiding the vitiated and pernicious air of its worst quarters. There are country places and retreats in the great cities like Chicago, New York, and San Francisco; better still, there are the growing centers of this immense land where, because of the youth of the people and the freshness of the environment, there is that love of liberty which so much conduces to the creative life. I recently returned from a long tour of the country for the purpose, in the main, of getting it into my vision and understanding; and the experience renewed that enthusiasm of my first days with Walt Whitman, and of the ode to which I have referred, for this country's possibilities in every realm of art. In Texas, for example, I seemed in the presence of so much vitality, so much interest in beauty and truth, that I could understand better than ever the present sterility of New England—as if it had expressed itself and then become as out of date as its soil. What may not come out of a State with a background as old as that of New England itself, close to the constantly discovered records and myths of the ancient Aztecs and the Mayas; and on her own soil looking back to Mexico, then to Houston, Crockett, and Bowie, then to the days of the Confederacy, and finally to a present wherein her cities are bursting with life and rioting in prosperity? Who that wants to write would go away from Texas in order to live beautifully and write beautiful things in southern France or in London? And one passes from this State to the desert, the mous -gray mountains, and the level valleys between; t the desert cities where the old gambling hall has given way to the observatory and the bandit retreat in the mountains to the biological laboratory; where all sorts of dreamers and scientists and scholars live under a crystal sky and feel not that there is nothing to write about.

So with California, with San Francisco chiefly, that city whose houses seem like doves perched on cliffs above the gold and purple of the ocean. Who will join hands with George Sterling to sing that city, which is not Rome, and needs no Horace, but which has beauty not beneath Rome and a story colorful enough for any hand! In 1847 all this land was waste, it was desert; and Webster, who impressed himself so mightily upon his time, and had so much to do with the political creed of Lincoln, saw the whole territory west of Missouri as a worthless desert—did all he could to prevent our acquiring it. When the Mormons were trekking across the West in search of a haven beyond the jurisdiction of the United States, the war with Mexico came on; and the Mormons were pressed into service in that war, thereby winning for the United States the very land to which the Mormons were marching in order to get away from the government. When they arrived in Utah the American eagle, having preceded them, was perching on the peaks of the Wasatchs. But they stayed and built Salt Lake City, and made the valley of the lake a vast expanse of wheat and grass, of flowers and fruit. Coming out of New England —for there both Joseph Smith and Brigham Young were born—how was it that they built a theater at once, laid at once the cornerstone of the present temple, and began to cultivate music and dancing so that today the city is excelled by none in America for intelligence and the love of art. For myself, if I were cribbed and confined in some village of Tennessee, I should go to Salt Lake City rather than to Sussex or Normandy.

Manifestly there is more in America to write about than any one has touched upon. Is there opportunity to write it? Is there the native gift to write it? Is there the right critical atmosphere? Whatever undermines a writer's vitality cripples his work. And of crippling things poverty is the worst. The spiritual effect of poverty is disastrous, though to a point it may stimulate. Beyond that it brings discouragement, with a lowered self-confidence and self-esteem. I believe that much good talent is snuffed out by the economic struggle; but I am not sure that it is more so here than in other countries, either now or in times past. It is perhaps true that since the scale of living is not so high in other countries as it is here, and the earnings of writers therefore higher, poverty here does bear harder upon artists than it does elsewhere. In any case, I plead for an adjustment of these conditions. I should like to see rich people turn from hospitals and churches, from the sick and from the mendicant, to the well and the strong—the builders of America—and give them a lift. And I should like to see good work become as profitable as sensational work is;

for our country is being civilized by those whose devotion and whose labors are not even respectably compensated—at least, not until after many years of sacrifice.

In order that artists may do their best work in America, I should like to see the critical tone deepened and heightened. It is nothing peculiar to America, nor to this day, that the gentle art of reviewing is complicated with every sort of commercial tangle, every sort of literary politics and propaganda. The strong man will survive against any sort of opposition, almost. But suppose that the constant and stupid dispraise of Dreiser, or before him of Whitman, had broken down that self-esteem and self-confidence which is the capital of any performer, whether he be a prize-fighter or a poet, and at the same time had deprived him of the means of life so that he could not physically bear the battle. Would America not have suffered one of the greatest possible losses? Justice and truth are a nation's divining wands, without which she can neither discover treasures nor keep them.

Poets and creative writers, whether they consciously mean to do so or not, are, in fact, engaged in the work of elevating the scale of feeling and acting, of increasing the sum of things which is called civilization. The satirist exposes absurdity and falsehood and attempts to shame them; the singer transmits the exalted moods which he has extracted from the world of society and nature about him in spite of the materialism with which they are burdened. The novelist portrays passion, ambition, cruelty, and hate as well as devotion, sacrifice, and love, in order that others may see what he has seen. All workers with pen or brush or chisel are logicians of the most delicate and exact methods, if they are really artists; beside them the reasoners in principles of law and statecraft and ethics are athletic logic-choppers.

Working in the midst of this scene called American, writers are bound to reflect what they see and feel, just as they are nourished by it, or irritated into expression on it, or pained by its spectacle. In a word, they are the products of the civilization from which they come; and even where they revolt from it they portray the thing which is rejected. One of the very best illustrations of this is Emerson; for in repudiating Puritanism he stated the obverse of that culture in terms of intellectual freedom from its restraints and superstitions.

Now, though I have said that an artist can live in America, I am compelled to record that I do not think highly of the civilization of America, or indeed of civilization anywhere in the world. Confining myself to America, I must say that it is difficult to define its moral standards when I consider its politics and its laws. Shouting the Declaration and the Constitution, we have committed grand larceny right and left in taking the Philippines and Porto Rico, in defining our attitude toward China, and in taxing without representation remote possessions in order to keep unharmed a thieving tariff. Our whole national life is one of falsehood, dishonesty, and hypocrisy. Monopolies control the means of life, and are specially armed by law to do so; and this bears doubly hard upon the thinkers whose minds are preoccupied with thinking for the race instead of getting something for themselves. Business is a form of larceny, and property is robbery. The railroads do practically what they choose; oil and coal and steel and sugar rule the domain—not thought, not beauty, not justice. We as a nation of merchants have made much of the common-law rule that the purchaser must beware what the seller sells—not that the seller must beware what he sells, and for what he sells it.

All this life of lying, swindling, and pretending is coupled with the loudest psalm-singing in the world, with the most bitter theological persecution in the world. The Rockefellers and their kind may fairly be said to be the rulers of the land—together with the beneficiaries of the commercial imperialism which they have created. And they are active in the trivial morality of prohibition and in the enforcement of laws made for them! They would not abolish the tariff or enforce the anti-trust act or enforce the amendments having to do with freedom of speech, the press, religion, and the equal protection of the laws. The churches, which feed upon the provender of the age, profit by the supremacies of the hour, showing by their daily activities that their motive is hate, not love; for they are in bitter quarrels with each other over such idiotic things as the form of baptism, and whether all are saved or only the elect; and whether there is a bodily or only a spiritual resurrection; and whether the Jewish reformer Jesus was born of a virgin or came into life as others have come. In a word, the churches today are what they were when Jesus denounced them, and told their elders and preachers that the harlots and publicans would enter the kingdom of heaven before they would. And this is our culture and our civilization. This is the culture against which the seers and the poets must make their fight, even while they live in its midst, and deny themselves, and find themselves hobbled and destroyed sometimes by its tyrannies. For the game of the church, the fundamentalists, the mercantile régime, is one of boycott; it is to starve out, to drive out, all who assail the existing order.

To test out this culture, this civilization, let us see how the community, the state, or the nation reacts to a given circumstance. Does it prefer to see a dominant figure kept up or brought down? Does it resent in the name of justice an injustice done to an individual, provided the career of that individual is a luscious sacrifice to the local theology? Will it drape its morality with the confiscated robes of a persecuted character? Will its products spurn the cliques and the factions that care nothing for the organic laws? Will it stand up courageously and truthfully for anything important and just? It will by exception, but not generally. And as to poetry, as to the product of the artist, what does it do? I have no complaint in my own case to make whatever, for my books of poems have been handsomely treated; but in spite of all this self-exalted talk by the 113,000,000 people of this land, how many care about poetry or care whether a poet lives or dies? On the average, a book of poems by a poet of established reputation will not sell 20,000 copies or 10,000 copies or 5,000 copies, but generally 1,500 copies or less. What is the matter? Where is this idealistic and spiritual nation? What is our civilization? Is it to be appraised in the light of the fact that the autobiography of a prize-fighter or a book of ephemeral short stories outsells a book of poems by a competent poet? Necessarily this must be the case. To lift the land from such a state is the work of the dreamers and the singers; when man is farther up the hill, this age will look in its spiritual life and reactions as the wooden plow and the hand flail look now to us.

THE LAST NEW ENGLANDER[1]

By H. L. MENCKEN

THE late Prof. Barrett Wendell, of Harvard, whose letters have been done into a stately volume by M. A. DeWolfe Howe, will probably go down into history as the last flower of the Puritan *Kultur*. Himself by no means a pure New Englander, for his surname was obviously Dutch, he yet had enough New England blood in him to feel himself wholly of that forlorn region, and he was accepted as a fit representative of it by all its tribal headmen. He was steeped in its tradition, and venerated its heroes. What came out of New England seemed to him to be virtuous and lovely, or, as he might have said, "gentlemanly"; what came out of the rest of the country was simply barbarous.

Nevertheless, Wendell was himself a walking proof that all he admired was passing in the shadows, for, try as he would, he could not squeeze himself into the old Puritan mold. Over and over again he would make an effort to do so, but always, as he struggled with the lid, a diabolical, iconoclastic mood would overcome him, and he would leap up and emit a ribald yell. Harvard, startled and un-

[1] From *The American Mercury* and *The Chicago Tribune.*

easy, never knew what to make of him. His principles were apparently impeccable; he was, in the current phrase, a consistent booster for the lost Golden Age, its glories and high deeds. And yet, whenever the answering cheer came back, he would make a mocking face and say something awful. The Cambridge campus is still warmed by those mockings. What saved him from downright infamy was the fact that, whenever they were actually in contempt of the Puritan *mores* and gnosiology, they were safely superficial—that is, they never questioned fundamentals. Wendell had a lot to say about the transient excesses and imbecilities of democracy, visible in his time, but nevertheless he believed in all the primary democratic fallacies, and even defended them eloquently. He was a tart critic of the whole educational process, and went to the length, in his own department of English, of denying it any value whatever; nevertheless, he remained a romantic Harvard man to the end of his days, and venerated *alma mater* with the best of them. He must have seen clearly that there was little sound and solid in New England culture, that the rest of the country had little need of it and would quickly surpass it; all the same, he clung to the superstition that the preposterous theologians of the early days constituted an intellectual aristocracy, and even wrote a book eulogizing the most absurd of them, Cotton Mather.

Wendell, in fact, was two men, separate and distinct, and they were often at war. One of these men was highly intelligent (though surely not very learned); the other was a romantic under the spell of a disintegrating tradition. The latter was the more charming, but often a prey to mere lyrical fancy. The picture of the American character that Wendell presented to gaping throngs in his Sorbonne lectures was a sort of fantastic chromo of the primeval New England character, seen through nine thicknesses of amber gelatine—in brief, a thing as bizarre as the accounts of the Revolution that used to be in school-books. "Fundamentally," he once said somewhere else, "we believe in fair play." It would be hard to imagine a more inaccurate saying. If any single quality, indeed, has marked off the Americano from all other civilized men since the start, it is his incapacity to purge combat of passion, his strong disinclination to allow any merit whatever to the other fellow—in brief, his bad sportsmanship. Our history is a history of minorities put down with clubs. Even the duel, during the few years it flourished in America, took on a ferocity unheard of elsewhere. Gentlemen, going out at daybreak, shot to kill. Aaron Burr was a thorough American; Hamilton was an Englishman. In other fields, Wendell indulged himself in similar sentimentalities. He reacted to the shock of the late war in the correct manner of a State Street banker. He succumbed to the Coolidge buncombe far back in 1920. Yet always the sharply intelligent Wendell hauled up and stayed the orthodox romantic. The tribute to him by Prof. Kuno Francke, quoted by Mr. Howe, is a tribute not only to a gentleman, but also to a man of sense. And even in the midst of his banal speculation whether Coolidge, after all, would not turn out to be "a Yankee Lincoln," he saw clearly the "small, hatchet-faced, colorless man, with a tight-shut, thin-lipped mouth"—in other words, the third-rate, small-town attorney, stuffed with copy-book platitudes and quite without imagination. He saw, too, the truth about Wilson, and stated it blisteringly in a letter to his friend R. W. Curtis.

Wendell's actual books, I believe, are now all dead, even his arbitrary and ignorant but highly amusing *Literary History of America*. His volume on Shakespeare, published in 1894, was admired by Sir Arthur Quiller-Couch and Mrs. Edith Wharton, but no one else seems to remember it. His novels and dramas are long forgotten. His *English Composition* was and is a school-book; he himself, in his old age, had doubts that it had accomplished even its pedagogic purpose. His political essays, once so salacious, now read like the heresies of the Jefferson era. What remains, then, of Prof. Barrett Wendell, A.B., LITT.D.? A great deal more, I believe, than a mere ghost. When, indeed, the roll of American literati is drawn up at last, and the high deeds of each are set down, it will be found that Wendell, too, did something, and that what he did was of considerable importance. In a few words, he helped to divert criticism from books to life itself—he was one of the first to see that mere literature is, after all, mere literature—that it cannot be understood without knowing something about the society which produced it. Even Poe, masterly critic that he was, overlooked this obvious and all-important fact. His discussion of books went on in a sort of vacuum. He had brilliant (and often sound) opinions about every technical problem imaginable, and about every question of taste, but only too often he overlooked the fact that his author was also a man, and that what the author wrote the man had first to think, feel, and endure. Wendell got rid of that narrow bookishness, still lingering in Lowell. He was primarily a critic, not of literary manners and postures, but of human existence under the Republic. There was no scholarly affectation about him, for all his superficial play-acting, his delight in impressing sophomores. He did not bury his nose in books; he went out and looked at the world, and what he saw there amused him immensely and filled him with ideas. In Mr. Howe's index the name of Longfellow appears but once, and that of Gilder but once, and that of Aldrich not at all, but that of Blaine is there six times, and after "Democracy" there are twenty-two entries.

It seems to me that this break with the old American tradition had its high uses, and has left its mark upon American letters. Criticism among us is vastly less cloistered than it once was. Even professors of the loftiest tone, if they would have themselves attended to, must descend from their ivory towers and show themselves at the sea-level. The aloof and austere spirit is now viewed with suspicion.

There are, I daresay, ancients who deplore the change. A natural regret, for it has made criticism vastly more difficult. But few deplore it, I believe, who know what literature really is—few, that is, who know the difference between mere intellectual prettiness and a body of living ideas.

As for Wendell's amazing contradictions and inconsistencies, his endless flounderings between orthodoxy and heresy, I believe that an adequate explanation of them is to be found in the compositions of Prof. Dr. Sigmund Freud, the Viennese necromancer. Freud, himself a Jew, discusses in one of his books the curious fact that jokes at the expense of the Jews are chiefly circulated by Jews themselves, and especially by the younger ones. Two Jewish drummers in a Pullman smoking-room fall into an exchange of such jocosities almost automatically. Why? Because, says Freud, they attain thereby to an escape from their Jewishness, which often irks them. It is not that they are ashamed of being Jews; it is that the Jewish practices of their elders are burdensome. They dare not revolt openly, for their sense of filial piety is strong, so they take it out by making jokes. By much the same psychological process, I believe, Wendell arrived at his curious mixture of contrarieties. Sentimentally and emotionally, he was moved powerfully by the New England tradition, and felt a strong impulse to defend it against the world. Intellectually, he saw clearly that it was in collapse around him—worse, that it had been full of defects and weaknesses even when, by his own doctrine, it had been strong. The result was his endless shuttling between worship and ribaldry. The last of the New Englanders, he clung pathetically to a faith which gradually succumbed to doubts. In his later years he thus stood upon a burning deck, whence all but him had fled.

Two things, for all his skepticism, he could never bring himself to admit formally, both obvious: first, that the so-called culture of Puritan New England was largely imaginary, that civilization was actually introduced into the region by anti-Puritans, and second, that when transcendentalism came in, the leadership of Puritanism passed from New England and went to the South and Middle West. To admit the truth of either proposition was psychically impossible to a man of his romantic feelings. Each, baldly stated, seemed to flout the local Holy Ghost. And yet both were true, and their proofs were visible at a glance. The first, I daresay, will never be granted formally, or even heard patiently, by any genuine New Englander. Only a short while ago Walter Prichard Eaton, a very able Puritan, was arguing eloquently that his blue-nosed ancestors were really lovers of beauty, nay, downright artists—and offering the charming old houses on Nantucket Island as exhibits. Unfortunate examples, alas, alas! The houses on Nantucket were not built until the Puritan theocracy was completely demoralized and impotent—until Boston had a theater, and was already two-thirds of the way to hell. And if they were actually built by Puritans at all, then it was by Puritans who had gone out into the wide, wide world and savored its dreadful and voluptuous marvels—Puritans who had come back from the eastern seas with gaudy silks in their sea-chests, and the perfume of strange gals upon their whiskers, and a new glitter in their eyes.

Orthodox history, at least as it appears in schoolbooks, assumes that the witch-burners and infant-damners had it all their own way in New England, even down to Revolutionary times. They actually met with sturdy opposition from the start. All of their seaports gradually filled up with sailors who were anything but pious Christian men, and even the back-country had its heretics, as the incessant wars upon them demonstrate. The fact that only Puritans could vote in the towns has deceived the historians; they mistake what was the law for what was really said and done. We have had proofs in our own time that that error is easy. Made by students of early New England, it leads to multiple absurdities. The fact is that the civilization that grew up in the region, such as it was, owed very little to the actual Puritans; it was mainly the product of anti-Puritans, either home-bred or imported. Even the school system, so celebrated in legend, owed whatever value was in it to what were currently regarded as criminals. The Puritans did not found their schools for the purpose of propagating what is now known as learning; they founded them simply as nurseries of orthodoxy. Beyond the barest rudiments, nothing of any worldly value was taught in them. The principal subject of study, first and last, was theology, and it was theology of the most grotesque and insane sort ever cherished by man. Genuine education began in New England only when the rising minority of anti-Puritans, eventually to become a majority, rose against this theology, and tried to put it down. The revolt was first felt at Harvard; it gradually converted a seminary for the training of Puritan pastors into a genuine educational institution. Harvard delivered New England, and made civilization possible there. All the men who adorned that civilization in the days of its glory—Emerson, Hawthorne, and all the rest of them—were essentially anti-Puritans.

Today, save in its remoter villages, New England is no more Puritan than, say, Maryland or Pennsylvania. There is scarcely a clergyman in the entire region who, if the Mathers could come back to life, would not be condemned by them instantly as a heretic, and even as an atheist. The dominant theology is mild, skeptical, and wholly lacking in passion. The evangelical spirit has completely disappeared. Save in a small minority of atavistic fanatics, there is a tolerance that is almost indistinguishable from indifference. Roman Catholicism and Christian Science are alike viewed amiably. The old heat is gone. Where it lingers in America is in far places—on the Methodist prairies of the Middle West, in the Baptist back-waters of the South. There, I believe, it still retains not a little of its old vitality.

There Puritanism survives, not merely as a system of theology, but also as a way of life. It colors every human activity. Kiwanis mouths it; it is powerful in politics; learning wears its tinge. To charge a Harvard professor of today with agnosticism would sound as banal as to charge him with playing the violoncello. But his colleague of Kansas, facing the same accusation, would go damp upon the forehead, and his colleague of Texas would leave town between days.

Wendell, a sentimentalist, tried to put these facts behind him, though he must have been well aware of them. There got into his work, in consequence, a sense of futility, even when he was discussing very real and important things. He opened paths that he was unable to traverse himself. Sturdier men, following him, were soon marching far ahead of him. He will live in the history of American criticism, but his own criticism is already dead.

OF CRITICS, AND HENS[1]

By W. B. Pressey

A CRITIC, who had lived all his life in the city, his profession, having been ordered by his where, of course, he had to live to practice physician to go to the country, went to his cousin's farm, fifteen miles from the railroad. His cousin, a very busy man, had no time for the talk the Critic wished since he was forbidden to write. "But," said the farmer, "it would be good for you to feed the poultry and gather the eggs." So the Critic took grain and went to the poultry yard.

In the poultry yard he came upon the most extraordinary hen, who, instead of retreating at his approach as the others had done, remained seated upon the ground, eyeing him insolently. The Critic, a little abashed, for he was unaccustomed to hens, said—for he had to talk, being a Critic—"Why don't *you* move?" To his astonishment the hen replied in the most polished accents, "I am creating, and must not be disturbed." "Ah," said the Critic, "I can understand that, though I am surprised to find such devotion to creation in a hen. But you may not know that I am a Critic, one who, while not himself creating, at least in the first instance, ex-

[1] From *The New Republic,* August 19, 1925.

plains and judges the creations of others. Upon such as I rests the responsibility of deciding which of these creations shall be preserved and which shall not, and of explaining why."

"Indeed," said the hen. "And may I ask how you can tell what should be preserved and what should not?" "I am glad," said the Critic, "to find some one, even if only a hen, to whom I may explain the principles of criticism. We Critics first set ourselves to comprehend what is the artist's intuition, that is, how he has obtained the material for his work and how he has given that material form. The form must fit the material perfectly, so that we may say of the work that it has style. If it has style, the beauty of the material may appear, but not otherwise." "You mention beauty," interrupted the hen. "Does beauty inhere in the material or in the style?" "In both," replied the Critic, "but especially in the style. Ugliness in subject may be redeemed by beauty in the manner of its representation."

"Would you say this has beauty?" asked the hen, rising and revealing a very white and handsome egg. "I see that you belong to the school of Brancusi," said the Critic, who was nothing if not modern. "You have produced a very interesting example of the ovoid tendency." "Has it style?" murmured the hen. "Distinctly," said the Critic. "In arrangement of both line and plane your work pleases. In color, though you lack contrast, you have succeeded by uniformity in establishing a mood which enables the mind to grasp more firmly the smoothness of your curves and the grace of your mass." "Thank you," said the hen. "But what was my intuition?" "It is obvious," the Critic replied, "that life presents itself to you demanding a shape, and that the shape in which you see life is ovate." "In other words," said the hen, "I make eggs because I see life in egg-shapes." "Precisely," said the Critic. "Do you really think I do?" asked the hen, eyeing the Critic sardonically. The Critic felt uncomfortable. He decided to be aggressive. After all, it was only a hen. "Of course you do."

"I am sorry," said the hen, "to find a human so wrong. You are carrying grain. I see life as grain and the struggle for grain. I see life as the rooster's love and his infidelity. I see life as the chance which gives me a beetle and leaves the guinea-fowl there only an ant. I see life as the destiny which drives me to making eggs. I do not see it as egg-shapes. For the shape of the egg is only the most convenient and economical form in which I may convey eggness, which is my way of expressing life. I can no more help it than you can help calling yourself I, if you are to call yourself at all. The lines and planes and mass of my egg do not matter; whether it has beauty does matter; but the fullness of its eggness determines whether it has beauty." "But eggness has nothing to do with art," said the Critic, desperately. "Then," replied the hen, "art has nothing to do with life. For life demands expression of its creatures, sometimes in eggness, sometimes in other ways. I understand you humans are addicted to other ways. But the way in which life demands expression is life to the artist, and if you criticize art you must criticize life, all the life included in the artist's expression of it. You have not tried to see the eggness of my egg; you have seen only the shell of my technique. As a matter of fact, the egg is a very bad egg." And she deftly broke it open with her beak.

"Now," said the hen, "is my egg beautiful or not?" But the Critic had gone.

THE FORTUNATE POETS[1]

By Agnes Repplier

Some years ago an English man of letters startled a Massachusetts audience by lecturing on "The Minor Poets of Australia." It was the presumption that minor implied a major which lent drollery to the title of the lecture; but in the speaker's able hands Australian verse resembled the "one class" steamers which carry tourists of moderate means across the Atlantic Ocean. There is much comfort on board these boats, and much content, because all passengers are on the same level; no first class luxury to dazzle, no third class squalor to annoy. All are second class alike, and the single standard saves them from the dissatisfaction which follows in the wake of comparison.

Now, I have for a long time past thought that the absence of great poets—an absence that has about it an ominous air of finality—is made less disconsolate by the amazing goodness of minor poets, of the rank and file of versifiers who show some measure of distinction, some fleeting moments of inspiration. We see scattered freely in newspapers and periodicals a mass of fugitive verse which is infinitely better than the fugitive verse of my girlhood. We

[1] From *The Yale Review,* January, 1926.

see also, and this is the most amazing aspect of the situation, a class of modest capitalists who buy this verse when it is reprinted in well-bound little volumes, and give it to their friends at Christmas time. Booksellers admit that such volumes pay their way; and Andrew Lang's sardonic suggestion that one method of growing rich is to abstain from publishing poetry has of late years lost its sting.

Those of us who are fancifully inclined have sometimes wondered what it must have been like to share the world with great poets, to waken in the morning and read a new-born poem, manifestly beautiful, and manifestly deathless in its beauty; just as now we waken in the morning and read that science has achieved a new and stupendous miracle in its endless task of collecting, preserving, and distributing the noises of the world. Should we have dilated with correct emotions, or should we have been "more than usual calm" in the face of our great good fortune? Well, on December the first, 1816, Leigh Hunt published in *The Examiner* Keats's flawless sonnet, "On First Looking into Chapman's Homer." Did English readers, who have always been faithful lovers of the sonnet, leap to recognition of this masterpiece? They did not. Even the customary readers of *The Examiner,* who were few enough, failed to note the new light on the horizon. In July, 1819, the architect, James Elmes, published in the *Annals of the Fine Arts* the "Ode to a Nightingale"; and, later, the "Ode on a Grecian Urn." Surely these manifestations of supreme beauty must have arrested instant attention, must have flashed their swift way into the heart and soul of England. Nobody gave any indication that this had happened. It is probable that "Casabianca," who made his triumphant appearance about the same time, was welcomed with more enthusiasm. When Wordsworth published his "Lines, Composed a few Miles above Tintern Abbey," the public, which is now so acutely, almost oppressively, aware of its perfection, never noticed it at all, never bought and never read the little book in which it made its diffident appearance.

The only tale of triumph I have to tell is one which the reader probably knows already. In 1845 Tennyson was thirty-six, and desperately poor, owing to the kind of insane investments which only a poet would dream of making. Monckton Milnes, afterwards Lord Houghton, asked Sir Robert Peel, then Prime Minister, to grant him a pension. Peel, after the immemorial fashion of Prime Ministers, replied that he had never heard of young Mr. Tennyson. Whereupon Milnes then and there read to him "Ulysses," that flawless and passionate appeal to the secret soul of man, bidding him forsake duty, and domesticity, and the much prized paths of peace, and fare forth into a perilous world. And Peel, who had lived all his life in the clutches of duty and domesticity, and who had just succeeded in materially lessening England's burden of taxation, was so moved by this glorious and disconcerting verse that he placed Tennyson on the civil list for two hundred pounds a year. For once the right man met the right poem with admirable results.

There are few such incidents to relate. It happens from time to time that a scrap of verse flung to the public awakens some chord in the public's unfathomable heart, and becomes famous overnight. Two instances that I can now recall are Kipling's "Recessional" and Mr. Edwin Markham's "Man with the Hoe." The splendid sweep and cadence of "The Recessional," no less than the sternness of its admonishment, compelled a hearing; while "The Man with the Hoe," that strange distortion of Millet's simple realism, preached the kind of a sermon which an uneasy world always delights in hearing. With two such examples of popularity before us, we can neither hope nor despair. We can never get beyond the maze of mystification in which the humors of the reading public entangle us.

A great impetus was given to the fugitive verse of England and the United States by the World War. It is an old and ever repeated axiom that the best war songs are written in times of peace, just as the best sea songs are written by insistent landsmen, and the best drinking songs by temperate poets. But we cannot class the war of 1914 with wars of the past. There was that about its ruthlessness and its splendor, its shame and its magnificence, which dragged men out of the rut of life, and fired them with strange ardors which they shall never feel again. They wrote with bursting hearts, and became for a little while greater than themselves. It was natural that Kipling, under the stress of strong emotion, should have recaptured his old incisive note:

> Who stands if freedom fall?
> Who dies if England live?

that Rupert Brooke, who was a poet, should have written his beautiful sonnets; that Alan Seeger, prophet and fighter, should have flamed into his unforgetable lines, "I Have a Rendezvous with Death"; that Vachel Lindsay should have expressed his sense of his country's deliverance in the last swinging verse of "Niagara." But by what miracle did Edith Wharton, past master of English prose and of cold irony, come to write the two faultless stanzas called "Belgium," stanzas of finished beauty and of noble understanding! How did it happen that an elderly, serene, peace-loving American gentleman like Mr. William Dean Howells should have been quickened into the praiseworthy rage which animates every line of "Passengers of a Retarded Submersible"? The very roughness of these verses, written after the sinking of the *Lusitania,* lends weight to their anger and their scorn; anger at a crime which surpassed all the crimes of our day, scorn of the callousness and apathy which accepted it as they might have accepted an earthquake or a tornado.

One other thing the war did for modern verse. It made it, for the time, intelligible. The despised versifiers of my youth were simple and explicit, plain sometimes to the verge of baldness. Their successors grew veiled and mystic, cloaking their meaning, if they had any, behind a confused medley of words. Now, only a great poet or a great prose writer can dare to be unintelligible. He must have something to give us which is worth searching for. Mr. Brownell says truly that Henry James's concern was to be precise, not to be clear. But Henry James was a great novelist. The precision he reached with infinite pains was a delicate precision, correct and distinguished. He never lost his own way in the mazes of his complex sentences, though we lose our way often. When the war came, he saw it with the terrible distinctness of the soldier in the trenches; and, like the soldier in the trenches, he died of the wounds it gave. There was that about this most devastating and glorious of all wars which defied confusion. Whether men sang of its devastations or of its glories, they sang with startling lucidity. It was no time for riddles.

Contemporary poetry, when readable, is a disturbing element in our lives because of its belligerence. This belligerence is twofold. It holds up to scorn the harmless versifiers of a past generation, and the weary old world of today. An anthology of *Poems of Revolt* has been recently published in England. *Poems of Complaint* would be as good a title. Poets are by way of thinking that their poetical predecessors and their contemporaneous legislators are equally worthy of reprobation.

They might be undeceived by a closer study of history and of letters; but the last thing any one of us seeks is enlightenment. The axiom "He snarls best who snarls first" sets people grubbing for grievances, which lie accommodatingly near the surface.

The clever group of Sitwells in England are good exemplifiers of poetic belligerence. They founded an asylum for fugitive English verse in an annual publication called *Wheels*. They have written some curious and very interesting poems, in which black lacquer seas, muslin clouds, and curdled sheepskin flowers divide our attention with the slow and lovely coming on of night, and dolphins

> Drunk with purple fumes
> Of wine-stained sunsets.

And they are the avowed opponents of all things that sin by popularity, such as humor, simplicity, and cricket. Yet Osbert Sitwell has founded a "Remember Bomba League," which shows that his mind moves in well-grooved channels; and Edith Sitwell, while justly reprobating the "Village Idiot School" of verse, permits herself to write of "chattering heat" and "purring greenery." It would be as close to nature and to realism to say barking rain and mewing mountains. As for cricket, it is something else besides a synonym for good form. It is sport, and a taste for sport may or may not be part of a poet's outfit. Shakespeare probably liked to play at bowls; Milton probably did not. Both wrote poetry, and it will be admitted that both wrote it well.

There is a fretful self-consciousness in the reiterated expression of dislike or contempt for earlier schools of prosody. Why should Mr. Ezra Pound, who has written some very good verse, allude to Sir Edmund Gosse as "a genuine antimacassar of the antimacassar period"? It is an ill-bred fashion of speech, and remote from critical. Sir Edmund has also written some very good verse, which, if more restrained and less forceful than Mr. Pound's, has as broad an intellectual girth. Why should an enthusiastic reviewer of Miss Marianne Moore's work (Miss Moore, it will be remembered, is the latest recipient of the $2,000 prize offered annually by *The Dial*) assure us that we will learn to take pleasure in her technique if we will only dismiss from our minds all memories of Tennyson? This seems a high price to pay for the enjoyment of even *The Dial's* prize poet, and why should it be necessary to pay it? We do not have to clear our minds of Dryden in order to read Keats. Why should we emulate Queen Anne, whose stock of amity was sufficient for only one person at a time, and who had to clear her mind of one friend before she could make room for another?

Once in a while, but not often, disparagement of a predecessor means disparagement of something which is closely akin to the disdainful modern who disparages. When Miss Amy Lowell jeered at the "beribboned trumpet" of Miss Louise Imogen

Guiney, she said an unworthy word of a poet whose fundamental qualities were curiously like her own. Miss Lowell had a broader sweep than Miss Guiney ever compassed, and a firmer control of varying forms of prose and verse. Her vigor and her versatility are alike unrivaled. But for all her freedom, and the glow and glitter of her lines, she is austere, scholarly, profoundly intelligent, and greatly valorous. To her Miss Guiney's austerity, scholarship, and valor should have made a sure appeal. If "The Kings" is too sharp a call to battle, too harsh a word for our eminently reasonable souls to attend, surely "The Knight Errant," written while Miss Guiney still felt the impetus and ardor of youth, can never lack a hearing:

Forethought and recollection
  Rivet mine armor gay,
The passion for perfection
  Redeems my failing way!

Give to my youth, my faith, my sword,
  Choice of the heart's desire,
A short life in the saddle, Lord!
  Not long life by the fire.

What a rebound from the gospel of today with its emphasis on a somewhat sluggish serenity, on peace at all price, and the great good-fortune of living out our full length of years, and dying in our beds of those complicated disorders with which nature rewards our caution. And who better fitted to feel its force than Miss Lowell, who superbly defied a discreet world in the verses entitled "Before War is Declared," published in the Boston *Transcript,* February 28, 1917. The contrast between the lovely silence of her room,

—the soft snapping of the fire,
And the round still glow of the lamp;

and the pictures of ruined France which she conjures out of the embers is given with all the force and ferocity which words can convey, and with no concession to our weakness, or to her own:

Men with frozen feet,
Blank with sleeplessness,
Peering through periscopes
At a waste country stark with burnt trees.
Men popping rifles at a gaunt horizon.
Wounded men lying in squirming earthworm tracts,
Waiting for the stretcher bearers.

And while she sees in fancy the wind-slanted aircraft darting like dragonflies through the black night, and hears the spattering machine-guns, suddenly

A log bursts, and the sparks flare up with soft explosions,
And then go out, one by one, without sound.

There is the same acute human sympathy in these scornful and sorrowful lines that we find in the most exquisite of all Miss Lowell's poems, "Patterns"; and more recently in "The Day that was that Day," which tells the story of a woman, broken, body and soul and mind, by the routine of toil without interest, of duty without spirituality, of domesticity without affection:

> I don't love nothing
> 'Cept the cat—
> An' cats is cold things to cling to,
> An' now mine's sick.

Cats *are* cold things to cling to. That is not their rôle in life. They are made to be loved, not to love; to receive homage, not to give it; to live by our side with wise attentive eyes, and their little cat souls as remote from us as if they were Buddhist saints rapt in contemplation on a mountain top.

What I miss most in recent poetry is the whimsical note which lent lightness and grace to generations of unheroic, unsentimental verse. By whimsical I do not mean absurd or nonsensical. I am not thinking of the *Ingoldsby Legends,* or of the "Jackdaw of Rheims," good though it is. I mean that touch, facile and debonair, which precludes all sense of moral responsibility, and, generally speaking, all sense of sympathy as well. Gray's "Ode on the Death of a Favorite Cat, Drowned in a Tub of Gold Fishes," is perhaps the most perfect example of this sportive vein in English poetry. It is flawless in treatment, and it is hard-hearted. But then Gray was, if not a great poet, a singularly good one; and he enjoys the peerless distinction of being the only English poet who never wrote a line too much. A more modern instance of the purely recreative mood is Peacock's "War-Song of Dinas Vawr." Peacock is distinctly a minor poet. His songs are scattered carelessly through his stories, and neither stories nor songs aim at impressiveness. "Dinas Vawr" flings loose from the standards of morality; but adheres closely to the standards of poetic art.

> We brought away from battle,
> And much their land bemoaned them,
> Two thousand head of cattle,
> And the head of him who owned them.
> Ednyfed, King of Dyfed,
> His head was borne before us;
> His wine and beasts supplied our feasts,
> And his overthrow our chorus.

There is little of this crisp and mocking verse today, though sometimes the spirit is caught for a moment, as when Mr. Edwin Arlington Robinson writes,

> Conscience always has the rocking-chair,
> Cheerful as when she tortured into fits
> The first cat that was ever killed by care.

And sometimes a word of consummate wisdom is flung to us so lightly that we half suspect we are being laughed at, as in Miss Louise Driscoll's warning note:

Oh, some there are that call you,
And some that bid you stay;
But if you want to hold a friend,
Let him go his way!

which embodies, in an easily remembered little verse, the wisdom of the ages. Marriage, as Mr. Bernard Shaw reminds us, suits a great many people, and its essence is fidelity. Friendship suits a few people, and its essence is freedom.

So much has been written and rewritten about new forms of versification that we are a trifle tired—not of the forms themselves, but of hearing them praised and belittled. It is easy to laugh at them, but there is danger that we laugh in ignorance. It is very easy to burlesque them, but parody, while a sharp weapon, is a blunt interpreter. On the other hand, nothing is less convincing than to be told that our ears are dulled with the tomtom of Georgian verse, and that our intellects are undermined by the "honorable mediocrity" of Georgian versifiers. A poet is free to choose his medium, a reader is free to choose his poet. Neither is going to be bullied or satirized into change of heart.

The worst that can be reasonably urged against unfettered verse is that while only experts can write it well, anybody can write it badly. There is no doubt that the difficulty of finding rhymes, the simple, despised tomtom rhymes, and the far greater difficulty of hammering out blank verse, did sometimes bring the old, bad poets to a close. Hence the consoling brevity of their work. No such obstruction stands in the way of the new, bad poets. Hence the disconcerting length of their effusions. We have an uneasy feeling that they could go on forever. Even the note of veracity, the refusal to smooth out wrinkles, and the quick, keen observation which distinguish the new, good poets, cannot always save them from fantastic imagery, and from the unhallowed pursuit of the obvious. Mr. Carl Sandburg's admired lines,

> The fog comes on little cat feet. . . .
> It sits looking over harbor and city on silent haunches, and
> then moves on;

are forced and artificial. Compare with them these two lines of Walt Whitman's,

> Surely whoever speaks to me in the right voice, him or her
> I shall follow,
> As the water follows the moon, silently, with fluid footsteps,
> anywhere around the globe;

and see what happens when a highly imaginative element enters into verse. For a man who began life with a reverent admiration for Martin Tupper, Whitman traveled far. It is to be forever regretted that his contempt for any known standard of taste—a quality which no poet is great enough to disregard—should appear to the unwary as indicative of strength. "There are those," says Mr. Brownell, "with whom self-expression merely means self-disclosure, and who set self-display before self-direction; fancying themselves the while gloriously unfettered, though appearing to the unsympathetic eye as merely unbuttoned."

The amount of verse published annually in England and in the United States would be incredible were it not so deservedly popular. It has a curious vocabulary, sometimes colloquial, sometimes vivid and full of color, sometimes loosening into slang, "the riotous medium of the underlanguaged." Its affectations differ from the affectations which were sadly familiar to my youth. Old-fashioned verse put up a bluff for profundity of thought. New-fashioned verse puts up a bluff for profundity of experience. It is the more interesting pretense of the two, and a trifle more convincing. From nearly every State in the Union come slim little monthlies, devoted to the publication of poetry. They look very small and frail, but they have vitality enough to keep themselves going. The first was courageously started in 1912 by Miss Harriet Monroe, and has achieved a well-merited success. Now we are told that Miss Monroe "reigns in Chicago as the 'autocrat of all the poetries,' " which is a pleasant thing to be. Publishers, we are also told, "welcome new poets," which is a pleasant word to hear. Anthologies are the order of the day. They lie, thick as the leaves of Vallombrosa, on booksellers' counters. Mr. Braithwaite's *Yearbook of American Poetry*—which grows noticeably stouter every twelvemonth—offers a well-appointed shelter for scattered and homeless verse. British poets earn American dollars by reading their poems in the United States. American poets earn English guineas by reading theirs in London and Liverpool. The *Detroit Free Press* is preparing future poets by setting up a "Young Verse-Writer's Corner," with an editor all its own, who corrects the children's verses, and publishes them "before and after" correction, like the advertisements of hair tonics. It will be remembered that when the two words, "Teapot Dome," were sufficient to throw the whole country into agitation, and to drive our legislators to the verge of frenzy, the august Senate was restored to good humor for a whole day by hearing Senator Heflin's clever parody on "Abou Ben Adhem," and Senator Lodge's inimitable lines on "Absolute Knowledge." These *jeux d'esprit,* which deserve to rank with Canning's rhymed dispatches, so delighted our law-makers that "Thalia's day" in the Senate was long recalled as an oasis of laughter in a desert of bickering. If music has charms to soothe the savage breast, poetry—or what passes for poetry—has charms to soften the irritability of the civilized.

Then come the prizes—prizes big and little, won periodically by poets, to the great joy and delight of their more exclusive admirers. There are critics who say that prize-giving demoralizes the arts, and there are critics who say that it is a healthy stimulus. On this point experts disagree; but there can be no shadow of doubt that prize-winning must be an agreeable experience. Miss Marianne Moore was warranted in looking upon *The Dial* prize as a triumphant vindication of her complex and difficult art. Miss Edna St. Vincent Millay, whose verse is as clear as crystal and as sad as life, won the Pulitzer prize in 1923. Mr. Robert Frost won it the following year. The great Nobel prize was awarded in 1923 to Mr. William Butler Yeats; and while all admit the grace and charm of Mr. Yeat's work, there are those who refuse to consider Mr. Thomas Hardy's pessimism as a sufficient barrier to this distinction. If the prize had been an English one, Mr. Hardy's attitude towards what he called "the dark madness of the war" might possibly have disqualified him. Like Viscount Morley, he felt, or at least he expressed, nothing but resentment at England's struggle for safety. It seemed to be part of his resentment against an imperfect, but not altogether worthless, civilization, which we cannot afford to let go until we are sure we have laid hands on something better. But I have never thought that the note of grim irony which Mr. Hardy strikes with such force detracts from the preëminence of his novels, or from the weight and beauty of his verse. His is no weak complaint, but an intelligent and bitter insight into the great sadness of the world. Cheerful he is not, but dignified he is, as all must admit who have read his often quoted "Epitaph":

> I never cared for Life: Life cared for me,
> And hence I owed it some fidelity.

It now says, "Cease. At length thou hast learnt to grind
Sufficient toll for an unwilling mind;
And I dismiss thee—not without regard
That thou didst ask no ill-advised reward,
Nor sought in me much more than thou couldst find."

This will never take rank in the hearts of men with Stevenson's "Requiem,"

Under the wide and starry sky,

perhaps the best-beloved little poem in the great realm of English prosody. A gay valor is at all times more winning than a grim philosophy, and the swing of Stevenson's lovely lines keeps them in our memories. One advantage the rhymed and rhythmic verse, the tomtom verse, if you will, has over modern competitors—we do so easily remember it.

And now to emphasize the one point I have desired to make in this paper—the great popularity enjoyed by poets of our generation. Not one of any real distinction has missed his mark. Who could have prophesied a ready hearing for Francis Thompson's ardent, exquisite, and fantastic verse? When Mr. Henry Traill wrote to Mr. Meynell, "A public to appreciate *The Hound of Heaven* is to me inconceivable," he but echoed the reasonable apprehension of every English critic. Yet fifty thousand copies of *The Hound of Heaven* were sold within three years of Thompson's death. When the first volume of collected poems was offered diffidently to the world, the world straightway bought it, and read it, and praised it with such warmth that Mr. Henley remarked somewhat sourly in *The National Observer* that the author had been attacked "by a most formidable conspiracy of adulation."

Everard Meynell says truly that this unlooked-for happening was not an isolated instance of success, but an illustration of the general welcome accorded to the poets. His mother, Alice Meynell, met with immediate recognition. The intensity of her spiritual insight and the careful beauty of her workmanship placed her high among the moderns. We can all remember how John Masefield bowled us over with *The Everlasting Mercy,* knocked us breathless and gasping into poetic spaces we had never known before, and which we surveyed, as soon as we recovered from our fright, with awe and admiration. Alfred Housman's *A Shropshire Lad,* that strange, seductive little book, with its German sentiment grafted on English soil, and its German melancholy breathed into English air, made its sure way into favor. Robert Bridges, who has striven less to gratify the public than any British poet, let alone any British laureate, of my day, has held his chain of readers steadfast and unbroken. From "faery lands forlorn" comes Walter de la Mare, singing of beauty and of grief. From the gray lands *North of Boston* comes Robert Frost, with more of grief and less of beauty in his poetic wallet. From the high seas and the white Afghan snows comes Henry Newbolt, chanting valorously. From the Sussex downs comes Hilaire Belloc, and from the "Smoke Nights" of the city comes Carl Sandburg. All have been honorably received, their books bought and read, their praises sung, their rival schools defended. Walter de la Mare says that we owe courtesy to living poets no less than reverence to the dead. We have given it, and given it gladly. Poets have been known to snub the public, but the public seldom dares to snub the poets. The Equator itself is not spoken of more respectfully.

What does this portend? Masefield, who has something of the prophet in his composition, is by way of thinking that it means the coming of a great poet. The time is ripe, he says, the signs are in the heavens; and it is on American soil that this poet will be born. I'd love to believe it, but I don't, because the genius of the age and the genius of the race—if we are a race—are developing along other lines. Science and finance—and it takes a deal of finance to give science a backing—rule the earth. The useful arts are costly arts, and the wealth of the world is theirs to spend for the ultimate good of mankind. But poetry blooms on the stony soil of Mossgiel where Burns plowed, and in the London garret where Chatterton starved and died. England was Merrie England when Shakespeare's comedies made it merrier; but England was sad England when Milton conceived *Paradise Lost*. Many a modern poet echoes Whitman's boast, and

> avowedly chants the great pride of man in himself,

which is invigorating as a cold bath is invigorating;

but not as a great moral truth, or as a great principle of beauty, is invigorating. Will the genius whom Masefield sees winging his flight earthwards fall on evil days, and be "the joy of an unhappiness which confesses itself"; or will he hark back to the lusty combativeness of a time when Marvell's call to play was like a call to battle:

> Let us roll all our strength and all
> Our sweetness up into one ball;
> And tear our pleasures with rough strife
> Through the iron gates of life?

Or will he pass earth by in favor of some other planet badly in need of genius, and leave us as we are, with no great note sounding in our ears, but with an antiphone of lesser voices stirring us to a sense of beauty? There is nothing disheartening in this prospect. If we can keep up a good supply of minor poets for everyday use, the great poets of the past will suffice for the exalted moments when we are privileged to read them.

DU CÔTÉ DE CHEZ PROUST[1]

By EDITH RICKERT

THE GUERMANTES WAY. *By Marcel Proust. Translated by C. K. Scott Moncrieff. Two vols. Thomas Seltzer, New York.*

TO A reader hesitating outside the strange landscape of Proust, one of the most alluring gateways—certainly from the Côté de Guermantes—is where the Red Shoes of the Duchess go twinkling over the page:

"I" am calling at the ducal residence. Swann comes in, superb in a "pearl-gray frock-coat," with "white gloves stitched in black," and carrying a "gray tall hat of a specially wide shape which Delion had ceased now to make except for him, the Prince de Sagan, the Marquis de Modène, M. Charles Haas, and Comte Louis de Turenne." When he laid this wonderful hat on the floor, it was seen to be "lined with green leather, a thing not usually done, because, according to him, this kept the hat much cleaner, in reality because it was highly becoming." "I" wondered whether in the old days he had not worn a clipped mustache or his hair brushed up

[1] From *The New Republic,* September 30, 1925.

vertically in front, for he seemed strangely altered. The fact was that he was mortally ill.

The Duchess came in—

> tall and proud in a gown of red satin, the skirt of which was bordered with spangles. She had in her hair a long ostrich feather dyed purple, and over her shoulders a tulle scarf of the same red as her dress. "How nice it is to have one's hat lined with leather," said the Duchess, whom nothing escaped.

No, nothing but the patent signs that her friend was dying.

To this annoying fact Swann would naturally not have referred; but pressed by the offended great lady to say why he would not join them in a trip to Italy in the spring, he was compelled to reply: "But, my dear friend, it's because I shall then have been dead several months."

How embarrassing for the Duchess! Swann politely reminded her that she must not let her concern make her late for dinner; but she "perceived in a vague way that the dinner to which she was going must count for less to Swann than his own death." As she hesitated the Duke cut the knot with an ax:

> "Come, Oriane, don't stop there chattering like that and exchanging your jeremiads with Swann; you know very well that Mme. de Saint-Euverte insists on sitting down to table at eight o'clock sharp . . . the horses have been waiting for a good five minutes. I beg your pardon, Charles," he went on, turning to Swann, "but it's ten minutes to eight already. Oriane is always late, and it will take us more than five minutes to get to old Saint-Euverte's."

The Duchess yields and lifts her red skirt to enter the carriage, thereby enabling the Duke to make the terrific discovery that she is wearing black shoes. ("But, M. Proust, this is incredible!" says the reader.) The Duchess, who hates a scene before Swann, gently insinuates that since they are late already . . .

"No, no, we have plenty of time. It is only ten to; it won't take us ten minutes to get to the Parc Monceau. And, after all, what would it matter? If we turned up at half past eight, they'd have to wait for us, but you can't possibly go there in a red dress and black shoes. Besides, we shan't be the last, I can tell you; the Sassenages are coming, and you know they never arrive before twenty to nine."

There you have it—pure essence of Proust—the whole episode, far more delicious than the excerpts suggest, contained within about thirty pages—essence of the Faubourg Saint-Germain, distilled with irony, and with no small tincture of human nature at large. And so adieu, for the time, to the feudal race of the Guermantes.

But with what, then, have we been occupying ourselves for eight hundred-odd pages of their story? We begin with impressions of life in Paris, mainly in the mind of Françoise, the old servant (about forty pages); spend an evening at the Opéra-Comique and are waved at by the Duchess de Guermantes (about thirty pages); go to visit her nephew, Saint-Loup, an officer in a garrison town, for the purpose of getting an introduction to the Duchess (about one hundred pages); return to Paris and have luncheon with him and his actress, "Rachel when from the Lord," go behind the scenes at a rehearsal (about forty pages); have tea with the Marquise de Villeparisis, meeting various grades and degrees of high life and entertained with much discussion of the Dreyfus Case until the Duchess herself enters and the Castle of Illusion topples to the ground (some one hundred and fifty pages); follows a brief episode with the degenerate Charlus, the Duke's brother, to be elaborated later (forty pages altogether); "my" grandmother has a stroke and dies (about seventy pages); the Duchess, no longer on a pinnacle of romance, invites "me" to dine with a distinguished company, including Royalty (one hundred and eighty pages); and "I" pay a call later to find out whether her cousin, the Princess, really intended for me the invitation to an "evening" which I had received from her (and do not find out until the next volume, as yet not translated).

These eight episodic blocks, welded together with incidents less developed and glimpses of other phases of Parisian life, make up the two volumes of this section of *Remembrance of Things Past.* It is obvious that they cannot be judged structurally until it is seen how they fit into the whole design. We have lived through the sensations of a child becoming aware of life in the delicious country town of Combray; we have been swung into the current of Swann's passion for the worthless Odette; we have shared the enchantments and disillusions of a growing boy in Paris and at Balbec by the sea; in this volume we have the romance and disillusion of a youth admitted to glimpses of high life in the world's most civilized society. We are warned by the titles of the works yet to come to us in English that we shall descend to lower depths in *Sodome et Gomorrhe,* and that after bitter personal disillusion we shall be rewarded with the clew to the whole process in *Le Temps Retrouvé.* Can we persist with unflagging courage to the end?

But wherein lies the difficulty? It is, at the very least, twofold. In the first place, as has been pointed out by Conrad, Proust, instead of presenting a synthesis of life, makes us follow him through all the mazes of an analysis—an analysis in which minutiae are magnified as if the author had somehow acquired a microscope attachment to his sensations and perceptions. In the second place, there are the sentences—Christmas stockings full of sugar-plums, it may be, but requiring to be taken in small bits to be digestible.

That the analytical method has been pushed to a degree before undreamed of, a few rough estimates will make clear. For example, in the forty-eight pages in Volume Two concerned with the grandmother's death, less than a dozen altogether are used to present the scene or the actors; and of these pages, about three would cover all the dialogue. The analysis, then, includes about three-fourths of the content. Again, in the great dinner scene, where little but description and dialogue would be looked for, at least two-thirds of nearly two hundred pages are concerned with the interpretation of the invisible. In a third passage tested, only about seven percent of a hundred pages consisted of anything but psychological analysis.

In the face of all this—this jungle of analytical sentences—why is there a Proust cult? Why do some of us, with an irritation that swells to exasperation, still read on?

If we read on, it is because we care about the truth, and we realize that this neurotic invalid somehow managed to capture certain elusive, strange, at times repellent, but undeniable manifestations of human life that have escaped others. Merely to have shown the continuity of character between a great feudal stock and the many branches of their stupid and corrupt descendants was something; to have traced the fluctuating feelings of adolescence was something; to have recreated the intense, fleeting sense-life of childhood was perhaps most of all; and these three worlds Proust has, by laying them bare, intensified, made us create for ourselves. If we succeed less in this Guermantes volume, it is partly through lack of tradition and familiarity with the material and partly through our failure, thus handicapped, to see the persistent irony which, like a concave lens, shows this great world of social life to be exceedingly small.

Time enough, when the last word has been put into English, to decide whether Proust was the supreme genius of his age, as many competent critics declare, or merely a clever psychoanalyst, or no more than a notoriety whom, as we know, Mr. George Moore cannot "stomach." But whatever we shall finally make of him, there are signs throughout his work that with him, not only was art a passion, but also, in all his patient tracing of the labyrinth of illusion, he expected to find in the heart of it some clew to the meaning of life. And as for the art itself, he conceived his writer Bergotte as dreaming of a patch of yellow wall in Vermeer's Delft as "of a beauty in itself sufficient." So, Bergotte reproached himself, he ought to have written; so that the phrase in itself would have become as precious as that bit of yellow wall under the brush of the Dutch master.

And Proust himself at times, with the skillful aid of Mr. Scott Moncrieff, is able to give us, not merely a phrase, but a paragraph as beautiful, as penetrating, as sufficient in itself as this on the grandmother dead:

> An hour or two later Françoise was able for the last time, and without causing them any pain, to comb those beautiful tresses which had only begun to turn gray and hitherto had not seemed so old as my grandmother herself. But now on the contrary it was they alone that set the crown of age on a face grown young again, from which had vanished the wrinkles, the contractions, the swellings, the strains, the hollows which in the long course of years had been carved on it by suffering. As at the far-off time when her parents had chosen for her a bridegroom, she had the features delicately traced by purity and submission, the cheeks

glowing with a chaste expectation, with a vision of happiness, with an innocent gayety even, which the years had gradually destroyed. Life in withdrawing from her had taken with it the disillusionments of life. A smile seemed to be hovering on my grandmother's lips. On the funeral couch, death, like a sculptor of the Middle Ages, had laid her in the form of a young maiden.

Here is nothing new, but a familiar thing deeply felt and shaped into words neither more nor less than fitting, not less beautiful in its way, perhaps, than the wistfully admired work of Vermeer. And it is for the sake of passages like this, embedded in *The Guermantes Way,* that those whose minds are sensitive to truth and beauty even when obscured by mortal imperfection, will read on to the end of all that Marcel Proust had to give.

THE UNCROWNED KING OF SUSSEX[1]

By Cameron Rogers

When Wilfrid Scawen Blunt, the uncrowned King of Sussex, died in his eighty-third year on November 9, 1922, there were but few of that vivid fellowship of his youth and manhood to observe upon it or to note the unfilled niche among the last of the great Victorians. Blunt, who had shocked these many times and had chidden them thunderously from afar off for their sinewed faith in imperialism and their heavy-footed stumbling among people who abhorred them; prophesying evil for England in the East and evil for England in Ireland; Blunt, the mad prophet of an enfranchised Islam and the aegis of Arabi, had after all outlived them as he had outhated and outsung them. They could never quite understand him. Perhaps in their halloing in the spoor marks of Cromer and Kitchener they never wished to, feeling that he was in some inexcusable way "a wrong un" though the kinsman of noblemen and himself one of the greatest gentlemen in England. In a manner incredibly magnificent he had betrayed his caste, wronged the salt of his own great Southern holdings, the coverts of Crabbet, and the Jacobean suzerainty of Newbuildings. He left England to ride abroad in the Saharan open upon a steel-thewed barb as

[1] From *The Saturday Review of Literature,* September 19, 1925.

arrogant as himself, to ride in a burnous as white as the sunlight, the handsomest face in Europe outthrust, urgent as a hawk's, to perceive the tyrannies and the follies of his countrymen in the land of his adoption.

To leave Sussex for a vast pagan household in the Sahara, pitched in the very shadow of the tomb of a Muslim Saint! Sheikh El Obeyd and Newbuildings! Monstrous. The man was a comedian. And yet El Sheikh El Obeyd became suddenly a noise in the land, and in the pitiless gaol of Khartoum another protestant welcomed his voice, though his own beat quite fruitlessly upon the ear-drums of a Grand Old Man whom certain of Her Majesty's Service who had fought with the emirs at Abu Klea and El Teb called in an evil levity Gordon's Old Murderer.

Blunt at Sheikh El Obeyd befriended Arabi, though he might not avert the punishment that crushed his crusade with the guns of Tel-el-Kebir. His convictions became a hail of little shafts that from the quivers of bookbindings made him a malison in the eyes of right-thinking England. And then he swept into England, and shortly therefrom into Ireland, where he opposed England with such glittering crescendoes that he passed into Kilmainham Gaol for a few months, as delighted as a child.

Ah, Blunt! Incurable case. And yet from his birth in 1840 to 1869, when the diplomacy of his country was bereaved of his services, he had been all that a landed gentleman of heritage and presence should be. Something in the eyes of his equally endowed contemporaries had then gone wrong. But what? Poet, diplomat, sculptor, author, sportsman, traveler, and a lover of many conquests, his were qualities sufficient, one might think, to guarantee sound British political views. But, alas, not so. Imperialism became in his mind a murrain laid upon him personally, a sickness to be delivered from and from which to deliver others. And he strove for this deliverance while his peers snorted with annoyance and fumed with a perfectly justifiable irritation.

And of course in the meantime he had married the granddaughter of Lord Byron, and there is no doubt he found reserves in the blood and bone of the Noels.

What a honeymoon and what a marriage. On foot, on horses, this vibrant couple made of the whole Orient their playground and of Africa their especial village green. Arabic was as their own language to them and in them, as in that other dark genius, Sir Richard Burton, the Bedawi strain seemed stronger than the Saxon.

Curiously enough, Blunt had but little profit or pleasure from the evening when he and Sir Richard came into each other's company. Sir Richard's fault, no doubt, since he cast those hypnotic eyes so dreadfully upon Wilfrid that the latter raised a navy revolver against him and threatened to pistol him if he did not at once desist. Yet in one way the two would not have made an ill-assorted couple.

Blunt labored his whole life long with a changing

mind upon matters spiritual. He had come under the influence of Newman, who, he would say, had wrought a miracle upon him. He had been more than once upon the point of a fervent and orthodox Catholicism, and then always he waited, wrestled anew with himself, and lived on beyond the extended hand-grip of the church. Islam beckoned and to his dear friend, the Grand Mufti, he more than once nearly made the profession of faith. He did not. Still he wrestled. One year of barren combat he determined to make an end of doubt and set out upon a journey of forty days to interview the chieftain temporal and spiritual of the Senussi, whose power went forth from Jerabub, near Tripoli. His guide was of the Senussi, and his pilgrimage lay among their fellowship, yet the convert-to-be was set upon and beaten, robbed and sorely injured, more, however, in his faith than in his body. So doubts returned again fourfold, and he wrestled and still wrestled.

In moments between this spiritual rough and tumbling, preaching, riding, and making love, he wrote. He wrote poetry that will live as long as anthologists exist to anthologize, such poetry as the first of that couple of superb sonnets:

O world, in very truth thou art too young;
When wilt thou learn to wear the garb of age?
World, with thy covering of yellow flowers,
Hast thou forgot what generations sprung
Out of thy loins and loved thee and are gone?
Hast thou no place in all their heritage

Where thou dost only weep, that I may come
Nor fear the mockery of thy yellow flowers?
O world, in very truth thou art too young,
The heroic wealth of passionate emprize
Built thee fair cities for thy naked plains.
How hast thou set thy summer growth among
The broken stones which were their palaces!
Hast thou forgot the darkness where he lies
Who made thee beautiful, or have thy bees
Found out his grave to build their honeycombs?

And certainly his prose will live as long as Ireland or the British occupation of Egypt are of interest to the world. But of the two it is his verse that is the more endurable. There had come quite early the *Sonnets of Proteus,* of which Oscar Wilde, in a review of *In Vinculis,* sterner ones written a decade or so later from Kilmainham Gaol, remarked with a pleasant smugness that not a few were shameful. Oh, the usage the "nineties" gave that word! In any case, they were love sonnets, for a multitude of loves inspired Wilfrid. Esther and Manon and Juliet and a many more. There is, for instance, for those who care to look for it, that translucent acrostic subtly entitled "A Cuckoo Song," to a young noblewoman who could not well have been more beautiful than her name.

Not all were in this vein, however. There is "The Wind and the Whirlwind," which blew into England out of Egypt clamant with an indignant warning and whose ending has proved not unprophetic:

Therefore I do not grieve. Oh, hear me, Egypt! Even in death thou art not wholly dead. And hear me, England! Nay. Thou needs must hear me. I had a thing to say, And it is said.

It was even nobly said, but it left nevertheless the nerves of the future Lord Cromer astonishingly unruffled. That this was so must have been a keen disappointment to Blunt, for he abominated Baring. In an elder day he would have called him out and run him through with a sense of great service to mankind, but custom in the closing decades of the nineteenth century hampered this solution. Invective was the only weapon in genteel usage, and though invective Blunt could use as a rapier, saber, or bludgeon with equal dexterity, yet the old fox remained unperturbed. In Blunt's journals we read of the eventual kill, however, and Wilfrid triumphant with the mask at his saddle-bow.

As the torrential course of his life bore him through the fifties he began to settle slowly back into the comely embrace of his Sussex properties and El Sheikh became more and more the Squire. There was the Arab stud of Lady Anne and the annual sales at Crabbet, where were assembled year after year men, women, and horses of the best blood in England. His contemporaries and his peers among the old landed gentry entertained a profound admiration for Blunt the host and great gentleman. They confounded this aspect not at all with the political one and though Arthur Balfour, Chief

Secretary of Ireland in 1887, refused Wilfrid permission to have his fur greatcoat in Kilmainham Gaol, he was observed to borrow it himself one nipping afternoon at Crabbet a short while later as he set out to view the stud. "May I just take this coat, Wilfrid?" How pleasant a request for Blunt to grant.

Indeed, many of them chose entirely to disregard what they considered a lamentable and incurable mania in a man whose heritage and ancestry was as illustrious and as rooted in the island tradition as those of the Percys themselves. Blunt's kinsman, for instance, the beautiful and brilliant George Wyndham, preserved during the whole of his lifetime great love and respect for Wilfrid, and when he was apprehended in the midst of astonishing rhetoric on the properties of that sinister nobleman, the last Earl of Clanricarde, he of the balas ruby bracelets and brutalized tenantry, and taken thence to gaol, Wyndham as who should say, poor lad, another seizure, allowed none of his affection to expire.

In those as in later days there was brave company at Crabbet and great dinners where Lady Anne at one end of the long long table, when she spoke to the guest upon her right or left, would in a gesture born of an enforced habit crane to observe if her words were approved by the squire, though no spoken syllables could carry a quarter of this distance to his ears.

But the granddaughter of Lord Byron of Rochdale died long before her storm-riding husband. The twentieth century found Wilfrid sadly depressed, with apparently but one pleasure in life, the harrying of Cromer, grown now of an apoplectic habit and pictured by Sargent "like a profiteer on one of his own packing cases."

George Wyndham the beloved died in his prime, and men of Wilfrid's own and older generation were missed daily from the august windows of Brook's or Buck's or White's, to be recalled only by tablets in the Abbey and the succession of their estates.

The war moved him, but not greatly. He still abominated imperialism, though the thunder of his denunciations had fled, spent, into skies dead years before.

And then there occurred the tragedy of Lady Anne's Arab stud, the great Crabbet stud, famous for two generations. His daughter, once the wife of the Honorable Neville Lytton and now the Baroness Wentworth, removed the stud by legal processes from his to her possession. A redoubtable lady by all accounts. Not filial, perhaps, but with the wills of Blunt and Byron so welded together within her character that the possessor of only one of them, handicapped by age and the utter lack of legal rights, could hardly hope to rout her. And so passed the jewel of his later days.

One morning in August, 1920, I drove from Greatham in company with Wilfrid and Alice Meynell to Newbuildings. We found Blunt like a high and ancient tower and clad in a flowing desert garment, superintending the inspection of a comely mare while the nephew of Chinese Gordon felt the slender forelegs and satin quarters. We passed into the Jacobean beauty of Newbuildings, where the neweled staircase and the Morris tapestry, the Chippendale and the Jacobean furniture and the pictures of his beloved horses, the Godolphin Arab, the Spotted Polish stallion, the Darnley Arab, and his own superb Mesaud, wrought an atmosphere that lapped one about like tangible stuffs, glowing and magical. We drank a very ancient white Burgundy and watched a pheasant single-foot through a little place apart where Francis Thompson had lived his last few pitiful days.

There was no tumult here of riven Egypt and tossing Ireland. Peace was inhaled and exhaled like a satisfying smoke. He was in his eighty-first year, and the men he had befriended or hated, protected or attacked, were all dead. Arabi was dead and Cromer, who had devised his ruin, and Kitchener, who had perpetrated the outrage of Omdurman. All dead, and the issues of their labors fast following them. In Newbuildings there was an extraordinary peace, a thing intimately connected with cadent sunlight and repose after hard work. He died unshriven by the church beyond whose walls he had spent a lifetime making up his mind to turn for the solution of all things to Rome. He desired no priest, no masses. He was buried in his own soil in the most beautiful woodland in the world, and the hares lollop by and the pheasants cukker the seasons through above his unregarding head. It is conceivable that the uncrowned king of Sussex, whose abilities were so many and so varied that they jostled each other in their rush for expression, deserves to share with Antony the spoken epitaph,

> There is nothing left remarkable
> Under the visiting moon.

THE HEART OF THE MATTER [1]

By ANNE DOUGLAS SEDGWICK

IN A recent much-discussed novel, *The Constant Nymph,* by Margaret Kennedy, when Tessa, the young heroine—over-young one feels her, for the maturity of the drama in which she is involved—has just died, killed, practically, by the blindness and carelessness of the man who loves her, and lies in the ambiguous foreign lodging-house to which he has brought her, after their flight from England and respectability, the sentence in which Miss Kennedy sums up her final contemplation of her heroine is:

> The night wind blew in, swaying the dusty curtains, and all the sheets of music on the floor went rustling and flapping like fallen leaves. A chill tempest, it blew over the quiet bed, but it could not wake her. She slept on, where they had flung her down among the pillows, silent, undefeated, young.

At the end of *Le Grand Meaulnes,* Alain Fournier's only novel—killed in the War as he was—Meaulnes's faithful friend and the faithful friend of Yvonne, Meaulnes's wife, carries her dead body down the stairs that are too winding to let the

[1] From *The Saturday Review of Literature,* August 8, 1925.

coffin pass, and the heart of his tragedy, and of Meaulnes's and Yvonne's, is reached as he says:

> Ce gout de terre de mort, ce poids sur le cœur, c'est tout ce qui reste pour moi de la grande aventure, et de vous, Yvonne de Galais, jeune femme tant cherchée—tant aimée.

And in another recent novel, *Mrs. Dalloway,* by Virginia Woolf, exquisite, aging Clarissa, at the end of her London day, in the midst of her successful party, is suddenly confronted with the realization of death. She goes into a still, dark little room and looks out at the night sky and sees the face of the old lady opposite looking out at her.

To detach such sentences, such incidents, from their setting, is to lift a sea-anemone from its pool, their significance and beauty leave them; but in their place, standing at the heart of a book, as the anemone stands in its transparent element, sea-water implicit in its every filament, they sum up not only the life of the book, but of its writer.

It is by such phrases and incidents that one remembers a novel, as the face of a friend may rise before us, at a certain moment, wearing a certain look that so reveals what we most love in them that tears come to our eyes as we recall it. They reveal the heart of a writer's feeling for his creation and are implicit in it from the beginning. From the beginning, I feel sure, Miss Kennedy saw Tessa on the bed, "silent, undefeated, young," and Mrs. Woolf saw Clarissa at the window and her unity with the old lady opposite to whom she had never spoken—the old lady who was going to bed while she was giving her party;—and Alain Fournier saw Yvonne in her blue velvet dress sown with silver stars, saw her dead hair, and felt her weight against her lover's heart. These are the things we never forget in a novel. They are often the seemingly insignificant things, like the mushrooms that the old peasant puts into his blouse for his wife, during the reaping in *Anna Karénine,* or like the vast stillness and splendor of the blue sky above the battlefield at which André looks up as he recovers consciousness, in *La Guerre et la Paix.* A biographer of Lévine or André would know nothing of the mushrooms or the sky, but to themselves such memories would be landmarks in their lives, the real inner life which is so very different an affair from the outer. Some one smiled then—it may not even have been at us—or did not smile; that was enough to alter the whole current of the river, and our landscape will never again be the same.

It is in a writer's capacity for feeling the significance of such moments and for finding the words with which to express it, and in which to sum up his whole theme, as with a closing chord, that we can best gauge the depth of his insight and the force of his mastery. Intelligence will not take its place, nor wit, nor even beauty. Some very great novels lack the quality I mean, Meredith's, for instance, and Henry James's. One recalls nothing in them as one recalls the face of a friend at that moment of unconscious revelation. Tears never risc for a phrase of Meredith's. Agile, penetrating, dramatically grave or tirelessly coruscating, he rarely seems to reach the heart of life and rest there, enfranchised and contemplative, though he circles round it with splendors of comment and display that are sometimes exhilarating and sometimes merely exasperating. Knowing so much about the heart, he is still singularly heartless. The capacity for feeling may not have lacked, but what did lack was the capacity for communicating it unalloyed by parade or gusto.

In Henry James a marvelous sensitiveness to each least impact of experience protected itself, one imagines, against life's heaviest blows by keeping the heart of reality at a distance. Reality alarmed as much as it fascinated him, and he only approached it when he saw it safely clothed in the complexities and preoccupations of super-civilization. Enchanting, absorbing as he is, lovable and often deeply moving, we do not feel that sense of tears for a single one of his situations or figures—unless it is the wistful little figure of "the Pupil."

Take a sentence at the end of *The Wings of the Dove,* and he never wrote a lovelier one, where Densher contemplates his memory of dead Milly:

> Then he took it out of its sacred corner and its soft wrappings; he undid them one by one, handling them, handling *it,* as a father, baffled and tender, might handle a maimed child.

There we have Henry James's art, and his heart, in fullest measure. Yet, lovely as the sentence is, we are not at one with it, or with Densher in his contemplation. Something comes between, making us more aware of its beauty and less aware of Densher and Milly; something palpably artful: the flavor of a pleasure in craftsmanship. The medium is still there, exquisite but untranscended.

How differently rings the end of the great chapter in *L'Idiot* where Rogogine has killed Nastasia, and Prince Muichkine—Léon Nikolaïévitch—sits beside him. I read the Russians in French, and any translation, of course, must give us the meaning divested of all the sound and shape in which its author clothed it, and sound and shape are an integral part, as we have seen, of the feeling they convey. Even so, what do we see and feel?

> Du moins, lorsque, quelques heures après, la porte s'ouvrit, ceux qui entrèrent dans la chambre trouvèrent l'assassin complètement privé de connaissance et un proie à une fièvre ardente. A côté de lui était assis sur le lit Léon Nikolaïévitch immobile et silencieux. Chaque fois que le malade commençait à délirer et à pousser des cris, le prince, aussitôt, lui passait sa main tremblante sur les cheveux et sur les joues pour le faire taire par cette caresse.

We are just helped to bear that; but it is almost more than we can bear, as it is almost more, we feel, for all his mastery, than Dostoevsky can bear, and its taste upon our lips, as of hyssop and vinegar, brings to our memory the scene of another crucifixion. Art is there, but art transcended, and emotion is there, mastered, and we have reached the realm of acceptance and contemplation. This sense of religion flows through all that Dostoevsky wrote, carrying him—and us with him—into strange complicities with depravity and madness; the feeling of the spiritual unity that binds men together and of the mystery that underlies their lives.

It is this quality, a mystical quality one may call it, which, in varying degrees, is implicit in all these haunting sentences, and we may recognize it in most unlikely places. Could any writer seem more unmystical than wise, cheerful, magnanimous Trollope, so prosaic, so pedestrian, so humorously acquiescent in the order of things as he sees it; yet what is it, again, but the sense of tears that overcomes us in *The Last Chronicle of Barset,* when Mr. Crawley (one of the great figures of literature), exonerated after his long martyrdom, says to Mr. Toogood:

> I do not as yet fully understand you, sir, being, perhaps, in such matters somewhat dull of intellect, but it seemeth to me that you are a messenger of glad tidings, whose feet are beautiful upon the mountains.

So exquisite in itself, so exquisite on Mr. Crawley's lips, with a savor of heavenly absurdity, who that finds the quotation in this setting could deny to Trollope the quality that is our theme? It brushes us, as with an angel's wing, at the end of François Mauriac's *Génétrix,* that sunny, dusty, dreary book, where the wretched, abandoned man feels, at dawn, the hand of the old servant, who has returned to him, laid on his head. It shines with love and pity through all that Katherine Mansfield wrote, and though the sober securities of Arnold Bennett's finest book—*The Old Wives' Tale*—give hardly a hint of it, do we not feel its breath in *Elsie and the Child,* in the extraordinarily touching scene where dear Elsie comforts her overwrought Joe?

One might wander among one's memories for many an hour applying the test and see never an answering ray, for it must be owned that there are great books that cast not one beam of this particular brightness. Flaubert and Stendhal dry our very heart's-blood and stop its beating: it is a dreadful brightness that we feel in them. The strange case of Marcel Proust leaves us in an uneasy uncertainty; perhaps it was his own; and we do not yet know whether his *Temps Retrouvé* is in some unpredictable way to resolve in a final justifying chord so much magnificent or loathly irrelevance. Some sentences, some descriptions—as of the church spires on the horizon in *Swann,* or the dead grandmother's face—its lovely youth recovered after the agony—make us feel that such magic must possess its own key. Yet we are left doubting; we are left even suspecting that in the vast labyrinthine edifice, covering ever more and more space, yet rising never by a span above its first levels, some torturing complex seeks to appease itself by a confession that is yet a constant duplicity.

Turning from all these, we may still own that many of the books we most care for and could not imagine ourselves without have none of the religious or contemplative quality. Jane Austen is tearless, yet we can read her forever. We may choose not to read Marcel Proust at all, and it is as difficult to reread *L'Idiot* or *Les Frères Karamasow* as to withstand twice in a life-time the shock, and surge, and appalling uplifting of a tidal wave; but *Emma* and *Pride and Prejudice* we can read every time we have the influenza. Sincerity, sobriety, security, these are also essential qualities in the making of a great writer, and she has them all, and with them her matchless, unhurried, tolerant humor. It is dangerous to feel much unless one is great enough to feel much, and wise and charming as she is, her glance would be the pin-prick to many an inflated emotion, though to many real ones she would be blind. The heart of the matter is not to be reached by any short-cut nor by ambitious effort or anxious esthetic theory, and to see her delicate fountain rising in its formal garden increases our distaste for the turgid floods that inundate the literary landscape, claiming to be clear lakes and mighty rivers.

THE SINGULAR—ALTHOUGH DUAL—EMINENCE OF RING LARDNER [1]

By GILBERT SELDES

THE KIND of reputation Ring Lardner enjoys today is exceptional in America. (Enjoys is, perhaps, not the word, for he is a man of a singularly ironic temperament; but if he cares for fame he can now have a double portion served to him.) He has become one of the most popular of our humorists, with a weekly syndicated article, a comic strip, and an inexhaustible market for "pieces" of any description. But he is, at the same time, admired by the *cognoscenti* for whom, in his long life as a writer, he has apparently never cared a snap of his fingers. While an odd million readers have enjoyed his work every Sunday in New York alone, his praises echo in *The Dial* (in America) and in T. S. Eliot's *Criterion* (in England).

This is a strange fate to overtake a popular humorist. Mark Twain achieved an Oxford degree and the praise of the professors of literature long after he had ceased to write his characteristic work. When *A Tramp Abroad* and *Roughing It* were popular, Mark Twain was despised by the Brahmins of

[1] From *Vanity Fair*, July, 1925. Mr. Seldes explains that the composition of this article preceded the publication of Mr. Lardner's fantasies.

letters as a "mere humorist." Nor did any one beat the intellectual trap-drum for Artemus Ward and Finley Peter Dunne in their heyday. Popular men in other fields have lately had some measure of appreciation; Chaplin, for example, is as deeply taken to heart by the intellectuals as by the masses. But literature has always been the last stronghold against the popular men—and Lardner has broken down every fortification.

Why? It is only eleven years ago that the letters of a busher began to appear in *The Saturday Evening Post*—those letters we remember as *You Know Me Al.* They seemed, on the surface, to be another effort to make fiction out of baseball and to use American slang for humorous purposes—nothing more. Two years later Lardner wrote a straight professionally humorous series of articles about a trip to Palm Beach. From then until 1920 he wrote stories of various sorts and an amusing book about his trip to the war areas. In 1920 he began publishing *The Big Town,* which, again on the surface, was an ordinary story of domestic life, with the slang a little changed in character. There followed other stories, deceptive in appearance. As far as I can discover, the only suggestion that Lardner was worth notice as a satirist and a writer appeared in *Vanity Fair* about two years ago, although it was probably earlier that H. L. Mencken appreciated the language Lardner wrote as contributions to his own work on *The American Language.* And now, in a uniform edition, Lardner calls forth the praise of the literary critics, even of the *avant-garde,* the Modernists. He is "an important figure in our national artistic output" and " has a fluent and finished technique"; he writes the American vernacular "like an artist" and is a master of character drawing. He is a satirist, an ironist, and the only American master of lunatic humor.

I quote these things from the critics not because they are in any way exaggerated, but because they are true and indicate the *kind* of reputation Lardner now has. As for explaining it, my guess is that one important reason for it is the new interest in purely American artistic phenomena which has developed since the war. Lardner is as native as baseball or corn-bread. You cannot export him or explain him—I have tried him on Englishmen, drunk and sober, and they actually cannot understand what he is saying. And this is true not only of the obvious things, his subject-matter and his slang; but of the hidden things, his characters and his rhythm. The imitators of Lardner imagine that a few cute misspellings and a few artificial phrases will give them the American language; he, however, knows better. He has written some of his finest work—the celebrated *Golden Honeymoon* and *Some Like 'Em Cold*—with hardly a slang word, yet they are in the purest American English, not British English, because their rhythm, the cadence or fall of the words, is the way we speak and the way we think. Take, for example, this paragraph from *The Big Town:*

> The hotel's got all the modern conveniences like artificial light and a stopper in the bathtubs. They even got a barber and a valet, but you can't get a shave wile he's pressing your clothes, so it's pretty near impossible for a man to look their best at the same time.

You can correct the grammar and spelling with a few strokes of the pen and not diminish in any way the American flavor, because the cadence is American; and you cannot do anything at all about that phrase at the end. Nor will the King's most kingly English conceal the give-away of character which the busher makes of himself in such a sentence as:

> All so I remember I told you to fix it up so as a hack would be down to the deepo to meet us tonight and you wont get this letter in time to tell them not to send no hack so I suppose the hack will be there but may be they will be some body else that gets off of the train that will want the hack and then every thing will be all O.K. but if they is not nobody else that wants the hack I will pay them ½ of what they was going to charge me if I had of came and road in the hack though I dont have to pay them nothing because I am not going to ride in the hack but I want to do the right thing and besides I will want a hack at the deepo when I do come so they will get a peace of money out of me any way so I dont see where they got no kick comeing even if I dont give them a nichol now.

Such passages are the work of a man to whom the structure of American speech is natural and sympathetic; American consists not merely of saying "thoid" for "third," but of *thinking* "I will wire you at my own expense the date of my wedding" and "I will punch a couple of their jaws when I see them," or "My sister Minnie—she married L. F. Wilcox, the tire people." Lardner has understood the habits of mind which "make" our speech, much more than our mispronunciations do.

And that is the essence of Lardner in every respect, because even his baseball series was not about baseball so much as it was about a character. As you read the letters, relishing their fun and appreciating their slang, there comes vividly to you the character of Jack Keefe, the busher: an ignorant and stupid fellow, a braggart and a coward, a stingy, sentimental fool. The traits of character are stroked in with the utmost delicacy until the whole figure is so rounded that whenever you see a pitcher in action you think of the busher. Baseball is quite secondary; Lardner might have made him a busboy or a race-track tout. He has hit the human and the universal; the rest is accidental.

In *The Big Town* Lardner develops three characters. One is the busher, grown wise and sardonic; the others are two women, the Mrs. and her sister, both foolish. In the process Lardner has sketched a section of American life which has since been done almost too frequently in the novels of Main Street, and never done so well. Here is his picture of a Long Island hotel:

> The men get up about eight o'clock and go down to New York to Business. They don't never go to work. . . .

When the women has prepared themselves for the long day's grind with a four-course breakfast, they set round on the front porch and discuss the big questions of the hour, like for instance the last trunk murder or whether an Airedale is more loving than a Golden Bantam. Once in a wile one of them cracks that it looks like they was bound to be a panic pretty soon and a big drop in prices, and so forth. This shows they're broadminded and are giving a good deal of thought to up-to-date topics. Every so often one of them'll say, The present situation can't keep up. The hell it can't!

By one o'clock their appetites is whetted so keen from brain exercise that they make a bum out of a plate of soup and an order of Long Island duckling . . . and they wind up with salad and apple pie à la mode and a stein of coffee. Then they totter up to their rooms to sleep it off before Dear gets home from Business.

This is, in part, the mood of *Babbitt,* but it lacks, fortunately, the tone of bitterness; Lardner's sour commentary seems to be wholly without personal bias, and that is why he can make fun of a thing and make his fun funny. It is none the less devastating; no more desolate picture of the lives of the merely prosperous has ever been done than the one that emerges from his books. And when he chooses a tragic theme, the materials never escape him. The story of "The Champion" makes you quiver with a rage which the author himself dispassionately seems not to share; in his latest story, "Haircut," published in *Liberty,* Lardner chooses to tell a story of a low and mean revenge (as a barber tells it all to a patron) as if it were all howlingly funny. It is obvious that, if he wants to, he can break our hearts.

This is very far away from the "funny man" of the Sunday papers—but the temper behind the work of Lardner is always the same. There is hardly a trace of good-natured humor in him, except when he is writing about people he knows and tells you that Irvin Cobb "is never happy except when amongst his books of which he has a complete set." Elsewhere there is always a touch of irony, a satirical slant, and a sardonic smile. And these qualities have joined with his fantastic imagination to produce his four "plays." Lardner has always written parodies; like all American humorists, he has depended on exaggeration to a certain extent. When he came to write these incredible plays there was no longer any check to his imagination; they were not meant to be played, nor, I understand, to be published. They are far more mad than anything in *Alice in Wonderland,* yet they give you the peculiar effect of being entirely logical. In *Taxidea Americana* the following conversation occurs:

PAT: I certainly feel sorry for people on the ocean to-night.

MIKE: What makes you think so?

The first act of *Clemo Uti—The Water Lilies—* is set on "the outskirts of a Parchesi Board. People are wondering what has become of the disc. They quit wondering" and sing:

What has become of the discs?
What has become of the discs?
We took them at our own risks,
But what has become of the discs?

and the play ends with:

SETHSO: Who is our father?
GETHSO: What of it? We're twins, ain't we?

His famous "I Gaspiri (The Upholsterers)" may be a parody of the Moscow Art Theatre plays as presented in argument and translation; but I prefer to think that it is also an attack of pure lunacy. Unlike the French *dada,* Lardner's mad fun is not willful; it is without deliberate intent to upset your mental processes. It has, in fact, the unnerving quality of seeming to be a little more logical than you are yourself, as if Lardner had made the unconscious in us speak while we were expecting mere superficial logic.

He has a boundless imagination—an American quality—and an apparently inexhaustible energy. It is hard to guess what he will do next, because America is not peculiarly receptive to the kind of fantasy he has been practicing in his recent plays. He could write a play which would be terribly funny and would knock all the conventional speeches, the stiff exits and entrances of our comedies, into a cocked hat; or he could combine his two great qualities, his clear-eyed observation of America and his gift of the fantastic, and write a novel. He may develop his occasional articles into an actual satirical record of American life, or keep them at the level of funny pieces. The things one is certain of are, however, good enough: he will always be entertaining; he will always indicate the presence of the temperament of an artist, and he will always be purely American. It is, thank Heaven, too late for him ever to change these three things.

IN BEHALF OF JOHN MASEFIELD[1]

By STUART SHERMAN

COLLECTED WORKS OF JOHN MASEFIELD. Vols. I and II, Poems. Vols. III and IV, Verse Plays and Prose Plays. *The Macmillan Company, New York.*

JOHN MASEFIELD has a grave musical voice, and when, with sharp little gushes of emotion, he reads "The West Wind" and makes one hear his lark singing "above the green wheat," I swear no sweeter song has been sung in my time or more soothing to a tired heart. Why should I not go on and say that I am not ready to sift him yet, because nearly all of his work, perhaps barring the adaptations from Racine, still seems alive?

This lean, sad-eyed master of song-craft, who has plowed Gloucestershire with oxen and the deep sea with ships, has given me more poetic pleasure than any other English poet living. Through his awakened personality I have felt mighty rhythms pulsing through forms of life that dissolve and decay; through waves that break, fields sown and harvested, foiled tragic lovers, hot races ending with blown steeds and fallen horsemen, and forlorn hopes ebbing out in blood-drenched, frost-bitten trenches by the Hellespont. His glorification of the invincible

[1] From *The New York Herald Tribune* "Books," January 10, 1926.

vanquished stirs me, I confess, profoundly. It is the inside story of human life. He tells it with swift, bright speed, and yet with a pathos which bites to the bone.

Without going through any critical processes, I have but to glance at the fifteen volumes which preceded this collected edition to my shelves to see that in the long race of this last twenty-five years Masefield has now for a decade or more been in the lead. My favorites of the old time, Stephen Phillips and John Synge, fell long ago into the blind cave of night. Masefield's immediacy and sincerity and fresh color are unfavorable to most of the others.

Thomas Hardy's ironical and mortuary musings in hobbling verse hold first place in the affections of some readers; but me they afflict with their monotonous insistence on the twenty-five gradations between green, gray, and black; take a pencil and collect all the adjectives in a hundred pages of his poems and you will feel as if you had spent a week-end in the House of Usher. Kipling's clarinet and Sir Henry Newbolt's bugles are trophies of old wars. Alfred Noyes affects me now like a playboy buccaneer dressed up for a summer pageant. Margaret Woods and Laurence Binyon still ring the chimes of Oxford sweetly. The antique moods of Walter de la Mare delight the ear and charm the heart. But the Irish ecstasies of A. E. generally leave me as cold at the center of my being as the fine technical exercises of Robert Bridges or the exquisite old Irish lace of W. B. Yeats.

Of course, I know that John Masefield has had his quarter century of productivity and his decade of fame, and that it is high time now for him to be slipping off the stage and leaving elbow room for the critics to haul the ascending stars into heaven. I know what the voguish critics are saying—that Masefield began with echoes of Kipling and Synge; that he spells Beauty with a capital letter; that the introduction of "closhy puts" and bar-room oaths into verse is no great feat once the trick has been suggested; that the tragedies are melodramatic through inadequate characterization; that the narratives are prolix; that the verse is padded with moral platitudes; that "lasted" is rhymed with "bastard," as it is by many speakers; and that throughout the works there is a culpable indifference to the poetic uses of the file, just as there is in the works of the Master of all Makers.

Some of this critical pawing is captious. Masefield's apprentice debt to Kipling in *Salt Water Ballads* and to Synge in *The Tragedy of Nan* was soon stricken off the score. The mature Masefield is nobody's echo. He is a figure as independent and original as any man can be who works, as all the great English poets have done, for the vital continuation of an ancient and splendid tradition. Obviously, he learned his craft of the masters. For the forms and instruments of his music his debt is immense, to Burns, Byron, Shakespeare, Spenser, and Chaucer. *The Everlasting Mercy* is, if you please, an English "Tam o' Shanter"; *The Widow in the Bye Street,* a modern *Troilus and Cressida; Reynard the Fox,* a resuscitation of the Canterbury Pilgrims; *Dauber* is Childe Harold or Don Juan gone on a fresh pilgrimage; and the chief sonnet sequence carries on the Elizabethan quest for the soul and the divine idea behind the shadows of things. But that a poet suggests such comparisons, while writing with sharp realism of his own times and out of his own experience, marks him not a slave, but an heir.

Some of these exceptions, however, are well taken, and Mr. Masefield himself would probably sustain them. In the heat of the race, he has not always avoided knocking the top-rail off the fence. In his brief introduction to this edition, glancing back over the performance of his generations, he says: "Often their work has been harsh, violent, and ill-considered." But their mission, he intimates, was not to gild the refined Tennysonian gold nor to paint the late Victorian lily white. Tennyson himself had kept an even balance between the native English tendency toward a robust rendering of life and the imported cult of artifice and technical finish. His imitators declined into a mere respectability, devoid of poetic courage or hope. The mission of Masefield's generation was to sally boldly into nature and restore vitality by reëmphasizing the native qualities: "character-drawing, humor, liveliness, and truth."

Certainly the apologist for Masefield should frankly concede his flaws and foibles to Mr. Squire and other parodists. He should take positive ground and defend him for the passionate expression of his tragic realism, his strength, and his sincerity. An English critic, Dixon Scott, moved to comment by *The Daffodil Fields,* began with a protest against the solemnity with which people take their poets. They, the poets, are just like other people, he would have us believe, not a race of "wilted priests," but "simple, jolly, frank, and friendly souls . . . engrossed in the grubby, glorious work of growing flowers." Well, a good many contemporary poets are like that. That is the trouble with their poetry. It is a kind of passionless floriculture. But John Masefield stands out as not in the least like that. Poetry has been in the place of religion to him; and he has served it like a priest—not with a linen ephod, but with Carlyle's "Baphometic fire-baptism."

In that interesting novel of his, *Multitude and Solitude,* there are many cutting observations on contemporary literature, and, in Roger Naldrett, there is a portrait of the poet's mind which we may accept as strikingly similar to that of its author. Roger declares that the Celtic love of the beautiful is "all buncombe." He finds the distinctive quality of Irish verse "in that kind of windy impersonality which one hears in their talk." "I maintain," he says, "that the Irish have no imagination. Imagination is a moral quality." Before he settles down to a literary life, Roger wishes to get the whole of himself involved and incandescent in the flame of his imagination. "I begin to think that a writer without character, without high and austere character, in himself, and in the written image of himself, is a panderer, a bawd, a seller of Christ. . . . Good God, Heseltine, it seems to me that a man should not be permitted to write a play before he has risked his life for another, or for the State."

Masefield's long narrative poem, *Dauber,* is ordinarily praised as a superb picture of the sea. It is that, but it is more than that. It is a superb picture of artistic dedication. It illustrates the author's sense of the means by which a moribund art may live again. Here is a man who desires to paint the "windy, green, unquiet sea," ships scudding before the wind, and the destinies of men whose ways are on the great deep. Nautical pictures he might make from models in his studio. To know the might and mystery of the sea, he must give himself to it as the saint gives himself to God. Three years before the mast, he hopes, will teach his hand to paint the living truth when he shows the landlubber how billows break and a ship goes up the wave. From the fore-topgallant yard, the dedicated dauber tumbles too soon to his death. But such prices the gods exact of those who mimic the Creator's art.

The point is that with Masefield literature ceases to be hypnotic, a dreamily recreative "escape from life." It becomes a probe to the quick of the spirit, stabbing us "broad awake." It becomes an exultant hymning and glorification of life, even while it rushes on catastrophe. I do not know whether he became a sailor in order to learn to sing, or whether he sang because he had been a sailor. But that fine poem about his great joys, *Biography,* is proof enough that the prime sources of his passion were not "literary." He loves the taste of his own days, bitter and sweet, and his physical immersion in experience: swimming, racing, the first glimpse of strange mountains; but heavy labor, too, in quarry and mill, roads tramped in the rain, the rough talk of peasant and sailor, the long road westward through the springing wheat, the comradeship of hard-palmed men following the sea,

> Whose feet with mine wore many a bolt head bright
> Treading the decks beneath the riding light.

The last line of this poem has been rather often quoted: "The days that make us happy make us wise." There is a good bit of Masefield in it. It is happiness, peace, and beauty which give a man new eyes and put "compassion" into his work. Yes, but reverse the saying and you have the other half of the poet's wisdom: "The days that make us wise make us happy."

In this world, a wise man learns to derive a great part of his happiness from discovering how much misery he can endure, how tough the human heart is, the blows it can take and still fight on, the wounds it can receive and still recover. I doubt whether any living poet save Thomas Hardy has meditated so deeply and so fruitfully on disastrous things as John Masefield. In his preface to *The*

Tragedy of Nan, a peasant drama written in 1907, he declares that "tragedy at its best is a vision of the heart of life. The heart of life can only be laid bare in the agony and exultation of dreadful acts. The vision of agony or spiritual contest, pushed beyond the limits of the dying personality, is exalting and cleansing. It is only by such vision that a multitude can be brought to the passionate knowledge of things exulting and eternal."

Among the tragic narratives I have a partiality for *The Widow in the Bye Street,* which many of the commentators rate below its deserts. It is notable for dramatic characterization. The title suggests that the interest centers in the mother, a figure treated with overwhelming pathos, though at the same time with an impartial disclosure of the jealous self-preservative elements in her affection for her son. A case might be made out for the central interest of Anna, who abides with singular vividness in my memory, dropping her spray of scarlet hips as a signal to Ern, and holding the dazzling light so that he may see to bash in Jimmy's face. Jimmy himself is, to my thinking, a pretty striking piece of characterization.

But there is a fifth person in this "sordid" affair, a fifth unnamed person, "exulting and eternal." She it was who made Jimmy desert his mother; she infatuated him with a harlot, she frenzied his arm to the murderous blow, she brought him to the hangman's noose, and among the ancients she was known as the divine Cytherea. Her defeat in the bloody squalor of these English circumstances was, I believe, for Mr. Masefield, one of the high interests of the occasion. Now many contrasted elements enter into the effect of this complete, symmetrical, and intense narrative—mother love, lust, jealousy, and murder; but the stinging beauty and terror of it depend, I believe, upon Masefield's vision of the authentic Cytherean casting her illusive radiance over a heartless drab.

This is not Anna whom he describes, hiding in the pastoral country after the execution of Jimmy—though it has her shape and name. This is the Cytherean illusion:

> There, in the April, in the garden close,
> One heard her in the morning singing sweet,
> Calling the birds from the unbudded rose,
> Offering her lips with grains for them to eat.
> The redbreasts come with little wiry feet,
> Sparrows and tits and all wild feathery things,
> Brushing her lifted face with quivering wings.

As W. H. Hamilton has pertinently remarked, there is something "fundamental in our poet's insistence upon another than the easy popular verdict on the unsuccessful." In his little book on Shakespeare, Masefield observes the Elizabethan dramatist's brooding sympathy with tragical kings, such as Richard II, who failed "because they did not conform to a type lower than themselves." Perhaps the idea is a little too subtle or too exalted for our common feeling that virtue resides with the victor and that the justice of a cause is to be gauged by its success.

But this notion of a moral splendor in the dead and defeated Mr. Masefield pursues through his tragedies: *Pompey the Great,* in which the hero has traits of resemblance to Woodrow Wilson; *Philip the King,* serene with religious faith after the destruction of the Armada, dismissing the tragic messenger with the thought: "In bitter days the soul finds God, God us"; the tragedy in Oriental mask called *The Faithful;* the noble tragic narrative of *Gallipoli,* in which fragments from the "Song of Roland" give the keynote; and so on through the two recent dramas dealing with the invincible "lost cause" of Christ.

To Masefield I think that the most beautiful and exalting thing in the world—the fairest form into which our transitory lives can flame, rushing into darkness—is the courage of men who have been faithful unto death. The heroic thrills him to his heart's core. Yet for him the World War was a long overshadowing agony, lit only by the blazing glory of human endurance. He followed the Red Cross to one of the most desperate battlefields to share its perils and to alleviate its miseries. These lines remind us in what mood men of peace in those days bowed to doom and

> . . . sadly rose and left the well loved Downs,
> And so by ship to sea; and knew no more
> The fields of home, the byres, the market towns,
> Nor the dear outline of the English shore.

> But knew the misery of the soaking trench,
> The freezing in the rigging, the despair
> In the revolting second of the wrench
> When the blind soul is flung upon the air.

From that tragedy Masefield returned with an immense and desperate compassion for the *animula*—God's waif, the human soul—poor, thin, little tenant of this falling house of flesh bewildered wanderer among his own juggernauts and thunders, along the roaring abysses of oblivion. The *Sonnets* dedicated "To My American Friends" in 1916 are an intensely realistic expression of a bitter quest, ending in the impersonally consolatory thought that

> The sun will rise, the winds that ever move
> Will blow our dust, and boy and girl will love.

Since the war Mr. Masefield has, I suspect, steadied himself by leaning heavily on the joy of people who do not think and feel deeply. In *Reynard the Fox, Right Royal,* and *King Cole*—outstanding narrative poems of these later years—friendly critics have hailed a recovery of that fluent, exuberant, creative energy, objective, dramatic and sensuous, which first astonished and delighted them in *The Everlasting Mercy.* Here are indeed high spirits and blithe scenes; sunlight and dew on English meadow and woodland; the barking of dogs; the excitement of horses; the pungency of the stable and the reek of the groom's strong pipe on the morning air; jolly, beef-eating, red-coated huntsmen;

English girls with roses in their cheeks; jockeys, farmers, hucksters, peasantry—all the countryside—gayly assembling for the old English sports, the fox hunt, the horse race, the traveling circus. Here are the bright speed, the galloping rhythms, the brilliant colors, the odor and zest of ruddy life.

One is tempted to say that the sensitive author of the sonnets and the lyrics, full of haunting cries and gushes of poignant sadness, has tossed his melancholy and the heartbreak of the *animula* into the west wind, and has voided the chamber of his personality in order to fill it with the ancient traditional emotions of the folk. It is one of many signs that John Masefield is a true poet of the taller sort, that he rises to a serene and joyous contemplation of the whole course of the "river of life" streaming down from Chaucer's time—with the eternal rhythm, and the fleeing waters that sparkle and pass. After sharp hunger, passionate seeking, nostalgia of the spirit, and tragic illumination, he has come to the clear high point from which Arnold described the full murmurous flowing of the Oxus to the sea. His personal feeling is discernible in the scene only in the softening of the light and in the almost inaudible undertone of compassion.

Lean'd on his fate, he gazes—tears
Are in his eyes, and in his ears
The murmur of a thousand years.
Before him he sees life unroll,
A placid and continuous whole—
That general life, which does not cease. . . .

"THE MIND OF THE RACE"[1]

By HARRISON SMITH

CHRISTINA ALBERTA'S FATHER. *By H. G. Wells. The Macmillan Company, New York.*

H. G. WELLS! It is a commonplace name, a name without flavor, curiously colorless and transparent, unlike Thackeray, Dickens, Hardy, Bernard Shaw, Arnold Bennett, Swinburne—a host of other names with substance to them. But a great man, a great writer is this Herbert George Wells, who is today fifty-nine years old, and who from his photos resembles a bristling Irish terrier more than ever; a little, defiant man, quite uninspiring.

Summer is over. In a few weeks the hills will be wine-colored again, and now as the season changes Wells presents the world with his fifty-third volume. Sometimes his books have come twice a year. Turn to the front of the new novel and read the titles that run far back into the adolesence of those of us who have earned the dignity of middle age. How they have entered into the mental texture of our present ideas of life! Mr. Wells discovered

[1] From *The New York Herald Tribune* "Books," October 4, 1925.

for us the age of steel and machinery—saw its social significance and translated it into fantastic stories which still remain the best that have ever been written in this realm which Jules Verne once penetrated. Think of the thousands of boys who have stolen away to libraries and have forgotten high school politics for *The War of the Worlds* and *The Sleeper Awakes*. Think of the serious young men in their first years of college back in 1910 arguing with downy hair on their flushed cheeks about *The New Machiavelli, Ann Veronica* and *Tono-Bungay* over their beer-mugs and in their dormitories—talking until dawn.

Recall, and blush if you must, the solemn discussions at summer hotels and on dark verandas with the flappers of those salad days, who formed a Greek chorus, and from the hammock swung a bored ankle while we talked to them of the social ideas of this new writer, and how we—we also were going to amount to something in this new and wonderful world which he painted. It was a world of limitless horizons, with people dashing about the bright skies in still uninvented airplanes, a democracy of the intellect, an international fellowship, a clean, bright, free existence. And still the flapper of 1910 swung her ankle, and back we came to the giggling moon and calf-love.

The old Wells of those days before the flood was always leading us by the nose—making us think of things that no one outside of sociological associations and scientific conferences ever bothered about. He was concerned with an amazing number of things; with what machinery was going to do for humanity and where modern education, democracy, and socialism were leading. He discovered the modern young woman in *Ann Veronica,* and in a measure prepared our minds for the unveiling of her legs and for her armed invasion of a still masculine society. He saw the evolution of marriage into a franker, cleaner system. He talked a great deal of the muddle and muss of the beginnings of the machine age and always pointed lucidly to the crystalline and limpid future around the corner. He foresaw the war. The fact that Herbert George often guessed wrong, that there was always some important element missing in his escapes into clearer living, is not important. It remains a fact that through his own work and that of the horde of writers who followed him he has entered into the mental processes of an entire generation of Americans and Englishmen. The reading, thinking part of the Anglo-Saxon world cannot get H. G. Wells out of its blood and out of its mind till those of us who are middle aged have been tripped up by the "hungry generation" pressing at our heels. One of Wells's pet phrases is "the mind of the race," and he has come extraordinarily close to achieving that sonorous title himself.

Let us turn back again and regard him in the midst of the war. There is a new note in Wells's voice—a touch of bewilderment. The familiar creaking earth began to accelerate its pace in 1914.

It fulfilled a few Wellsian prophecies almost immediately—the airplane, tanks, modern warfare with entire populations engaged, social changes, etc. And then it began to run ahead of its prophet—an express train, and a little defiant man with a bristling mustache tearing after it. He wrote *Mr. Britling Sees It Through,* an extraordinarily interesting revelation of his own frame of mind, and, incidentally, perhaps the best bit of propaganda produced in England during the war.

But, alas! our astrologer was no more. Departed his divining power, his magic! He began to rake up old ideas, polish them, and discover new Utopias. "The world needs a new Bible," proclaimed Herbert George, and proceeded to write its history, beginning with its birth from the sun. What gigantic energy! It is true again that historians and geologists have picked a few holes in it, but for the most part its majestic fabric remains intact. We have our new Bible now, and by turning over its pages can find what a great novelist thinks of Napoleon and Kublai Khan. This Gargantuan job, which would have been any professor's life work, if, indeed, any university could possibly have given it birth, hardly interrupted his stream of ideas. He spent three months in Russia and wrote a book about the world's greatest revolution. In one novel Wells discovered God; and in another he told us what was wrong with education; another tangled itself in psychoanalytical love. Amazing virtuosity! Wells was as interesting as ever, as agile as ever, as brilliant as ever. But there was some element missing. You see, Mr. Wells had never caught his train. The youths in college with the incredible numerals of 1924 on their banners were discussing Mencken, Shaw, Lewis, and a score of other gods over their bootleg whisky and on verandas with the latest model of streamline flappers.

But not Mr. Wells. Then came brand new Utopias from Mr. Wells, in which clear-eyed goddesses and youthful Apollos talked with charm and eloquence of freedom and denatured love against a background of garden cities and combed, thornless landscapes. But irony has no place here, for what religion has offered us more benign Nirvanas than Mr. Wells has created for us on our own earth? He has even seen the end of life's ugliest sin, which is death. And all within our grasp if we would but seize it and if humanity could but drop its dirty ancestor, the ape, whose existence Mr. Wells proves so finally in his history.

Now comes his latest novel, and any one who believes that because the prophet has failed he is any the less a novelist may correct his error by reading *Christina Alberta's Father*. It is about a certain Mr. Preemby and his daughter, Christina Alberta. If you have read *Mr. Polly, Love and Mr. Lewisham,* or *Kipps,* you do not have to be told much more about Mr. Preemby than that he was the widower of an extraordinarily energetic woman who ran and owned the Limpid Stream Laundry in a dingy section of London. Mr. Preemby was just about as efficient as a newly hatched chicken; a downy little man with an immensely overdeveloped mustache and a habit of blowing through it and saying, "H'hrmp!"—a pathetic and yet somehow a very lovable human being. There was a fantastic side to him, too. He was always muddling around with esoteric ideas, thinking about Atlantis and reincarnation—a victim, in fact, of the mental rubbish that so many weak but imaginative minds are nourished on. It was this side of him that made him insist on painting a Swastika on the outside of his wife's blue laundry vans. But his daughter loved him, just because he was dear and muddle-headed and used to like to pretend that they were themselves "Atlantides," descendants, in other words, of the drowned continent.

Early in the novel Mrs. Preemby dies and turns loose on a hard and overpopulated world this little man and his flapper daughter. Christina, needless to say, is made of different stuff. In fact, you find out, as she does herself later on, that she isn't even his daughter. Christina has been barging about London before her mother's death, getting her hair cut short and her skirts still shorter, and discovering art, scraps of education, and how to talk with appalling frankness of the things that used to be whispered behind one's hand. She introduces her father to a modern studio, where the reader meets an extraordinary variety of innocent Bohemians. And then, since the old man is quite obviously wretched there, she abandons him in a first-rate boarding house in Bath.

After a week of this Mr. Preemby discovers that he is the reincarnation of Sargon, Ruler of the World. He is not actually insane, but all of his theosophical fancies have at last come to roost in one great delusion which broods over his mind. The result is naturally catastrophic. After several amusing adventures in which he announces to "his people" the coming of their lord and ruler, Sargon the Great, he is, of course, shut up in an insane asylum. Christina is desolated. Her father has disappeared, and the shock is sufficient to reveal to her that the messy love affair in which she has become involved is a stupid violation of her own honesty.

An engaging young writer, one Bobby, who for two years has been unable to write more of his novel than its title page, becomes interested in the little mustached man who is sheltered for a few days in Bobby's boarding house on his inevitable progress to the asylum. While Christina and several of her new intellectual friends are trying to discover how they can persuade the State that Sargon the Great is not insane, Bobby proceeds to snatch him out of bedlam by the simple process of kidnaping him and running off with him on a motor bicycle. At this point Bobby meets Christina and falls very naturally in love with her. Also, it is sad to relate, at the same point Mr. Wells's novel begins to go to pieces. He is not willing to let well enough alone, to tell this simple and charming tale, to present the laundress's widower with such deft skill that one can see the little man sitting in his chair and "H'hrmp"ing through his mustache, and to create a girl of 1925 who is every bit as real and intriguing as was Ann Veronica in those old days when women threw stones through London shop-windows. Mr. Wells must tack some sort of Utopia at the tail of this novel, as if he were a minister pointing a moral to his sermon. I do not mean that the book does not turn out satisfactorily. Mr. Preemby dies; his daughter discovers a real and very satisfactory father, and Bobby is put off without marriage. But it is too bad that one has to wade through a score of pages of rather rambling philosophy about "the new world," "the Mind of the Race," etc., etc., as a climax to a novel which no other man in England or America is capable of producing.

MADAME DE SÉVIGNÉ IN THE COUNTRY [1]

By Logan Pearsall Smith

In traveling across France the train sometimes passes a formal park, through which a great avenue, opening its vista for a second, reveals at the end of that perspective the mansard roofs and stately façade of some seventeenth-century château; and in the imagination of the traveler this little glimpse may awaken the thought of the great age of French history—that vainglorious reign, so famous in arts and arms, of Louis XIV, the *Roi-Soleil.* To an American or English traveler at least there may be something pompous and cold in the vision, thus suddenly evoked, of this vanished France; he may not be able easily to imagine what the personages were really like for whom these parks were laid out and these stately houses erected. But, on the other hand, it is possible that our traveler may feel himself curiously at home in this period—more at home there, indeed, than in the democratic France of the date of his railway journey. Many of the inhabitants may seem to him like long-acquainted friends, with the very texture of whose minds he has become familiar, learning in long days of delightful conversation the things they liked and laughed at,

[1] From *The Dial,* July, 1925.

the problems they puzzled over, and with what fears and hopes their thoughts traveled along those avenues to the Court and the wars.

Thus to reverse the time-process, thus to be transported back into the actual life of a bygone epoch, requires a spell, a necromancy we might call it, more potent than that of history: the chroniclers, the historians, and even the memoir-writers of the *Grand Siècle,* can at most enable us to see it, so to speak, from without—to look in, as through gates of gilded iron, upon that formal region. If then our Anglo-Saxon traveler can enter there at ease, can feel himself happy and at home in that society, it must be because a more intimate access, a more personal introduction, has been his privilege: he must have made the acquaintance, and have won the friendship, we may safely hazard, of the lady of genius who stands ready with her golden key to open that escutcheoned gate to those who love her. This magic instrument, the wand which this enchantress wielded (though without the slightest consciousness of its power) was nothing more than the feathered quill with which Mme. de Sévigné scribbled her almost countless letters to her daughter—letters which, in spite of their old dates and spellings, come to us across the centuries like contemporary documents, and read indeed as if they had been written hardly more than a day or two ago. With almost all the upholstered figures of past epochs it is a constant effort to believe that they once actually existed, did once indubitably breathe the air and walk in the sunshine of this earthly scene; but with Mme. de Sévigné, so limpid is the sound of her voice, so lively her glance, so inextinguishable the spirit of life that shines and sparkles in her letters, that we find it hard to believe—we cannot really believe—that she has been, for more than two centuries, dead.

When we get to know her best, at the beginning of her correspondence with her daughter, Mme. de Sévigné was approaching the age of fifty, but her face still retained the coloring of girlhood; she enjoyed, she said, the fine blood that ran so agreeably and lightly through her veins, almost believing that she had discovered some fountain of perpetual youth—for how otherwise could she account for her splendid and triumphant health? This "divine Marquise," with her fair complexion, her blue eyes and golden hair, was a lady of rank and high distinction, who was famous for her wit and grace and beauty. She played no insignificant part in the society of her time, and her biographers have for the most part written of her as a woman of the world, a great lady of Parisian society, a wit and *raconteuse* of worldly gossip. The temptation, indeed, to write of this aspect of her life is a strong one: she loved the world, and appreciated in a curiously conscious way all that was magnificent in the stately age she lived in—the rejoicings for victories, the pomp of great marriages, and the splendor of Versailles as it shone new-built and brilliant in contemporary eyes; the torches and gold costumes of the fêtes there, the confusion without confusion of the courtiers and music, the stately figure of the Grand Monarch, and the triumphant beauty of his mistresses, with their thousand ringlets, their lace and pearls. How diversified everything was, how gay and gallant; and surely, she said, writing before its disastrous eclipse, never had there been a star so brilliant as the King's!

But interesting as is Mme. de Sévigné's account of the Court and fashion, she herself is more delightful than any good society—the "fine creature," as her English lover, Edward FitzGerald, called her, was, as he said, all genuine, "all Truth and Daylight"; and it is the picture she unconsciously gives us of her own frank, generous-hearted nature, her "good Sense [to quote FitzGerald once more], Good Feeling, Humor, Love of Books and Country Life," which is the greatest charm of this correspondence. *"Rien n'est bon,"* she wrote, *"que d'avoir une belle et bonne âme; on la voit en toute chose comme à travers d'un cœur de cristal";* and this sentence might form the best motto for the many volumes of her correspondence. We see into this crystal heart perhaps most clearly in the long letters written in the solitude and leisure of her country days. Although her home was in Paris, she had a retreat at Livry, in the midst of a forest not many miles away. Sometimes in the spring she would drive thither in her coach and six, merely for the afternoon, to refresh her spirit with the young green of the trees and the songs of the nightingales; and often she would live for weeks or months there, especially in the autumn, finding in that autumnal forest a solitude, a melancholy, and a silence which, she often felt, she loved better than anything else in the world.

But much the greater number of her country letters were written from the family estate in far-off Brittany, where long periods of her life were spent. First of all she describes the journey from Paris, partly in her coach by road, and partly with the coach on board a sailing boat and floating down the Loire; and these journeys are so vividly reflected in the magic glass she carries with her that we remember them almost as intimately as if they had been journeys of our own. Sometimes she would travel alone in the company of her uncle, the old Abbé, with whom she lived, sometimes with friends who were making the same journey; and she often recounts the conversations with which they filled the long hot days of driving. Often, too, she would stop at the country houses of friends on the way, and, with her coach drawn into the coach-house, her horses resting in the stables, she would pay long visits at these great *châteaux,* with their avenues and terraces and fountains, bored or pleased, according to the company she found in them. But sooner or later these journeys, with all their fatigues, and with their accidents, for her coach would sometimes upset and land her in a ditch—they were strange things, long journeys, and if one remembered them one would never travel, but God made one forget—she would arrive on her own estates and drive up the avenue to her own *château,* where she would find awaiting her the business affairs and social duties which belonged to her position as an important territorial personage and the mistress of a great estate.

The *château* of Les Rochers lies about four miles from the town of Vitry, and no great distance from Mont St.-Michel. The house, the formal gardens, the woods with their great avenues, remain as they were when she lived there; the orange trees in their tubs are her orange trees; the clipped limes are the limes she planted; and the room in which she wrote her letters, with its table, its portraits, the bed of yellow satin, embroidered by her daughter, is now as she describes it in her letters, fresh and gay, and almost untouched by time. We are familiar not only with Les Rochers, but with the society of the neighborhood—a society, as she regarded it, of tiresome and pretentious people, whom she was always trying to avoid. Some critics have greatly blamed her for her contempt of the provincial *noblesse,* which was, they say, so superior in moral qualities to the high and fashionable society of Paris and the Court in which she delighted; but posterity can hardly reprehend with much enthusiasm the aristocratic disdain to which we owe so amusing a picture-gallery of provincial bores, each of them touched off with a light and witty malice which makes us understand why her intimates found such a delight in her company that, as one of them declared, he at least would hardly care to go on living without her, *ne sachant avec qui rire finement.* She was much beset by these unwelcome neighbors, who would come to call so often, or even to stay in the house for longer visits; but she consoled herself with the philosophic thought that bad company was after all better than good—it was so delightful to have it go! The departure of tiresome guests—what could be a greater pleasure? she would ask her daughter. *"Je me ménage les délices d'un adieu charmant,"* she writes of some visitors staying in the house, describing later on how exquisitely the sound of their departing coach-wheels had refreshed her blood.

But a great part of the time Mme. de Sévigné was more or less alone at Les Rochers with her uncle, the old Abbé, who helped her manage her affairs. One of their main occupations was the improvement of the property: each of them had a band of workmen; the Abbé loved to build, and was always wandering out to look at the chapel he was erecting, while his niece had a passion for planting trees. She would be sometimes out, early in the mornings, up to her knees in dew, marking out new plantations; and each time when, after an absence, she arrived again in Brittany, she would hurry out to see her avenues, marveling at the growth of the trees she had planted, the long shadows they cast, and how much greener they were than the trees near Paris. Was it their nature to be so green, she wondered, or was it the freshness of the Breton rains? There is indeed a charming breath of the forest in these old letters, and it is somewhat surprising to see this fine lady, who so dearly loved all that was gay and amusing and brilliant in the elegant and opulent society of Paris, suddenly transformed into a kind of woodland creature, spending, even in the winter, long days in the silence and solitude of her forest paths; to see her looking like a *loup-garou,* as she said, and dressed in an old coat and an old straw hat, planting with her workmen oak-trees in the rain.

That love of wild nature which we regard as a modern passion, that blending of mood and landscape which so deeply colors our modern consciousness, is generally supposed—and supposed with much truth—to date from the time when sunsets and lakes and woods and mountains first mirrored themselves, with all the splendor and richness of their coloring, in the romantic eyes of Jean-Jacques Rousseau. But Rousseau had his predecessors: there were lovers of nature before his birth, and among them Mme. de Sévigné, with her passion for trees, must be counted; for although, like her contemporaries, she was blind to the beauty of lakes and moors and mountains, and although her woods were not the savage and dark forests in which Chateaubriand entombed his inexplicable despair, but arranged plantations, with mottoes on the trees, and dry and pleasant walks, and labyrinths, and artificial echoes; yet her melancholy delight in the solitude, the mystery, the *sainte horreur,* as she called it, of these lofty groves, her passion for wandering at night in their dark recesses, were moods of *romantisme avant la lettre,* as the French call it. Nor have any romantic writers of a later period noted with greater sensitiveness the changing aspects and hours of forest scenery; the frosty stillness of winter days, with faint sunlight making the distance dim and misty; the beauty of the leafless trees in March, with a confused noise of birds that foretold the spring; the triumph of May with the nightingales; the coolness of the woods in torrid weather, the sweetness of the summer nights there, with their soft and gracious air; the beauty of the sunsets at the ends of the great avenues, or the enchantment of the moon, silvering the shadowy spaces of their long perspectives. *"Nous avions entendu un cor dans le fond de cette forêt"*—we rub our eyes: can this haunting sentence have been penned, so long before Alfred de Vigny's birth, by a lady of fashion in the bewigged reign of Louis the Fourteenth?

A foreigner who might attempt to define for himself the charm of these seventeenth-century letters, although he might not be able to analyze into its elements this liquid and harmonious French, flowing on through volume after volume with the inexhaustible vivacity of a fountain of clear water, could not but note the felicity of the many translucent phrases which mirror with such limpidity the woodland lights and shadows, as they colored Mme. de Sévigné's meditations and tinged her varying moods, while she paced those avenues, hour after hour and day after day. Heaven only knew, she said, what thoughts she didn't think in that Breton forest: there were pleasant memories and hopes and day dreams; and there was a great spectacle of contemporary history, which she watched from her woods, and over which she moralized with unfailing interest. She liked great events, great changes of fortune pleased her; and there were certain strokes of Providence which, although they took her breath away, delighted her with their suddenness and grandeur.

But the general conclusion of all her thoughts was a sad one; almost all her meditations led to a melancholy moral. Kings, and the lovely mistresses of kings, princes, and courtiers, as she thought of them in her somber forest, all seemed to her examples of human misery and weakness. And none of these actors, playing their parts, great or small, on the world's stage, was contented; and not one of them—and she found in the thought a melancholy kind of consolation—was really happy. And she herself? For her too there were many black thoughts lurking in the forest which she tried to hurry past without regarding. Her humor was indeed a happy one; she was easily amused, and could accomodate herself, she said, to almost anything that happened; and all that was essentially cruel in human conditions, the mockery of hope, the swift passing of time—the very shadows of the great trees she had planted reminding her that she too was growing old—even the nearness of hideous and degrading old age, and of death, which she feared and hated—all this she could bear without repining; it was the common lot. But thus to be growing old and perishing so far from the person she loved with so strange a passion—this was a thought to which neither religion nor philosophy could reconcile her; nothing could cure her bitter tears.

Mme. de Sévigné's letters to the daughter she loved with this vehemence of passion have so much the character of love-letters that many readers have been repelled from them by the tiresome monotony which seems inseparable from effusions of this kind. There is indeed in all extreme affection an element of unreason—a divine madness, it may be, but still a madness—which disconcerts us: the elixir of love is a divine potation, but it is most serviceable for literature after it has been tempered and transfused by art—decanted, it may be, into the crystal chalice of a lyric, or cooled in the ornamented jars of a sonnet-sequence; and impetuous love-letters, fervid with the ebullitions of unmoderated feeling, are apt to pall, in the end, upon the unenamored reader. Even Edward FitzGerald, who in his later years became so devoted to his "blessed Sévigné" that he composed, as a labor of love, a big dictionary of the places and persons mentioned in her letters, confesses that he had been kept aloof from them for many years by "that eternal daughter of hers"; and others of her admirers cannot but be wearied at times by her praises of Mme. de Grignan's perfections and her laments over their ever-recurring separations, especially since posterity has enviously, and perhaps unjustly, agreed to look upon this Countess as an unamiable and sophisticated prig, who was by no means a worthy object of so ardent a maternal passion.

But then they remind themselves that this fine excess has after all its pathetic beauty, and that without its inspiration Mme. de Sévigné would never have written these golden letters, in which she made use of all her resources to amuse and entertain not only her daughter, but posterity as well—gathering the pick, as she said, of all the baskets, the flower of her wit and thoughts and eyes and pen. And after all, they remember, the poor lady, unlike most lovers, was more or less aware of her own folly, and tried to moderate its vehemence and vary its expression in a hundred humorous and graceful ways. Still it was her song, as inevitable and natural to her as the nightingale's descant; and she repeats its phrases over and over with the musical reiteration of that woodland chorister. *"Ah! la jolie chose qu'une feuille qui chante!"* she wrote of the nightingale in a phrase which has become famous; and as she reiterates her longing for the being whose image was her inseparable companion, her voice echoes from the formal forests of seventeenth-century France with something of the pathos and beauty of that fabled parent's musical lament. For the thought of Mme. de Grignan was, she said, the center and depth of all her meditations; around it everything else slid and vanished; and should ever, by some miracle, that thought desert her, it would leave her like a wax figure, hollow and empty and with nothing within. So all day long, and day after day, her imagination, out-distancing the swift couriers who were carrying her letters to the South, would wing its way across the breadth of France to the terraces and triumphant view of that great mountain castle in Provence, where, amid an uproar of music and guests and servants, and a perpetual storm of wind, the lovely philosophic Countess lived and reigned.

Mme. de Grignan piqued herself upon her mastery of the modern and fashionable philosophy of Descartes; her mother was of the older, more human, and homely school of Montaigne, whose essays she was so fond of reading; and curiously enough she remains, with Montaigne, one of the human beings of the past with whom posterity is most intimately acquainted—being indeed, as FitzGerald said of her, much more living to us than most of the living people whom we see about us. Writing long ago those hasty epistles to which she attached not the slightest importance, letting her pen gallop at its will with the reins upon its neck, as she set down amid her woods her meditations on mortality and on the cruel lapse of time, which was bearing her away, with all she loved, so swiftly upon its resistless stream, yet in her very complaints of his invincible power she was, though she had no notion of it, splendidly triumphing over this old enemy. And indeed Time himself, busied as always with his great work of ruin and obliteration, has for once proved himself a chivalrous opponent, turning away his scythe to preserve with delicate care the slightest records of Mme. de Sévigné's moods and fancies. Many writers have longed for durable renown, laboring with no success to win an immortality in the thoughts of succeeding ages; but this splendid gift of Fame was vouchsafed to Mme. de Sévigné in answer to no request of hers. That easy, graceful, smiling defeat of oblivion, that effortless and unconscious victory, we might almost call it, over Death, which is the magic and marvel and the ultimate interest of her writing, was the outcome of a genius she never knew she possessed; nor had she indeed the slightest notion that, in a life in which nothing happened, she was turning into immortality everything she touched, weaving out of her ephemeral thoughts a delicate but enduring tissue which has proved untarnishable by time. And amid the destruction of so much of ancient France, the scene and background of her country meditations still remains, with its formal gardens, its architecture, and the great avenues of its environing forests, so inviolate, so unblemished by the ineffectual and defeated years, that the tourist from another age who makes a pilgrimage to Les Rochers will almost ask himself at last, with a kind of eerie wonder, whether he may not be himself more of a ghost than the spirit he has come to visit—an evanescent shadow or *revenant* out of the chaos of a future much more doubtful than the immortality of that lifetime which is destined to outlast his own—that golden past which shines in these unfading letters, and seems indeed actually to gleam before his eyes, illuminating the circle of sunny space within the enclosure of those Breton woods.

ASSAULT UPON THE POETS[1]

By CHAUNCEY BREWSTER TINKER

After all, what is Parnassus but the slope of a mountain?
—*Old Play.*

EARLY in the morning of July 28, 1814, Percy Bysshe Shelley, an unknown young poet, and Mary Godwin, daughter of that preposterous philosopher, William Godwin, ran away together, leaving behind them, in Godwin's home in Skinner Street, London, a startled and indignant family. Their flight to Calais was thrilling but uncomfortable. Mary left her father's house at four o'clock in the morning, accompanied by her stepmother's daughter, Jane (or Claire) Clairmont, who, being bored in Skinner Street, had decided to run away too. The girls joined Shelley at the corner of Hatton Garden, and the three of them drove off together in a post-chaise. It was, as Mr. Beers has said, "one of the most sociable elopements that one remembers to have read of."

The day proved to be sultry, and Mary more than once felt faint. It was necessary to rest at every stage of the journey. Shelley was divided between anxiety for her health and terror lest pursuers should overtake them. At Dartford they therefore took four horses in order to outstrip pursuit. Be-

[1] From *The Yale Review,* July, 1925.

fore four o'clock in the afternoon they were in Dover, where Mary refreshed herself by a bath in the sea. It was deemed unwise to wait for the night packet to Calais lest their elders overtake them; so Shelley, after time for consideration, went about interviewing customs-house officials and bargaining with sailors. It was a beauteous evening, calm and free—what could be more delightful than to cross the Channel in an open boat? The seamen assured Shelley that a crossing could be made in two hours, and Shelley, who had never crossed before, believed them. The small boat which he hired to convey them was ready by six o'clock. The baggage was to come by packet.

It was not long before the young people saw the sands slowly recede behind them. There was little wind, so that the sails flapped in the languid air; but with nightfall a violent swell began, and a fresh night-breeze soon produced a heavy sea. Mary fell sick, and passed the night in restless slumber, reclining on Shelley's bosom. He was himself so exhausted that it was with some ado that he could support her weight. Claire appears to have shifted for herself. At moments Mary roused herself to ask her young lover how far they had gone, and to receive the dismal answer each time, "Not quite half way."

There was no improvement as the hours passed. The moon sunk behind a red and stormy horizon, and the fast-flashing lightning became pale in the breaking day. Suddenly a thunder-squall struck the sail, and the waves rushed into the boat. And then, as so often in his short life, Shelley, who could not swim, prepared himself for a death by drowning. Even the sailors regarded the situation as perilous, if we may trust the words of Shelley himself: "I had time in that moment," he wrote later, "to reflect and even to reason upon death; it was rather a thing of discomfort and of disappointment than of horror to me."

At last the sailors succeeded in reefing the sail. The wind changed, and their boat drove straight ahead into the harbor of Calais. Exhausted with fatigue and sickness, Mary walked with her companions across the sands to the hotel, safe now from wind, wave, and relatives.

Such is the story of Shelley's elopement, which has been told by a score of biographers, and will be told again by a future score. Every reader now knows the story from *Ariel.* But not every one knows that the first person to tell it in print was Mary herself. In 1817, less than three years after the event, she and Bysshe compiled and published a modest little volume, entitled *History of a Six Weeks' Tour,* most of which deals with a later trip to the Continent, but the opening sections of which, written by Mary with some help from Shelley's journal, recount that earlier journey of 1814 and the Channel crossing which I have just narrated. My account is largely composed of phrases and sentences drawn from the *Tour* and from Shelley's journal.

But there are other accounts, or rather reminiscences, of the flight. Years later, when Shelley was no more, the scene (as my friend Professor Peck has pointed out to me), makes its appearance in Mary Shelley's novel, *Perkin Warbeck,* at the point where Richard, Duke of York, is leaving Scotland with Katherine:

> It sufficed for their two full hearts that they were together on the dark wide sea; the bright sky above, and calm upon the bosom of the deep. They could ill discern each other in the shadowy twilight; a dream-like veil was cast over their features, as sleep curtains out the soul, so that we look on the beloved slumberer, and say, "He is there, though the mystery of repose wraps me from him"; so now darkness blinded and divided them: but hand clasped hand; he felt that one existed who was his own, his faithful; and she rejoiced in the accomplishment of the master-sentiment of her soul, the desire of self-devotion, self-annihilation, for one who loved her.

Far more remarkable, however, is the reminiscence of the event from the pen of the poet himself. In that volume of supreme lyrical splendor which Mrs. Shelley gave to the world in 1824 under the title of *Posthumous Poems of Percy Bysshe Shelley,* there is a highly characteristic ballad (so Mrs. Shelley later called it), named "The Fugitives." In a later edition of her husband's works, she classed it among "Poems written in 1821"—that is, seven years after the events of which an account has been given. The elopement is viewed across a vista of seven years, so that it should surprise no one to discover that distance has altered the scene very considerably. When a poet's imagination has played over an event for seven years, we may expect it to glow with new color and a larger significance.

I

The waters are flashing,
The white hail is dashing,
The lightnings are glancing,
The hoar-spray is dancing—
Away!

The whirlwind is rolling,
The thunder is tolling,
The forest is swinging,
The minster bells ringing—
Come away!

The Earth is like Ocean,
Wreck-strewn and in motion:
Bird, beast, man, and worm
Have crept out of the storm—
Come away!

II

"Our boat has one sail,
And the helmsman is pale;—
A bold pilot, I trow,
Who should follow us now"—
Shouted he—

And she cried: "Ply the oar!
Put off gaily from shore!"—
As she spoke, bolts of death
Mixed with hail, specked their path
        O'er the sea.

And from isle, tower and rock,
The blue beacon cloud broke,
And though dumb in the blast,
The red cannon flashed fast
        From the lee.

III

"And fear'st thou, and fear'st thou?
And, seest thou, and hear'st thou?
And drive we not free
O'er the terrible sea,
        I and thou?"

One boat-cloak did cover
The loved and the lover—
Their blood beats one measure,
They murmur proud pleasure
        Soft and low;—

While around the lashed Ocean,
Like mountains in motion,
Is withdrawn and uplifted,
Sunk, shattered, and shifted,
        To and fro.

You will detect at once the differences between the ballad and the facts out of which it springs.

Claire Clairmont, for instance, has disappeared, and the elopement has become a quite conventional *fuite à deux,* if I may use the phrase. And of course there is no mention of sea-sickness, or of Dover, Calais, or the Channel. The poem is like Thomas Campbell's ballad, "Lord Ullin's Daughter," which had been published in 1809, and must have been quite familiar to Shelley:

By this the storm grew loud apace,
  The water-wraith was shrieking;
And in the scowl of heaven each face
  Grew dark as it was speaking. . . .

The boat has left a stormy land,
  A stormy sea before her,—
When, Oh! too strong for human hand,
  The tempest gathered o'er her.

It is as though Shelley, with the memory of that night of July 28-29, 1814, in mind, had, in imagination, cast himself and Mary in the rôle of the "chieftain to the Highlands bound" and that fair Lord Ullin's daughter. Or, to state it in another way, he had divined from his own experience the poetic truth in the old romantic ballad of the eloping lovers. But, you see, for biographical purposes, the poem is negligible. No biographer, so far as I know, has cited it in connection with Shelley's elopement. To do so, indeed, would be to court misconception. If the poem has any value apart from its own sweetness and intensity, it is not in recording the mere events of life, but in revealing the subtle and elusive relations between the facts of biography and the fabric of poetry.

But let us return to the three fugitives. Later in the morning, Shelley, who was resting in the hotel, was informed that "a fat lady had arrived, who said that he had run away with her daughter." This was Mary's step-mother, Mrs. William Godwin, formerly Mrs. Clairmont, that unlovely being in green spectacles who has been immortalized by Charles Lamb's hatred of her. She had crossed on the night packet, like the luggage. She wanted her daughter, Claire Clairmont, back again, and she appears to have been willing to take Mary home with her, too, if she would consent to come, though it was not her chief mission to separate the young couple. Her husband had imposed an odd restriction on her, that she should not see Shelley himself, intending, I suppose, thus to administer a snub to the young disciple who had ventured to put into practice the radical theories that he had learned from Godwin himself. Be this as it may, Claire spent the next night with her mother, but was not persuaded to give up her trip. Fancy being asked to turn back, having just set foot for the first time in your life upon the continent of Europe! So Mrs. Godwin had to go home alone, "without a word," having, like so many parents in such stories, accomplished nothing at all. But the pursuit of this fat lady who (let us hope) was wearing her green spectacles, furnishes just the touch of low comedy appropriate to an elopement, that strange mixture of passion, peril, and fun. Mrs. Godwin plays no rôle of vast importance, yet who would spare her from the story?

And does Mrs. Clairmont appear in "The Fugitives"? Assuredly not. The mother (or stepmother) is not usually the pursuer in romantic ballads, but remains at home in a state of prostration. It is the father who should pursue, and it was her father whom Mary Godwin feared. So did Lord Ullin's daughter:

> "O haste thee, haste!" the lady cries,
> "Though tempests round us gather,
> I'll meet the raging of the skies,
> But not an angry father."

Where, we may therefore like to know, was William Godwin? O reader! he remained among his books in Skinner Street. And does he therefore make no figure in our heroic ballad? Assuredly he does. He wears a heroic mask over his dull features; but he is Godwin nevertheless. The father of the fleeing lady appears at the very end of the ballad to curse his undutiful child and devote her to the raging waves. To Shelley, I suppose, in the excitement of his *enlèvement,* that silly old man seemed to be arrayed in all the terrors that are conventionally assigned to outraged fathers. Even the anger of a Godwin must have seemed formidable to the fugitives. If one were engaged in an elopement, however unromantic its actual circumstances, it would be quite impossible, I submit, to avoid all romantic thoughts. A conviction of heroism would steal over one. In the glow of success one would seem to be a very Lochinvar, making off with another man's bride, heroically, in the nick of time. At least the emotions of Young Lochinvar would be more intelligible than ever before! And so, seven years after the events, Shelley set it all down, supplying the lack of a rival bridegroom by boldly creating one. Here is the conclusion of "The Fugitives," which I have withheld for a moment:

IV

In the court of the fortress,
Beside the pale portress,
Like a bloodhound well beaten,
The bridegroom stands, eaten
By shame.

On the topmost watch-turret,
As a death-boding spirit,
Stands the gray tyrant father,
To his voice the mad weather
Seems tame.

And with curses as wild
As e'er clung to child,
He devotes to the blast
The best, loveliest, and last
Of his name!

This ballad, which may well have been a gift to Mary Godwin as its "only begetter," blends the facts of the elopement, reminiscences of older poems, and the poetic fashions of Shelley's day in no insignificant way; and its study may serve to illustrate once more that uttermost mystery by which genius fuses the realism of life into the speed and splendor of poetry. To a biographer, in search of the unadorned facts of life, the little poem might seem like a ludicrous perversion of the events. But happily the poem is its own *raison d'être,* which certainly does not require for its appreciation the elaborate analysis to which it has just been submitted. It would be well for Shelley if his poems could eclipse the story of his life, and so, in far distant times, they may do; but just at present "his futile, unhappy career" (as Mr. Beers has called it) has fascinated the reading public. M. Maurois' *Ariel* is a very readable book —has it not been a first seller?—but it hardly mentions Shelley's poetry. Perhaps we ought to concede that it has at least the merit of leaving untouched a subject which the author does not understand. French interpretations of Shelley's lyrics may, no doubt, be spared. But this is not the worst of the matter. The success of *Ariel* will establish a style of writing by which the lower levels of biography will be made so amusing that readers will hardly be won to lift their eyes to the hills and the infinite skies above.

We are in for it now. As a result of the popularity of M. Maurois and of his ironical English predecessor, Mr. Strachey, we must brace ourselves for a rushing flood of these novelistic biographies.

Hardly an author of the nineteenth century, except Alfred Lord Tennyson, can hope to escape. Somebody is sure to do Burns before the year is out, for as a philanderer he surpasses Shelley and even Byron, and, for a love-story such as his, readers may even consent to be drawn back to the eighteenth century. Rumor has it that M. Maurois himself will write on Disraeli. Miss Alice Brown has put Charles Lamb into a play. We have had from Professor Harper a fine biography of Wordsworth, but nobody has yet tried to make it over into a novel. Still you never can tell. That illegitimate daughter of Wordsworth's may very possibly appear in fiction to take posthumous revenge for the sins of her sire. Miss Lowell has given us a more serious biography of Keats than some of her readers expected or desired, but her publishers try to win the public by announcing on every copy of her book that she has "the verve of a novelist." Now that is unfair to Miss Lowell, for she has deliberately declined to write a mere story about Keats; but somebody else will seize the opportunity. Fanny Brawne will serve for the heroine in some highly psychological story. And Byron! Well, it is clear that the biographers are by no means done with him. M. Boutet de Monvel has just produced a life in French, and Mr. Desmond MacCarthy promises one in English. Mr. Harold Nicholson has written a brilliant and careful book about Byron's last days, and Miss Mayne has revised her *Life of Byron*. The publishers of the latter assure the public, on the dustwrapper of their book, that Miss Mayne is "an adept at the analysis of character," and has "the instincts of a novelist." Let us not pause to speculate on the emotions with which a Lockhart or a Trevelyan would read such words.

It is going to be very interesting to see how Byron's reputation fares under the repeated attacks of the biographers. It has, for instance, always been customary to regard Byron's services to Greece and his death at Missolonghi as an act of atonement, a heroic and redemptive, if catastrophic, climax. Fine things for Europe, politically, came of it—so much is admitted by Mr. Nicholson in his study of the last stage of Byron's career. But as we read his book, *Byron: the Last Journey,* it becomes almost impossible to preserve any shreds of hero-worship. "For Byron," says Mr. Nicholson, "this Greek venture was the last chance . . . there was really nothing else for him to do." La Guiccioli had become a burden and her father a ludicrous nuisance. There had been civic troubles in Ravenna and, later, in Pisa, and these had put Byron out of sorts with Italy. He wanted to be off. He had thought of America and of "Bolivar's country." He was known as a radical and the friend and protector of radicals. One has to live up to one's reputation. And then there was that Cockney journalist, Leigh Hunt, and his pack of dirty children. The noisy Hunts were a legacy from Shelley, as it were. In Greece there would at least be no Hunts. Byron had long ago assumed the rôle of philo-Hellenist—

had he not written about Greece in "Childe Harold"? Had he not written the "Corsair" and the "Siege of Corinth" and the "Isles of Greece"? He had also got into correspondence, as the Devil would have it, with the Greek Committee in London, and they expected fine things—impossible things—of him. Before he knew what he was doing, he was obliged to go. He once said of himself that his eyes never opened to the folly of his undertakings until retreat (at least with honor) became impossible. So it was, says Mr. Nicholson, an "irresolute and dyspeptic little man, who, on that July evening, limped gloomily up the gangway of the *Hercules*."

Even Byron's appearance at this time was unheroic. His thinning auburn-gray hair fell "in wisps" over his collar. It was still curled, to be sure—by his valet—and drenched with oil. There was nothing godlike about him any more. He was incontestibly middle-aged, tired, and irritable. He was in no state of health for heroism or for prolonged diplomacy. He was destined to have an epileptic fit in Greece. He was suffering, as an autopsy later proved, from enlargement of the heart, and there was some sort of trouble with the brain and with the sutures of the skull. And Greece! Greece was a land of bickering, dominated by those paltry men who flourish in time of war. Also there was a thirst for British gold—greed, everywhere greed, and a wish to lead Lord Byron to the shearing rather than to the slaughter. It was all a hopeless mess for one who had come thither for action and a splendid gesture. There were mud and sewage, flies and stench and fever—a confusion of tongues as of Babel and a confusion of plans as of Bedlam. By the middle of February Byron, says Mr. Nicholson, "had realized that the only thing he could do for Greece was not to run away."

Now it was in the midst of all this that, on January 22, his birthday, Byron produced one of his greatest lyrics. It is commonly called his last poem, and bears the title, "On this Day I complete my Thirty-sixth Year." A portion of the poem is printed by Mr. Nicholson in his account of the horror of Missolonghi. These are the only verses quoted in the entire book.

The sword, the banner, and the field,
 Glory and Greece around me see!
The Spartan, borne upon his shield,
 Was not more free.

Awake! (not Greece—she *is* awake!)
 Awake, my spirit! Think through *whom*
Thy life-blood tracks its parent lake,
 And then strike home!

Tread those reviving passions down,
 Unworthy manhood!—unto thee
Indifferent should the smile or frown
 Of beauty be.

If thou regret'st thy youth, *why live?*
 The land of honourable death
Is here:—up to the field, and give
 Away thy breath!

Seek out—less often sought than found—
A soldier's grave, for thee the best;
Then look around, and choose thy ground,
And take thy rest.

Upon these verses Mr. Nicholson makes no comment of his own, although he does give the brief remarks of Gamba upon Byron's determination to stand by the expedition. But Mr. Nicholson's artistic purpose in quoting them is clear. He wants to emphasize the pathetic contrast between the soldierly lines and the sordid realities of life. But for once his art betrays him. The stanzas play havoc with the biography. For suddenly the apparition of Byron is before us. Here is the man himself. Here is the explanation of the Greek expedition that has eluded us all along. Such was the emotion in the heart of him, the impulse and motive of everything, burning on, unquenchable, under the dirt and disease, the quarrels and the greed. Who that lived through the years 1917-1918 shall fail to understand?

To some, no doubt, the poem seems ludicrous enough. There were swords and banners in plenty about Lord Byron, but no field on which to employ them. It was precisely and accurately the trouble that there was no field. A soldier's grave was easier to sing about than to find, though Death, in his ironical fashion, was hanging over the poet as he wrote. It is all very poetical to talk about choosing one's ground and taking one's rest; but life moves along its dull and commonplace round. The biographer, as Chorus, stands by to remind us that the poor victim's bones were to find no resting place in Greece, but, after autopsy and embalming and coffining, were to be shipped to England for interment at Hucknall Torkard.

Suppose we go to the extreme of cynicism and deny the poem the grace of sincerity, have we injured it? Have we so much as breathed upon its perfection? Suppose that the biographical test proves the poem to be a tissue of falsehoods, what of that? Is it not still the very voice of the warrior—or the voice of one who would fain be a warrior? Is it not true to Byron's dreams, dreams that haunted his mind long after they had departed forever from lesser men? I cannot feel that a biographer has discharged his responsibility to Byron unless he detects in this poem some indication of the motive and meaning of Byron's last days.

If some one finds here evidence of Byron's tendency to pose, I should not think of denying the charge; for I do not know how poetry is to dispense with such posing. By what principle of criticism are we compelled to reconcile a poet's dreams with the events of his life? It is not the object of poets to lead lives or write poems that shall provide good material for the biographer. It is a poet's office to enter imaginatively into the experiences and emotions of other men and then to reconstruct and supplement them creatively. Call this posing if you will. It is, in any case, the creative process. Poets are constantly guessing at and divining experiences which they themselves have had only fragmentarily. In the poor scraps and shreds of experience they see, though dimly at first, the outlines of a vaster, more universal and significant event. *Ex pede Herculem.* Thus their actual experiences are forever taunting them, as it were, with the thought of what might have been or what ought to have been. They fall to dreaming and posturing and idealizing—to writing poetry, in short. The process is usually accompanied by a profound melancholy arising, in some sort, from the discrepancy which the poet feels between the rounded and finished experience which he sees imaginatively and the mortifying realities about him.

Byron's tendency to pose accounts, in some degree, for the intense humanity of his poems. The value of the famous "Byronic pose" is to be gauged not by its likeness to Byron, but by its likeness to human nature. To feel in superlatives and wear a brow of misery; to halt between eagerness and weariness; to be considered indolent, casual, and wicked, yet on a sudden to be capable of heroisms—or gentleness; to win the world with your bravery and then to repudiate it with an epigram as a bauble not worth the holding; to retire to the wilderness to taste one's renunciation and to long for home ("a home, ah me! what home?")—all this, I suppose, is "Byronism." But it is also human. A fig for a man who cannot indulge himself with the dream of being Napoleon or Conrad or Cain! He will prove but a poor lover of poetry.

Hence there are two pitfalls which beset the path of biographers. The first is the temptation to work back from the poems to the facts out of which they were kindled. It would be as difficult to resolve the foliage of a plant into the soil and sunshine which have entered it. The second is to accuse the poet of insincerity because his accounts of himself do not fit the facts as biographers discover them. I would not for a moment wish to be understood as protesting at the record and interpretation of those facts; but I should hope that the critic would realize that in the interpretation of poems they are to be used with the utmost caution.

That the mere facts of Byron's life are likely to mislead the critic of his verse I cannot doubt, for it was he who defined his poetry as the dream of his sleeping passions. He did not compose his verses, then, in a tempest of passion. To Murray he explained that his passions must be dormant before he could write, or, rather, before the creative tendency, the shaping power of his dreams, could commence. To trace dreams back to the actualities of life is (for all but psychologists and soothsayers) a perilous task. How is a critic to say whether or not a poet's work is dramatic in quality or a transcript of reality, when the poet is busily erasing the differences between the two?

What, for instance, is the bereavement to which

Byron refers in his lovely song in the "Hebrew Melodies,"

Oh! snatch'd away in beauty's bloom,
On thee shall press no ponderous tomb;
  But on thy turf shall roses rear
  Their leaves, the earliest of the year;
And the wild cypress wave in tender gloom. . . .

Away! we know that tears are vain,
  That death nor heeds nor hears distress:
Will this unteach us to complain?
  Or make one mourner weep the less?
And thou, who tell'st me to forget,
Thy looks are wan, thine eyes are wet.

Nathan, who wrote the music for the "Hebrew Melodies," inquired of the poet in what manner the lines referred to any scriptural subject. "He appeared for a moment affected—at last replied, 'Every mind must make its own references; there is scarcely one of us who could not imagine that the affliction belongs to himself.' " Here, then, is the poet's advice, to make our own references, to see in the poem a sentiment or an experience of universal import, appropriate to our individual needs. What Byron's peculiar bereavement may have been—if any—is of small significance to the reader. Since it is a Hebrew melody with which we are dealing, it may not be inappropriate to remark that lovers of the Psalms have always used them as Byron would have us read this song of his; they have made their own associations. The Twenty-third Psalm, the "Miserere," and "De Profundis" have proved permanently responsive to human needs. Scarce one reader in a thousand knows (or cares to know) anything about the origin of the Psalm. One of the Psalms, "In Exitu Israel," has actually become associated with Easter rather than with the historical event to which it refers. The Psalms have gathered round them a glittering corona of associations which were hopelessly beyond the ken of the author. Byron's song has nothing to lose by our ignorance regarding its origin. It would perhaps be fortunate for the poet if our ignorance could be extended to the origin of other poems.

To "Fare Thee Well," for instance. Byron's descendants have insisted upon bringing him into court, or rather upon keeping him there, so that now we know, or think we know, a great deal more about the famous separation than it is well for anybody to know. One doesn't even feel sure how much of the evidence it is decent for one to read. I feel a half guilty, half fascinated interest. I stagger through it, wondering why it has all been printed—and why I am reading it!—startled, bewildered, unconvinced, shifting from one view to another, and uncomfortably aware that no jury is going to give in a verdict at the end. If it be true that Byron committed the crime of incest, a good many utterances about him will no doubt have to be altered. But I should like to submit the view that we can, if we will, keep his poetry untainted and meaning to us very much what it did before. Byron is, I am aware, the most personal of poets and in his poems often seems to be contributing to that particular discussion of his private affairs which happens to be current at the moment. But let us not forget that all this is in the romantic style. I imagine that at some future time this personal note may come to be regarded as the great nineteenth-century convention by which poets were recognized as poetical. If they had, in every instance, completed the creative act and all connection between the original impulse and the final product had been obliterated, the poets would have escaped the perils to which they are now exposed. Their ideal portraits and dramatic sketches are now considered as so many likenesses of the artist, and the picture is judged by a photograph of the sitter. It would be far wiser to look in the pictured countenance for its resemblance to ourselves.

There are, I imagine, many literally minded folk who feel that if Byron wronged his wife, the poem, "Fare Thee Well," must be worthless. From the beginning it has been called worthless. The world of 1816 received it with shrieks of indignation. Wordsworth courteously asserted that it was "wretched doggerel, disgusting in sentiment, and in execution contemptible." But posterity has differed in its estimate.

> Fare thee well! and if for ever,
>   Still for ever, fare *thee well:*
> Even though unforgiving, never
>   'Gainst thee shall my heart rebel.

Would that breast were bared before thee
  Where thy head so oft hath lain,
While that placid sleep came o'er thee
  Which thou ne'er canst know again:

Would that breast, by thee glanced over,
  Every inmost thought could show!
Then thou wouldst at last discover
  'Twas not well to spurn it so.

Though the world for this commend thee—
  Though it smile upon the blow,
Even its praises must offend thee,
  Founded on another's woe:

Though my many faults defaced me,
  Could no other arm be found,
Than the one which once embraced me,
  To inflict a cureless wound?

Yet, oh, yet, thyself deceive not;
  Love may sink by slow decay,
But by sudden wrench, believe not
  Hearts can thus be torn away.

It is the mark of the creative mind that in the very midst of its experience it begins to dramatize its sorrows. The mere fact that one has sinned and that there is nothing to be said in defense of one's conduct, does not prevent one from learning, by that very experience, how an innocent being would feel in the circumstances, and, having learned it, the creative tendency is to cast it into verse where such an innocent victim may forevermore find language for his sorrow.

This is one of Byron's lyrics which has usually been regarded as the product of the very passions which it rehearses. This, at least, one is inclined to think, gives evidence of feelings in no dormant state. Byron himself said the tears fell fast over the paper as he wrote, and Thomas Moore added that the manuscript was "blotted all over with marks of tears." But when the first draft of the poem was sold at Sotheby's some years ago, Mr. E. H. Coleridge examined it for tear-marks, but found none, and much merriment among commentators has resulted. "'Tis pity," sighs Mr. Paul Elmer More; but why should Mr. Paul Elmer More sigh? Poets do not weep as they write dramatic lyrics, and even if they did, the verses would be much more valuable than the tears.

As a preface to the verses when they appeared in the volume of 1816, Byron quoted some beautiful lines from Coleridge's "Christabel," which are of special importance to our present consideration:

> Alas, they had been friends in youth,
> But whispering tongues can poison truth:
> And constancy lives in realms above;
> And life is thorny; and youth is vain;
> And to be wroth with one we love
> Doth work like madness in the brain. . . .
> But never either found another
> To free the hollow heart from paining—
> They stood aloof, the scars remaining,

Like cliffs, which had been rent asunder;
A dreary sea now flows between.
But neither heat, nor frost, nor thunder,
Shall wholly do away, I ween,
The marks of that which once hath been.

It is not my purpose to speak of the origin of these lines, but simply to point out the way in which Byron read them. To him they had no special connection with Sir Leoline and Roland de Vaux of Tryermaine, the separated friends in "Christabel." In the lines he saw mirrored himself and Lady Byron. From the time when he first saw Coleridge's lines in MS. they must have seemed as though written for him. The exact origin of the lines, whether in the sundered affections of Coleridge and Wordsworth, or some other relation of Coleridge's life, could have meant nothing to Byron as he copied out the lines for a preface to his own lyric. Coleridge had given deathless expression to a form of remorse which we all experience at some moment or other, and which Byron was now feeling with all the intensity of his passion.

And what is to prevent the reader from going to Byron's lines as Byron went to Coleridge's, for an expression of emotion which is peculiarly applicable to his own needs? It was because Byron felt that they had that powerful appeal within them, I suppose, that he could not destroy them, that he could not even refrain from publishing them.

As I think of the sins of Byron (which, after all

is said, are a matter between Byron and his God) and of the shadow which they may cast, temporarily, over his poetry, I am reminded of the fame of a later poet, which was suddenly blasted into infamy, so that for years his very name was not to be mentioned among the respectable. But the world soon found that it could not so easily dismiss its quondam favorite. He was, it appeared, something more than "an esthetic sham." Room had to be made on library shelves for the "Ballad of Reading Gaol" and *De Profundis*. The righteous and hysterical folk who had thrown their volumes of Oscar Wilde into the fire had to go out and buy new ones. The horror gradually died away, and we could again read Wilde without thinking of his crimes. It is a comforting lesson that we learned. The revelations and the scandals pass. Time blows the chaff away at last. The gossips and the story-tellers rise and reign for a moment, and then, like Moore and Medwin, they cease to be. The poetry remains.

EMILY DICKINSON[1]

By Charles K. Trueblood

I

In Emily Dickinson there seems to have been much of the visionary; if not in the general understanding of the word, then at least in the meaning that her imagination inclined to the form of inner vision rather than inner hearing, or other of the interior analogues of sense. Her verse-world, so brilliant and so intense, seems yet in a characteristic way, a world of soundless contemplation, of "quietness distilled," interrupted rarely, and perhaps only on her own terms, by small low sounds, or those falling gently on the ear, from far off. Not that she was without images of things vividly heard or felt, but that such images were not so frequent in comparison to images of things vividly seen, and when they did occur their vividness was more apt to be achieved by visual than by auditory or other figures; as, for example, her "blue, uncertain, stumbling buzz" of the fly, or her wind as "tufts of tune," or as "caravans of sound." Again, she found, it seemed —for certainly she could communicate—a particular pleasure in vivid stillness, such as the silence of noon on certain summer days, or the soundless

[1] From *The Dial,* April, 1926.

streak of a falling star, or the noiseless brilliance expressed in her conceit of butterflies "leaping off banks of noon, plashless as they swim." This distillation of temperament into vision, this brilliant quiet, might perhaps be more apparent if one contrasted her poetry with, for instance, the verse-world of Masefield, so thronged with the rich torturous riot of every sense. Yet in such contrasts we should be on guard; it is easy to make too much of a phrase. But if we accept the phrase with enlarging qualifications, if we understand it as only a hint of characteristics which may be more than the words can denote, or as a tentative bearing taken in surroundings where all is somewhat evanescent and transcending, then it may be of value in pointing at the great delicacy and great force which seemed to coexist in her individuality.

The combination of great delicacy and great force tends, no doubt, to be self-destructive in a serious sense; and we are not without indications that it was so with her. In temperament particularly, delicacy and force might be considered to consist of the same thing, namely, feeling; delicacy relating to the subtlety of the incitement, and force to the depth of the resulting emotion. And that she possessed both such force of heart and such exquisiteness, there is much evidence, subtle as well as obvious. . . . It is evident in that pleasure in contemplation, un-invaded by the disturbing messages of the inferior senses, that delight in brilliant quiet, which has already been noted. It is evident in all that one may suppose as to the explanation of such an attitude, and deduce from the belief that her poetry, like other very original poetry, is the image, not of random thoughts or idle observations, but of fundamental wish, central to mental being. It is most of all obvious in the shrinking and reluctance with which she met the most usual and ordinary, even the most affectionate and tender, of human contacts.

Her shrinking was no gesture. It became an avoidance and a flight. Her involuntary reluctance grew with reiteration into deliberate escape. It passed into gossip, and from gossip into legend, in which it became sufficiently fantastic, one gathers, to furnish reason for an authoritative biography. Turning through this biography, the *Life and Letters,*[2] one has the impression that she fled the world because she felt indeed that it was too much with her. And taking at its face value, as in fact we should, the description therein of her sensibility—from which it appears that the burning of a neighbor's straw shed more played upon her than an earthquake would upon the average person—we may indeed consider that she escaped from circumstance because it too rollingly echoed in her mind. Yet here again we might well be on guard. For while we can accept this truth of her as far as it goes, we may find, if we trace the growth of her inwardness both forward and back, that the truth so stated is not quite all the truth. The ivory tower aspect of

[2] *Life and Letters of Emily Dickinson.* Edited by M. D. Bianchi. Houghton Mifflin Company; Boston.

her seclusion is perfectly intelligible as a refinement upon the general world, as a preservation of treasures of feeling from an excess of irrelevance, as a great factor, no doubt, in contribution to the purity and flowering of her rare poetic instinct. Yet perhaps this seclusiveness was but the outer appearance of an inward bias which not only began much earlier and deeper, but also, in the end, went much farther. Her solitude, one comes to feel, began long before it became obvious, and went much deeper than was ever apparent. And her rare subtle knowledge of the interiors of the spirit, which we now so much remark upon, was perhaps derived from the length, as well as the sadness and the intensity, of her dwelling there.

Her solitude must indeed have dated, in some part, from the time she began temperamentally to be more than a child. It seems reasonable to think it began in her relation to her family, that is, really her relation to her father; for the family all dwelt, though they seemed not to have been aware of it, in the shadow of his personality. He was a man of gentle feeling, great intelligence, but tremendous primness. The last, perhaps, was his marking trait, for the public encomiums of him betray a general impression of immense respectability. As a young man he had signed his kindly frosty letters to his fiancée as her "most ob't servant, Edward Dickinson." And his portrait rather confirms the tale. We see a handsome man of eminent look, but with that perhaps unconscious austerity in lips and brow and carriage of the head which strikes with awe, not alone the hearts of sinners, but how much more those of the ingenuous and the timid. A culprit could, in imagination, feel himself slipping, slipping, hopelessly, down the smooth cold sides of that austerity—unless help were vouchsafed from above, as often it was, except in reprehensible cases; yet none would have dared hope for it.

But on the one marked character at the Dickinson hearth, the force of his respectability was imperfectly effective. In Emily there had been early apparent the sparkle of more than ordinary question. It was timid Emily, alone of three hundred girls in the Mt. Holyoke Seminary, who publicly and victoriously defied the regimen of Mary Lyon on the question of whether Christmas Day should be spent with fasting and prayer at the seminary, or in celebration at home with one's family. It was Emily, in the seemly Dickinson household, who enjoyed irreverence, and who grew offhand with accepted revelation, and saw in the austerities of the public God merely an infinitude of tedium. It was Emily, only, who could write whimsically to herself, regarding the God of her own solitude:

> I hope the father in the skies
> Will lift his little girl,—
> Old-fashioned, naughty, everything,—
> Over the stile of pearl!

With the growth in force of so much individuality, what of the forbearing, but massive and immovable, respectability that was Edward Dickinson? Could he understand a mind so like his, in some ways, and so different? And what if he could not? Would there be submerged collision? and with what result? Or if there were no collision, what became of the opposition? Force does not evaporate; and as to the growing fact of her force and the established fact of her father's force, or the family force, there could be no doubt.

Adjustment to one's world is generally thought to consist either of remaking oneself or of remaking the world. But it seemed that she did neither: she moved to a brilliant and subtle solitude leagues within. Without shrinkage, but rather with an increase of her mental and temperamental powers—or perhaps one should say an increase in their effectiveness—a process of withdrawal inward began, which, it seemed, never quite ended.

Her interiorization gained impetus from what is usually understood to have been its main cause; this was her encounter with love. It took place in 1853, her twenty-third year. She was, during this year, in Washington and Philadelphia with her father, who at the time was a member of Congress. In Philadelphia she met the man, whose name is not revealed, with whom she fell in love; he was married. When she realized the state of her feeling, she fled back to Amherst, where he followed her. The biography relates that one day

Sister Sue looked up from her sewing to see Lavinia, pallid and breathless from running, who grasped her wrist with hurrying hand, urging, "Sue, come! That man is here!—Father and Mother are away, and I am afraid Emily will go away with him."

But it does not appear that the contemplated moral succor was required for Emily. The Dickinson generations, it seemed, had already spoken in her blood. She went on with life in her father's house, showing no outward mark of this crisis except an "unexplained picture in a heavy oval frame of gold," hanging on the wall of her room, and an increase of turning from the world, which soon, no doubt, became apparent enough. "To the faithful," she wrote, "absence is condensed presence. To the others—but there are no others."

Now, one would think, she sought the rare inner air of spirit; and it was now, perhaps, as the turmoil of the actual died upon her ear, as she found in some degree the distance, the silence, the light, the "bright detachment" which she sought in anguish, it was now that her poems began, as the private day-book of her heart; for she intended most of them, it seemed, for no other eyes. They mark rememberably the character of her solitude for force and delicacy. Could such tumultuous precision have been achieved otherwise than through her characteristic visionism, so powerful and yet so far from gross? In it only, perhaps, was the full force of a great temperament to find an expression utter and complete, tremendous and yet delicate. Indeed, such burning filigree may mark out for us, as well as anything can, how much more discriminated, how much more useful to the mind and heart, how much greater the world of vision can be than the worlds of the other senses; and how much more we should choose it, if a choice were to be made.

Perhaps it is because this was the direction which her brilliant, silent vehemence took; perhaps it is because her retreat inward was to the bright observatories, and not the dark recesses of spirit, that her utterance shows so little of the morbidness which often accompanies the growth inward of mental being. In the deepest mazes of her solitude, it seemed, touch was brilliantly kept with the exteriors of the actual, by the clearest, the finest, and, for her, the most characteristic of the senses. Perhaps the great vitality of that contact by vision is the essence, in part, of her poetic originality. "The eye begins its avarice," she wrote, and the words may have more than their immediate meaning. Her individuality, apparently, made its impress upon her world especially through vision; through vision she exercised her abounding share in that fine lyric tyranny, which makes the poet's whole world the private possession of his personality.

It may have been a phase of this visionism, existing in her love of contrasts, and coupled with an arch humor, which was at the core of her characteristic whimsical charm. It is best shown in a species of inverse hyperbole, a favorite mode with her, in which the lion and the lamb are made to lie down together, in which things strange and vast are put in the same figurative company with things homely and small. She likes to speak of "Vesuvius at home," of God as "a noted clergyman," or as "Papa above," of the storm winds as "dogs defeated of a bone," of Eden as "the ancient homestead," or that "old-fashioned house we dwell in every day," of her own being as a tiny craft among "stately sails," oblivious alike of its presence and its absence. These things, possibly, were only whimsicalities, but perhaps they were more, too. Since the poet cannot but draw his own likeness, and project the properties of his own feeling into what he describes, was there, in this inverse hyperbole, not only whimsicality, but—what was another phase of her delicacy and her shrinking—an effort to make the gross world less strange and painful by stamping it with the character of her own vision, by figuring it in the terms of her own experience?

It was thus perhaps that she rebuilt her world, of treasured and familiar things, deep within, and distant from fearful circumstance. Built too, seemingly, of the substance of vision, it was as powerfully yet lightly wrought as she could make it. But the more she built its loveliness, the more she was contained within it. And since with so vital a temperament, the creative substance must have been almost continuously forming, in a sort of reverberation to the delicate pronouncements of the senses, the progress of her imprisonment must indeed have been steady. How keenly she became aware of those unseen bars is only too evident in her great lyric longings for escape; and the escape in this instance is a far different thing from the old escape from circumstance. It is the prison of herself from which she now wants extrication. One sees it first, perhaps, in her whimsical longing for namelessness:

> How dreary to be somebody!
> How public, like a frog,
> To tell your name the livelong day
> To an admiring bog!

Or perhaps it first appeared in the wish, implied more than a few times in her poetry, to be absorbed in a sympathetic force greater than herself, or as great in a different way. And as the inward tendency progresses, one begins to discern its characteristic final forms. That brilliant inner prison is becoming too confining. From longing for namelessness, one observes the progress to longing for greater freedom. "What," she wrote,

> What if I file this mortal off,
> See where it hurt me—that's enough—
> And wade in liberty?

For that indeed is finally the sole escape for those who are too much caught in the prisons of themselves.

Strong as was this lyric prison, it was yet based in other things outside her personality. It was, in fact, only a slender mansion in her father's house.

And when, in June, 1874, her father suddenly died, a strange, unthought-of night fell indeed on her cherished "bright detachment." If he had not understood her temperamentally, or perhaps in any way, he had yet never intruded, and he had shown an immense if prim tenderness, in which she and the others of his family had long dwelt. How much he must have been in that household we can only imagine, except as we have it vividly said in his daughter's poem:

> We learn in the retreating
> How vast an one
> Was recently among us.
> A perished sun
>
> Endears in the departure
> How doubly more
> Than all the golden presence
> It was before!

And from her manner of speaking in numerous poems of life, death, the grave, and eternity, it seems evident that this loss tore a ghastly breach in her inner citadel. In these poems there is not the old note of longing, which was yet so airy and so alive; there is not the whim in the description of the wind as having "no bone to bind him," which was also her description of her own wish-to-be. This quietism is not so brilliant or so poised for soaring; instead there are deep painful looks at the exteriors of our mortality, in those final moments when the frost is mantling in the clay. Instead, as elsewhere in her poems, of looking forward to the beginning of the bodiless, there is here rather an overmuch of the ending of the body. Instead of the privacy of the breeze, here is the privacy of the low dwelling. The idea of escape seems to have metamorphosed into the idea of refuge, and one cannot be sure but that the note of refuge—in the tomb—was the note on which she ended. It is indeed a possible conclusion to inwardness.

That her exquisite vision should have dwelt so steadfastly, so powerfully, and so often, on the conclusion of our poor clay is perhaps one of the most formidable of the objections to calling her a mystic, as has been done—loosely, one would think. Would the dead flesh have looked so stricken if she had not been of "that religion which doubts as fervently as it believes"? Indeed, in calling her a mystic are we not blurring the outlines of her characteristic effect? Is not to call her a mystic to deny, in a way, her unequaled general sensitivity? The mystic is but too often polarized by his sustained and indiscriminate ecstasy. But not in all her life was she so polarized. Does not the immense value of her poetry lie in the fact that, rather than mysticism, it is the rarest of lyric asceticism? Is not that the secret of the strange, fine intelligence of the heart, and the comfort that so many have found in her, so many of the stricken? When has stoic's metal been struck to a more exquisite chiming?

II

Consistent with the delicacy and the force of heart which were noticed as so characteristic of her individuality, there appears as perhaps her principal literary quality a certain lyric incisiveness, a bright, passionate brevity, a sensitive immediacy of word to thought. In poetry one grows accustomed to think of incisiveness as often secured by discreet abrasure; of the brevity in question as a studied brevity, for which the faculties required may be merely intelligence and fine attention; and of immediacy as the product of much choosing. Yet in her case the reverse seems true. For her, apparently, to think and write pointedly, briefly, and with the happiest immediacy of word to thought, was as natural as to feel powerfully.

There is, in her verse, an obvious absence of studio finish. . . . She was evidently inattentive to the more or less "artistic" arts of metrical and phrasal music, and appears readily capable of letting the verse-scheme of a poem, and even the syntax, stumble or scramble, in a curious carelessness of everything but the flash of vision and the gold of phrase. What she says seems always said with the choicest orginality, but not always with poetic fluency, or even much attempt at it. And while it perhaps should be remembered in this connection that most of her poems were written strictly for herself, often probably as the notes of her thoughts, the marginalia in her private book of experience, which she had no idea that others than herself would ever see, it still does not seem certain that the result would have been widely different had she been writing formally and for publication.

These oddities of structure and finish seem to betray the fact that a poem of hers is almost wholly first thought and not after-thought. Compare her work with that of A. E. Housman, who dealt with many of the same themes, and some of the difference due to after-thought should appear. The verse of Housman, direct and piercing as it is, seems yet to reflect multiplied exclusions, and a final simplicity that has been minutely wrought. The poems of Emily Dickinson seem to reflect simply the direct feelings of a profound heart. They seem less works of infinitely considered art, in which the effort has been guided to achievement by a subtly taught sense of poetic effect, than merely the spontaneous motions of a rich sensibility phrased with natural immediacy in language which, if irregular, is of sparkling definition.

There was, of course, nothing merely wandering about her poetic effort. However wholly from the heart her poems may seem to come, no one who much reads them can escape the impression that poetry, in her hands, becomes in good share a mental magic. Her trenchant measures are as free from the dwelling unction of the merely sensuous as they are free from the mere piecing out of insight. The penetrating phrases into which her thought and feeling are sharpened are set down with a close economy that sometimes has the effect of extreme, fine dryness. And as significance is the substance of her force, so her verse follows the forms of wit as much as the forms of sense. Her poems might indeed be called epigrams. They might be called conceits, too, being often so whimsical, and so edging on quaintness in their originality; they might be called conceits, that is, were they less fervently intended. And whether conceits or epigrams, they seem always at the key of the often intangible matter, and have not only general pointedness but specific point.

To the service of her feeling she brought, perhaps as corollary to her characteristic inner vision, a rare and singular sense of words. Words, to her, were a festival; and she spent, as the biography notes, hours with the dictionary. And since there are not many of her single words that would not have been feasible and usual in ordinary intercourse, we can reasonably imagine that she must have been finding again the hidden, vivid textures in old meanings, restoring for herself the lost edges of ordinary expression, searching out the forgotten but astounding faces of customary words. It strikes one, too, that she had very positively that tremendous command of "things used as words," which, to Emerson, so marked the authentic poet. And to this command, one cannot forbear thinking, her escape from circumstance added, curiously, much strength and nourishing. Is it too much to suppose that when she contracted her existence, she increased, in certain ways, its depth and height? that when she then looked at the things of her lessened life, it was more than before with the remarkable eyes of the imagination? that she then erected the familiar objects in her round of deeper days, with powerful lyric conviction, into symbols of far things? In her verse noon does not always mean merely noon; it seems sometimes to stand for the possibilities of a greater glory. Nor are storms seen from covert merely storms seen from covert; they call up thoughts of the refuge foreverlasting, even if that refuge be only the grave. It is not to be contended, surely, that symbolism achieved through so rich a temperament cannot add a weight to words.

Not only by symbolism, which seems a thing so elemental and so directly of the heart, but by her figures of speech, the products of her sense of similarity, her acute visualizing mentality, did she add strength to her verse. Her characteristic figure, perhaps, was metaphor, and it is apparently in the quality of her metaphor, and in the fact that not only her metaphor, which outstands, but all the smaller parts of her poetic utterance are made of the same vivid, chiefly visual substance, that her extraordinary poetic distinctiveness lives. Filled with the clearest colors and the most consummate lights, her poetic speech seems alive, to its smallest parts, with its special sparkle. Where is to be found a figurative note like hers in its combination of delicate brilliance and trenchant quaintness, its piquancy and its sincere fervor? It sets a mode in imagination that could found no fashions, for its secret is not detachable. Here, indeed, we are as close as we shall get to the language of her individuality; and here we must rest merely with observing the force of spirit evident in its lightest terms. It recalls again that her poetry was not professional; that it was but a means by which she constructed her "bright detachment," and partly lightened a weight of thinking.

It must also have been, in the same direction, a laying up of the treasures of comprehension, of her deep knowledge of the interiors of the spirit, gained, evidently, with so much anguish. In her poems, said to have been found, for the most part, copied on note-paper, and laid away, tied with ribbon, in little bundles, each of six or eight sheets, one can refresh his feeling and thinking, secure that in what he thus comes back to, he will find no waning of choiceness. This brilliant understanding of the heart and its suffering, this great sensory delicacy, is rare essential wealth, proof against tarnish. It is seldom that one finds surer gold.

LUCIFER FROM NANTUCKET[1]

An Introduction to "Moby Dick"

By Carl Van Doren

I

The age which produced *Moby Dick* failed to recognize its features in that stormy glass. Recognition has had to come from an age so different that it is obliged to view the book as a document of the past and to take its delight in qualities which, though essential to Melville, were only incidental to his main design. Whaling is now history. So, too, though more likely to be revived again, are such concerns as Melville felt for the plight of the soul voyaging through oceans of terror and doubt on the mortal quest for immortal certainty. But in Melville's day both matters were almost in the news.

New England, turning from her rocky pastures, had sought the more hospitable acres of the sea and had brought the art and science of whale-catching to a pitch never equaled before or since. In this the island of Nantucket led the chase. "The Nantucketer," says Melville, "he alone resides and riots on the sea; he alone, in Bible language, goes down

[1] From *The Century,* August, 1925.

to it in ships; to and fro plowing it as his special plantation. *There* is his home; *there* lies his business, which a Noah's flood would not interrupt, though it overwhelmed all the millions in China. He lives on the sea, as prairie cocks in the prairie; he hides among the waves, he climbs them as chamois hunters climb the Alps. For years he knows not the land; so that when he comes to it at last, it smells like another land, more strangely than the moon would to an Earthsman. With the landless gull, that at sunset folds her wings and is rocked to sleep between billows; so at nightfall, the Nantucketer, out of sight of land, furls his sail, and lays him to his rest, while under his very pillow rush herds of walruses and whales."

This, of course, is poetry, but it is founded upon what in 1851 was a matter of common knowledge. Not only New England, but all the northeastern United States, sent its imagination habitually to the Pacific with the whalers. Inland youths followed their instincts to the ports and set sail upon vessels which, after abominable voyages, came home reeking with blubber. Men who stayed behind wished they might go with the greasy Argonauts and listened to their yarns wherever a returned whaler used his tongue. California invited in another direction, and Kansas held forth the promise of adventure. But the sea still filled a great part of the horizon of escape. It was the highway leading out of monotony. It was the purge of desperate moods. "With a philosophical flourish," says the narrator of *Moby*

Dick, "Cato throws himself upon his sword; I quietly take to the ship." For tales of such prudent suicide there was an abundant audience. Melville could write in the confidence that many others would have shared his impulse and would be interested in his lore. He knew that a whole body of tradition had grown up, particularly along the seaboard, and that it had prepared the soil for his huge epic. Indeed, he attached his fable to a creature already fabulous. There had been talk of a white whale, known to earlier chroniclers as Mocha Dick, which had lived for years as a dangerous Ishmael of the deep and which, though it had eventually been conquered, might easily be chosen as a symbol of the unconquerable perils of the whaler's calling. Of Mocha Dick Melville must have heard, or he would not have chosen for his whale a name so near that of its prototype. And about it he assembled a mass of erudition which he would hardly have dared to assemble in an age to which the facts would most of them seem, as they seem to the present age, remote and quaint.

Something very Yankee in Melville enabled him to take full advantage of his confidence in his public. Though a transcendentalist, he was also a sailor and a scholar, and he wrote his book as if to make all its rivals unnecessary. It is, among other things, a treatise, packed with details. He knew he had no easy task, exact knowledge of his theme being then what it was. "The classification of the constituents of a chaos, nothing less is here essayed. . . .

My object . . . is simply to project the draught of a systematization of cetology. I am the architect, not the builder. . . . I have swum through whole libraries and sailed through oceans; I have had to do with whales with these visible hands; I am in earnest; and I will try." He classifies whales, and names them. He pauses in his narrative to tell ancient stories or to deny mistaken rumors. He describes the manners of his beasts not only when they are in conflict with their pursuers, but, so far as he can learn, when they are at peace in their own affairs. Only a little less systematically does Melville undertake to portray the manners of men when on whaling voyages. He explains the construction of their ships, the discipline of their ordinary routine, the methods of their fierce assaults, their treatment of their prizes, the devices which comfort their hours of leisure, the punctilio which governs the society of ships in the whaling fields. He hits off the characters of the men who are brought together in such a venture, reports their speech, and catches up items from their previous careers to fill in the picture. He comments upon the antiquities and landscape and habits of the Pacific.

Often enough his information is interruption, so far as the specific plot is concerned; but Melville never intended to work along one straight line. The universe of whaling is his stage, and its activities all contribute to his plot. *Moby Dick* must be read, in part, as *The Anatomy of Melancholy* is read, for its illustrations and incidents, for its wonder and laughter. When, for instance, Melville touches upon mastheads, he has a cheerful fling through time to prove that "the business of standing mast-heads, afloat or ashore, is a very ancient and interesting one. . . . I take it, that the earliest standers of mast-heads were the old Egyptians; because, in my researches, I find none prior to them. For though their progenitors, the builders of Babel, must doubtless, by their tower, have intended to rear the loftiest mast-head in all Asia, or Africa either; yet (ere the final truck was put to it) as that great stone mast of theirs may be said to have gone by the board, in the dread gale of God's wrath; therefore, we cannot give these Babel builders priority over the Egyptians. And that the Egyptians were a nation of mast-head standers, is an assertion based upon the general belief among archaeologists, that the first pyramids were founded for astronomical purposes; a theory singularly supported by the peculiar stair-like formation of all four sides of those edifices; whereby, with prodigious long upliftings of their legs, those old astronomers were wont to mount to the apex, and sing out for new stars; even as the look-outs of a modern ship sing out for a sail, or a whale just bearing in sight. In Saint Stylites, the famous Christian hermit of old times, who built him a lofty stone pillar in the desert and spent the whole latter portion of his life on its summit, hoisting his food from the ground with a tackle; in him we have a remarkable instance of a dauntless stander-of-mast-heads; who was not to be driven from his place by fogs or frosts, rain, hail, or sleet; but valiantly facing everything out at last, literally died at his post. Of modern standers-of-mast-heads we have but a lifeless set; mere stone, iron, and bronze men; who, though well capable of facing out a stiff gale, are still entirely incompetent to the business of singing out upon discovering any strange sight. There is Napoleon; who, upon the column of Vendôme, stands with arms folded, some one hundred and fifty feet in the air; careless, now, who rules the decks below; whether Louis Philippe, Louis Blanc, or Louis the Devil. Great Washington, too, stands high aloft on his towering main-mast in Baltimore, and like one of Hercules' pillars, his column marks that point of human grandeur beyond which few mortals will go. Admiral Nelson, also, on a capstan of gun-metal, stands his mast-head in Trafalgar Square; and even when most obscured by that London smoke, token is yet given that a hidden hero is there; for where there is smoke, must be fire. But neither great Washington, nor Napoleon, nor Nelson, will answer a single hail from below, however madly invoked to befriend by their counsels the distracted decks upon which they gaze; however it may be surmised, that their spirits penetrate the thick haze of the future, and descry what shoals and what rocks must be shunned."

II

At the same time, neither such embroideries as this nor the rich substratum of fact in *Moby Dick* would alone serve to make the book the masterpiece it is. Well above them both stands the plot. It might, in another handling, have been simple. It might have been farcical. Ahab, the captain of the *Pequod,* has lost one of his legs in an encounter with Moby Dick and has vowed to have revenge. In the imagination of Melville, transcendentalist as well as sailor and scholar, the matter became a tragic, even a cosmic, issue. On his own cruise he had, he seems to hint, begun to brood over symbols. "Lulled into such an opium-like listlessness of vacant, unconscious reverie is this absent-minded youth by the blending cadences of waves with thoughts, that at last he loses his identity; takes the mystic ocean at his feet for the visible image of that deep, blue, bottomless soul, pervading mankind and nature; and every strange, half-seen, gliding, beautiful thing that eludes him; every dimly-discovered, uprising fin of some undiscernible form, seems to him the embodiment of those elusive thoughts that only people the soul by continually flitting through it. . . . There is no life in thee, now, except that rocking life imparted by a gently rolling ship; by her, borrowed from the sea; by the sea, from the inscrutable tides of God. But while this sleep, this dream, is on ye, move your foot or hand an inch; slip your hand at all; your identity comes back in horror. Over Descartian vortices you hover. And perhaps, at midday, in the fairest weather, with one half-throttled shriek you drop through that transparent air into the summer sea, no more to rise for ever. Heed it well, ye Pantheists."

And if the matter was cosmic to Melville, so was it tragic, as it would have been to any contemporary transcendentalist. An obscure distemper gnawed everlastingly at the core of Melville's peace. His unsettled youth had, it seems, been due to a natural rebellion which sprang from his animal spirits. Then, after his return to land, he had grown more speculative. The traces of his speculations it is now impossible to study in detail, but their general tendency is clear. They move all in the direction of disillusionment. He looked for a friendship which should combine a perfect fusion of the friends with a perfect independence of the persons involved. He looked for a love which should be at once a white rapture and a fiery ecstasy, at once a flash and an eternity. He wanted to find life profound and stable and yet infinitely varied. He set himself to reduce the mystery of the world to a single formula, and then to master the formula. In all these things he had been, inevitably, disappointed. Nor was he able to explain his disappointment by reasoning that he must have given too docile a belief to the lessons of idealism. Instead, he clung to his own values and gradually made up his mind to the notion that diabolism was rampant in the universe. How else could he account for the estrangement of friends and the numbing of lovers, for the insecurity and boredom of life, for the multiplied and obstinate riddles of the cosmos which he inhabited? In Ahab he found an opportunity to project his own drama. Once Melville had hit upon this central scheme, he could elaborate it with violent thought, as he elaborated his setting with piled erudition.

Ahab is the Yankee Faust, the Yankee Lucifer. Another of his Nantucket kind, accustomed to the dangers of his occupation, might have been expected to regard the loss of his leg as a mere accident for which nothing could be blamed. Still another, accustomed to the doctrine of predestination, might have been expected to regard his loss as the will of God, working mysteriously, yet somehow righteously. But Ahab, created in Melville's image, cannot be reconciled by either of the orthodoxies in which he has been bred. As he cherishes his mad hatred within him he becomes aware, by its hot light, of depths below depths of fury. "Ahab, in his hidden self, raved on. Human madness is oftentimes a cunning and most feline thing. When you think it fled, it may have but become transfigured into some still subtler form. Ahab's full lunacy subsided not, but deepeningly contracted; like the unabated Hudson, when that noble Northman flows narrowly but unfathomably through the Highland gorge. But, as in his narrow-flowing monomania, not one jot of Ahab's broad madness had been left behind; so, in that broad madness, not one jot of his great natural intellect had perished. That before living agent, now became the living instrument. If such a furious trope may stand, his special lunacy stormed his general sanity, and carried it, and turned all its concentered cannon upon its own mad mark; so that far from having lost his strength, Ahab, to that one end, did not possess a thousand-fold more potency than ever he had sanely brought to bear upon any reasonable object." No wonder, then, that Ahab, in his narrow-flowing monomania, has raised the white whale to a dignity which alone could justify this rage. "That intangible malignity which has been from the beginning; to whose dominion even the modern Christians ascribe one half of the worlds; which the ancient Ophites of the East reverenced in their statue devil;—Ahab did not fall down and worship it like them; but deliriously transferring its idea to the abhorred white whale, he pitted himself, all mutilated, against it. All that most maddens and torments; all that stirs up the lees of things; all truth with malice in it; all that cracks the sinews and cakes the brain; all the subtle demonisms of life and thought; all evil, to crazy Ahab, were visibly personified, and made practically assailable, in Moby Dick. He piled upon the whale's white hump the sum of all the general rage and hate felt by his whole race from Adam down; and then, as if his chest had been a mortar, he burst his hot heart's shell upon it."

And no wonder, too, that Ahab carries his desire for vengeance to lengths which for his creed meant blasphemy. He vows to know the cause of his misfortune and to pay back blow for blow. He is in absolute rebellion against whatever god or godless chaos has wrought this havoc upon him, against whatever it is that Moby Dick represents, against whatever is outside the wall within which mankind is hemmed. "How can the prisoner reach outside except by thrusting through the wall? To me, the whale is that wall, shoved near to me. Sometimes I think there's naught behind. But 'tis enough. He tasks me; he heaps me; I see in him outrageous strength, with an inscrutable malice sinewing it. That inscrutable thing is chiefly what I hate; and be the white whale agent, or be the white whale principal, I will wreak that hate upon him. Talk not to me of blasphemy, man; I'd strike the sun if it insulted me. For could the sun do that, then could I do the other; since there is ever a sort of fair play herein, jealously providing over all creations." "The prophecy was that I should be dismembered; and—ay! I lost this leg. I now prophesy that I will dismember my dismemberer. Now, then, be the prophet and the fulfiller one. That's more than ye, ye great gods, ever were."

Thus Ahab, lifted by his fury to a sense of equality with the gods, goes on his long hunt. Like Jonah, stifling in the belly of the whale, the prisoner of the universe fumbles for the whale's proud heart, to destroy it. Nor is Ahab alone. He commands a little world, men of all races and all colors, and ruthlessly employs them to weight his blow. Gradually, as he withdraws them from the land where they were free creatures, he infects them with his horrid will. In the end they are all welded into one fist and one harpoon. The *Pequod,* which insolently sets sail on Christmas day, becomes an entity, one consolidated will insanely questing for a black grail, as if parodying some holy quest. For all its earlier delays, the story increases its tempo as it advances, and grows sulphurous at the close. The gods, disturbed upon both their upper and their nether thrones, invoke, it seems, thunder, ocean, and the hugest of the brutes of creation to put down this impious man who has tried to crowd so close upon their secrets. Moby Dick, white and silent, still inscrutable, turns upon his enemies and sinks their ship before he glides away, unharmed and unperturbed, to other business. The *Pequod* goes down, a skyhawk nailed to her mast. With her, for the moment, sink the hopes of man. Evil is God.

III

How far Melville meant *Moby Dick* to be a symbol cannot now be discovered. "I had some vague idea while writing it," he told Hawthorne's wife, "that the whole book was susceptible of an allegoric construction, and also that *parts* of it were—but the speciality of many of the particular subordinate allegories were first revealed to me after reading Mr. Hawthorne's letter which, without citing any particular examples, yet intimated the part-and-parcel allegoricalness of the whole." The spiritual similitudes of the story had their origin, it cannot be doubted, in Melville's bitten soul. Ahab is created with such passion because Melville was nearly, or felt that he might have become, another Ahab. Thus explained, the problem becomes less difficult. Melville had inherited the smooth creed of a respectable Christianity, with its neat schemes of rewards and punishments and its nonsense about the beneficence of the universe toward mankind. He must have noted exceptions to these pretty rules while he was cruising through the Pacific, but he appears to have noted them as specific cases without generalizing from them. On dry land again, settled down to writing about his adventures, he had begun to reflect upon the world at large. "I am like one of those seeds," he said, "taken out of the Egyptian pyramids, which, after being three thousand years a seed and nothing but a seed, being planted in English soil, it developed itself, grew to greenness, and then fell to mold. So I. Until I was twenty-five, I had no development at all. From my twenty-fifth year I date my life. Three weeks have scarcely passed, at any time between then and now, that I have not unfolded within myself. But now I feel that I am come to the inmost leaf of the bulb, and that shortly the flower must fall to the mold."

Writing to Hawthorne in the midst of *Moby Dick,* Melville thus reviewed the seven years since he had felt himself to be alive. Like various other young men of his decade, he had got his vitalizing touch from transcendentalism. It had poured fire into his veins. It had lifted him into a sense of wider human and divine horizons. It had also given him to believe that the center of those horizons, if not they themselves, lay within his own soul. But transcendentalism really transvalued few values. Carlyle still bellowed strenuous old prejudices, and Emerson went on lifting his sweet voice in hymns of hope and compensation. Melville could not be satisfied. Though both his earlier and his later doctrines taught him that the cosmos had a meaning, and that the meaning was simple and good, his experience denied that conclusion. In the world itself he had found a thousand malevolent contradictions. Blind chance, heedless of the interests of men, seemed to rule there; and blind chance, Melville thought, could come from nothing less than the activity of the devil. And where within his own self, he asked in vain, were those serene, virtuous regions about which he had heard? His own heart was a region of storms and cross-currents. The deeper he went into it in his reflections, the more he was horrified by the fierce things he perceived there. Only a little more, and he could imagine himself a mad Ahab, fixed in a wild rebellion, setting out to scour the unfathomable universe which had wronged him and against which he had vowed a devastating, supernatural revenge. Nor was it merely the Lucifer in Ahab which Melville comprehended. He saw him also, in some degree, as Faust, bound to get at the truth though it should blast him. With two motives of this power, Ahab could look forward to no peace but that which might come from supreme triumph or total annihilation.

This was Melville's state. For all his realism, he had never arrived at the idea that perhaps the universe has no meaning at all, or that it has many meanings, all equally satisfactory to different finite intelligences. As to the dark impulses which he found within himself, he had never understood that they were the survivors of functions and processes in which human nature had engaged in the ascending millenniums since it was mere protoplasm fighting its way out of the primal mud. Melville was in the plight of a geographer who, though his observation had taught him that the earth is round, was trying to calculate its area and survey its surface on the hypothesis that the earth is flat. He was in the plight of a philosopher who was trying to lay down a moral system without taking into account that third dimension of morals, which is otherwise known as history. Whatever Melville's first-hand knowledge of the world which he wanted to chart, he could not free himself from his bondage to the formulas by which he had been taught that the world could be charted. Between his knowledge and his inherited formulas arose the conflict which muddied the stream of his own life. The conflict, however, begat Ahab.

IV

Readers who have expected less of the universe than Melville did, and have therefore been less disappointed, are likely not to find their imaginations stirred as they might once have been by Ahab's vow and quest. His blasphemy no more shocks them than would the shrieking of an angry child. They study the methods of his madness without being greatly touched by its causes or results. Consequently, they often find the talk of the chronicle towering too high. The language seems to have something reckless about it, something a little hollow. It rants occasionally, like the language of certain of the minor Elizabethans who are praised, but tiresome. None of the characters of *Moby Dick* is required to restrict itself to the tongue of nature; the tongue of rhetoric very often is enough for Melville. What he produces is an immense miscellany. One passage may be pure comedy, another may be encyclopedic information, another may be mighty poetry, another may be transcendental raving. A classical disposition may well feel lost in such a torrent. Whoever enjoys himself most in the romance must get his enjoyment from its tumult and variety. Indeed, only a fairly heroic reader can take this voyage. It represents Melville at his peak. He is here neither as easy as in "Typee" nor as furious as in "Pierre," but his qualities are in that working combination which reveals him most thoroughly. Savage energy, ceaseless curiosity, nipping irony, desperate brooding, strange, full-lunged mirth, ultimate pessimism—he weaves them all into his pattern. Over it rises the smoke of his wrath, vexed and blasphemous.

Perhaps every reader must, with whatever first

introduction or first impression, make the rest out himself. Fortunately, there is more to *Moby Dick* than its transcendental meaning. There is more than its variety of details. In its own enormous way, it marches. "Call me Ishmael," the narrator says in the first sentence, thus cutting himself off from the ordinary, friendly world. He goes to New Bedford, takes up with a cannibal harpooner, joins the crew of the *Pequod,* and is at sea before he realizes the purposes of Ahab. They become evident to him but slowly. In the interval, while the ship makes its way to its fields of action, Ishmael has time to expound the technique of his calling, and to describe the characters who are practicing it with him. Even on the Pacific the *Pequod* cannot go directly to its mark. It must move through dull delays, while the illusion of its single, unavoidable aim gathers strength. Its path crosses that of many another vessel, and they hail one another and exchange the news of the ocean till there has been woven of their crossings and communications a solid fabric of knowledge concerning all that goes on there. Finally, when it comes to the struggle with Moby Dick, the mad captain and his fated crew have built up such anticipations that this seems to be the focus of the universe, whether the struggle be actual or symbolical. As Ahab has drawn his crew after him, so the *Pequod* seems to be drawing, in the allegory, all the other ships afloat. The spirit of all whalers, the spirit of all sailors, yes, the spirit of all dauntless men, seems matched against the spirit of resisting, malicious nature personified in Moby Dick. At the crash, nature proves eternal as well as unassailable, and the fable comes to an end in the vortex of a drowning world. And with an art hardly to be noted elsewhere in the entire work, Melville instantly ends his story. "Now small fowls flew screaming over the yet yawning gulf; a sullen white surf beat against its steep sides; then all collapsed, and the great shroud of the sea rolled on as it rolled five thousand years ago." Had he been everywhere willing or able to let his materials in this fashion speak for themselves, *Moby Dick* would need no introduction.

CAN CRITICS BE GENTLEMEN? [1]

By Arnold Whitridge

Not long ago a reviewer for one of the weekly papers criticized an author for being too much of a gentleman. His book, a collection of literary essays, was interesting enough, but it suffered from a certain lack of sympathy. The author, to use the reviewer's own words, "was a gentleman first and a literary critic second." The article went on to expatiate upon the fundamental incompatibility of the two species and finally concluded by warning the "gentleman" that he must either mend his ways or resign all aspirations to literary distinction.

The tone of the reviewer was so confident that for a moment we hardly ventured to question his reasoning. Indeed, if he had not protested so much we would willingly have let him have his way. Perhaps it was the extra ounce of conviction that aroused our suspicions instead of stunning us into acquiescence. It occurred to us that, after all, the Temple of the Muses should be open to all worshipers, without regard to race, creed, or color. By what right was this arbitrary sign, "Gentlemen Not Admitted," blazoned above the door? Was it an inevitable symbol of the times? Nobody likes a

[1] From *The Forum,* November, 1925.

perpetual loser, and for the last hundred years the gentleman has been losing all along the line. Democracy, if it has not actually hustled him out of politics, has made him step lively to keep up with the crowd. Not content with this success, it appears that democracy is now bent on hounding him out of the broad domain of literature, whose gallant walks have refreshed his spirit for so many hundred years.

It is not the purpose of this essay to play the cynic or to lament a lost cause. No doubt it is true, as Talleyrand says, that those who did not live before 1789 can never know what society really means, but in any case, what we have lost was an exotic flower that must inevitably have withered in a new environment. Without speculating further on the delicate perfection of the good old days, let us examine the gentleman and try to determine his inherent limitations as far as the appreciation and understanding of literature is concerned. Obviously we must consider the gentleman at his best. The most hardened Tory would not maintain that a fox-hunting squire was *ipso facto* a judge of literature. Nor is the possession of evening clothes an infallible guide to critical acumen. Tennyson once grumbled that Browning would die in a dress suit, and if the unmitigated atmosphere of the drawing-room is injurious to the poet, it is not likely to be healthy for the critic. The point would hardly be worth making were it not that a taste for society and the race-track is so often mistaken for the essential attributes of a gentleman. Such qualities, of course, are entirely irrelevant. Let us grapple with the issue as it is, not as it appears to the prejudiced and the class-conscious. Does the gentlemanly instinct of reticence, taste, decorum, whatever we choose to call it, tend to falsify the literary judgment?

"Literature," says Cardinal Newman in one of his glorious passages, "does not argue, it declaims and insinuates; it is multiform and versatile: it persuades instead of convincing, it seduces, it carries captive; it appeals to the sense of honor, or to the imagination, or to the stimulus of curiosity; it makes its way by means of gaiety, satire, romance, the beautiful, the pleasurable." What can the gentleman oppose to such all-compelling variety? We admit at once—nothing. He who undertakes to condemn whatever may not conform to his private code of morality must be prepared to jettison an invaluable cargo of masterpieces. A sinless literature in a sinful world is on the face of it inconceivable. To the best of our knowledge it is the fanatic, a very different creature from the gentleman, who judges literature by purely ethical standards. To withhold Rabelais from the public libraries because a few small boys delight in extracting his pornographic plums would be as fatuous as it is to legislate against alcoholic liquors because a few men choose to make beasts of themselves. Literature and law are alike in that they cannot cater to the abnormal man.

It is the peculiar merit of the gentleman that, far

from imposing his own standards upon literature, he contrives to keep himself out of the way. "Men are forever vulgar," says Ruskin, "precisely in proportion as they are incapable of sympathy." The adjective "genteel" has unfortunately warped the true meaning of gentleman. An air of finicky refinement fits the imitation well enough, but the genuine article instinctively recoils from shams. Sympathy, freedom from callousness, the ability to sense a situation—these are the qualities that mark the gentleman, and these, we maintain, are also qualities that distinguish the best literary criticism. In theory, at least, we believe that everybody, radical and conservative alike, will admit the overwhelming importance of sympathy. It is the dearth of this one quality that keeps the body of literary criticism so slight. Hack writers who flit gracefully from politics to sport, and from sport to literature, succeed temporarily in making us accept such substitutes as intimacy or facility, but in the long run posterity will disown these interlopers.

From the practical point of view, however, insistence on sympathy involves us at once in a host of difficulties. If it is to mean more than mere lazy tolerance, sympathy necessitates intense imaginative effort. *Marius the Epicurean,* for instance, could only have been written by a scholar who brought the whole weight of his intellect to bear upon the beauties of paganism. Matthew Arnold's *Essays in Criticism* represent, aside from anything else, a fine departure from the narrowly insular attitude of his contemporaries towards the literature of the Continent. Both critics no doubt have their limitations. Walter Pater's passion for beauty, Arnold's insistence on the saving grace of culture, neither of them covers the whole field of literary endeavor. In a word, Pater and Arnold were human beings and not demigods. But will any irresponsible reviewer have the effrontery to maintain that they were hampered by being gentlemen? Whatever virtue they possessed as critics was due to the disciplined yet sympathetic intellect which we have tried to show is the hall-mark of every gentleman of education.

Sympathy, even though it be founded on a rock-bed of wide reading, never of itself made a literary critic. The quality of sensitiveness, which we have referred to already as the absence of callousness, is at least equally important. Mr. Chesterton's delightful remark on the electric light signs of Broadway will perhaps illustrate our meaning. "What a wonderful sight," he is reported to have said, "for those who can't read." This constant awareness of vulgarity or beauty, of the genuine or the artificial, can hardly be deliberately acquired. It is the critical sixth sense without which the soundest judgment may go astray. The novelist may thrive without it, the poet often becomes tongue-tied because of it, but for the man who aspires to qualify as a critic it remains the one inevitable prerequisite.

Sensitiveness, whether we like it or not, cuts both ways—towards pain and towards pleasure. Once we adopt the armor of indifference, a perfectly legitimate defense to all but the critic and the gentleman, the two extremes are automatically eliminated. It is one of nature's most inexorable laws that one cannot become oblivious to the ugly without at the same time losing a feeling for the beautiful. The dreadful effects of callousness are nowhere better illustrated than in the pages of that popular favorite, the etiquette book. The man of the world may dismiss these handbooks on good form as being frankly ridiculous. He may even find them mildly amusing. The picture of the twentieth century *bourgeois gentilhomme* struggling to ape the manners of Fifth Avenue possesses an undoubted elemental humor, which further attracts the Pharisee by titillating his sense of social superiority. The critic, however, is not so easily entertained. Beneath the unconscious satire he recognizes the essential beastliness of these travesties on society. If the younger generation is going to be brought up to consider the niceties of table decoration as the criterion of good manners, then indeed it is time to join the chorus of croaking pessimists in their lament over the degeneracy of the times. This is a question of sensitiveness rather than morality, and here again the critic and the gentleman march side by side.

At their best they have yet another quality in common. We have called it intuition, the ability to sense a situation. Walter de la Mare has divided the poetic imagination into two distinct kinds: "The one divines, the other discovers. The one knows that beauty is truth, the other proves that truth is beauty." We do not wish to make exaggerated claims for the critic, but we maintain that there are moments when he approaches the poet in his faculty for divination. It is perhaps more usual to consider criticism as a rigidly intellectual process, as something entirely removed from the fine frenzy of the poet. If we are prepared to accept a relentlessly scientific conception of criticism, then indeed our theory of intuition falls to pieces. Criticism can never be more than partially scientific. When every item of information has been collected, when every ambiguous passage has been unraveled, the critic still has the bulk of the work before him. Sheer analysis, however profound, does not constitute criticism any more than a knowledge of chess automatically makes a man a military genius. Something must happen before the chess champion can hope to follow in the footsteps of Marshal Foch. He must have learned, among other things, that the science of war involves more than the calculation of chances and the cool exercise of reason. So, too, literary criticism refuses to be confined to the dispassionate method of the laboratory. Creation is after all the driving force behind every act, and the critic must feel the goad no less than the poet or the musician. Otherwise he will fall into the German error of making books instead of writing them. What is it that galvanizes the dry bones of scholarship into the living creature we call criticism? What is it that distinguishes the erudite papers of the Modern Language Association from Francis Thompson's essay on Shelley?

More than anything else we believe it to be the quality of intuition—the quality that divines, that wings its way to the heart without climbing the weary road to the understanding.

It may well be asked why we assume that the gentleman possesses this rare quality in common with the critic. For the moment, we must content ourselves with a glittering generality. The gentleman's view of life is more panoramic than that of the man in the market-place. Whatever his handicap in the study of literature, he is blessed with one tremendous advantage. He looks upon literature as his own patrimony, not as a private garden of which he must ask the key of some college professor. Books are not a pleasant refuge to which he betakes himself in moments of despair; they are the inseparable companions which are forever supplementing his own narrow experience. Now this business of intuition, of which we have made so much, is not as supernatural as it seems. The man who correlates his reading and his observation will soon be credited by his friends with extraordinary powers of divination. When asked to explain a certain opinion he may merely shrug his shoulders. Nevertheless, we trust him as we do the expert consultant who, when called upon to give his reasons for a rather unusual diagnosis, replied abruptly, "No reasons, merely a clinical hunch." But to the men who know him that clinical hunch is enough.

Having done full justice and perhaps more than justice to the gentleman's qualifications for criticism, let us return to the original charge made against him: that he is constitutionally incapable of understanding genius. What *rapport* can there ever be between the artist, with his impossible table manners and his still more impossible emotionalism, and the impeccable, close-lipped, self-contained apostle of good form? We have deliberately chosen the two extremes, and yet we do not believe that even between these two understanding is hopelessly inconceivable. It may well be that the gentleman shudders on his first plunge into Bohemia. The first time that Andrew Lang met Stevenson he took an instinctive dislike to him. One glance told him that Stevenson was an affected aesthete, but eventually they became the best of friends. Supposing they had never met after the first unfavorable encounter, Lang might still have reveled in *Treasure Island*. Why should it be taken for granted that the gentleman cannot appreciate a work of art without admiring the character of the artist?

As long as we are embarking upon the troubled waters of art and morality, we may as well make for a storm-center at once. Is it possible for the gentleman to approach the subject of Oscar Wilde dispassionately? Here, if anywhere, his standards of decency might be expected to deaden his literary sympathy, but again we suspect the difficulty of being more apparent than real. Nothing can obscure the shimmering brilliancy of *Lady Windermere's Fan*, and nothing can atone for the degenerate taint in Oscar Wilde. It is not the gentleman who finds it necessary to rummage old newspaper files for accounts of the trial on the plea that he is making a comprehensive study of Wilde's plays. The gentleman takes the best and ignores the worst without pretending that the worst can in some way be palliated on the vague score of genius.

And now let us forget the gentleman, or rather let us consider him not as a strayed reveler from the *ancien régime,* but as the incarnation of rarefied common-sense. Though genius chafes at his criticism, is he not usually right after all? There are certain avenues to literature which your man of commonsense will not tolerate. One of them is the approach via illegitimate children. Just at present literary criticism is suffering from what the French call *fureur de l'inédit.* By all means let us have the documents on Wordsworth's French daughter, but preserve us from those sentimentalists who look for her influence in every line of his poetry. Instead of assuming that scraps of unpublished matter are necessarily interesting, it is well to remember that the assumption lies just the other way. The homage paid to unpublished documents is one of the diseases of modern scholarship. This year being the hundredth anniversary of Byron's death, it is perhaps worth suggesting a nice piece of entirely useless research. There has so far been no authoritative list of the women he seduced in Venice during the year 1816-1817. Such information can be of no conceivable interest to anybody, but if ever discovered it will probably be hailed in some quarters as a distinct contribution to Byroniana.

No doubt common-sense can be reduced to absurdity, like any other virtue. We have tried to vindicate it from the attacks of its opponents because, at the moment, the champions of the bizarre are more than usually loud-mouthed. God forbid that we should live in a society so standardized that eccentricity dare not show its head. There will always be a need in a democracy for splendid saints and splendid sinners. Whatever the form of government, mankind keeps its interest in "the dangerous edge of things." It is well that eccentrics should flout the dictates of common-sense, but they must not invoke the very deity they have defied. Garibaldi would have raised few recruits if he had based his appeal on the promise of a bonus when the Austrians were defeated. "Let those," he said, "who wish to continue the war against the stranger come with me. I offer neither pay nor quarters nor provisions; I offer hunger, thirst, forced marches, battles, and death."

The man who can sound that note without being theatrical is not often met with in any age or in any country. When he appears men will follow him, whatever their walk in life. So it is with literature. Genius always leaves havoc in its wake. The value of sound literary criticism lies in its ability to recognize impostors. It does not tolerate national prejudices, it is not concerned with capital or labor. Above all, it abhors that miserable class-consciousness that seeks to confine genius to one stratum of society.

THE ALL-STAR LITERARY VAUDEVILLE[1]

By EDMUND WILSON

THE WRITER of this article is a journalist whose professional activities have been chiefly concerned with the American literary movement of the last fifteen years. He has written reviews of the productions of that movement and worked on magazines which were identified with it; he has lived constantly in its atmosphere. And he feels sympathy with all its manifestations, even with those of which, artistically, he disapproves. It is to him a source of deep gratification that literature has been "sold" to the American public and, on principle, in the face of alien attack, he will stand by even the least intelligent, the least disinterested, of its salesmen: he has served in that army himself. But it has recently occurred to him that, to consult frankly his own taste, he really feels only the mildest interest in most of the contemporary literary goods which now find so wide a market, and that he is disaffected to the point of disgust by the publicity service which has grown up in connection with them. He has come to realize that it is scarcely possible nowadays to tell the reviews from the advertising: both tend to convey the impression that masterpieces are being manufactured as regularly and as durably as

[1] From *The New Republic,* June, 1926. This article was originally published anonymously.

new models of motor-cars. In the early days of the present era, the reviews of Mencken, Hackett, Dell, and Untermeyer set an example of honesty and boldness. Today, these critics, having got the kind of literature they want, are apparently perfectly content; and most of the reviews are written by people who have not attempted to go further. The present writers on American literature all have interests in one phase or another of it: either the authors know each other personally or they owe each other debts of gratitude or they are bound together by their loyalty to some common cause. And almost all forget critical standards in their devotion to the great common causes—those of an American national literature in independence of English literature, and of contemporary American ideas as against the ideas of the last generation. Even Stuart P. Sherman, once so savage in the opposite camp, has become as benevolent as Carl Van Doren and now occupies what has perhaps become, from the popular point of view, the central desk of authority, to which each of the performers in the all-star circus, from Ben Hecht to Ring Lardner, steps up to receive his accolade. The present writer has, therefore, for his own satisfaction, for the appeasement of his own critical conscience, attempted to draw up a candid statement of his convictions in regard to his contemporaries, not merely in disparagement of those whom he thinks overrated but in justice to those whom he considers admirable. If he succeeds in irritating one editor or reviewer, in an atmosphere where now for some time complacency and moderation have prevailed, he will feel that he has not written in vain.

To begin with the contemporary American novel —which is commonly assumed to be our principal glory—I must confess that I cannot read our novelists. We compare our fiction to English fiction and conclude that we have been brilliantly successful in this field; but the truth is merely that the English novel is just now at a particularly low ebb. We have no novelist of the first importance, of the importance of James, Joyce or Proust; or of that of Balzac or Dostoevsky. Dreiser rightly commands our respect; but he writes so badly that it is almost impossible to read him and, for this reason, I have difficulty in believing in his literary permanence. To follow the moral disintegration of Hurstwood is to suffer all the agonies of being out of work without being rewarded by the esthetic pleasure which art is supposed to supply. Sinclair Lewis, with a vigorous satiric humor, has brought an indictment which has its local importance, but, when one has been through *Main Street* and *Babbitt,* amusing as they are, one does not feel any appetite to read further novels by Lewis: they have beauty neither of style nor of form and they tell us nothing new about life. Joseph Hergesheimer, though he can tell a story, writes nearly as badly in a fancy way as Dreiser does in a crude one: the judgment of him that I most agree with is the remark attributed to Max Beerbohm, "Poor Mr. Hergesheimer, he wants so much to be an artist." Cabell, though a man of real parts, is, at his worst, a case of the same kind: *Beyond Life* I consider one of the most obnoxiously written books I have ever read. *Jurgen* certainly had its merits: it was well planned and curiously successful in the artificial evocation of the atmosphere of primitive folklore. But, except at his moments of highest imaginative intensity, which are neither very frequent nor very intense, Cabell is intolerably insipid. His genealogies and maps of Poictesme bore me beyond description and the whole Poictesme business strikes me as the sort of thing with which ingenious literary schoolboys sometimes amuse themselves. I dislike also Cabell's southern sentimentality, which leaves him soft when he thinks he is most cynical; and I always feel that, in the impression he gives of living and working in a vacuum, he furnishes a depressing illustration of the decay of the South since the Civil War. Willa Cather is a good craftsman but she is usually dull. In spite of a few distinguished stories, she suffers from an anaemia of the imagination and, like that other rather distinguished novelist, Zona Gale, is given to terrible lapses into feminine melodrama. Waldo Frank writes in a never quite satisfactory style which combines Joyce with the Hebrew prophets. At his best, he touches tragedy and, at his worst, embraces melodrama. He possesses a real poetic sensibility and is refreshing in so far as his vision is different from that of any one else; but, in his novels, where we hope to see him stage a drama, he is usually content to invoke an apocalypse. I consider Jean Toomer's *Cane* better in literary quality than Frank's *Holiday*. I feel more interest in Dos Passos and Fitzgerald than in any of the writers mentioned above: they are younger than the others and one does not feel that one knows so precisely what to expect of them. Dos Passos is ridden by adolescent resentments and seems rather given to documenting life from the outside instead of pursuing the authenticity of experience; but, though, like that other documentator Lewis, he is far too much addicted to making out systematic cases against society, he is a better artist than Lewis and has made steady progress in his art. Scott Fitzgerald, possessing from the first, not merely cleverness, but something of inspired imagination and poetic literary brilliance has not till recently appeared to know precisely what he was about; but with *The Great Gatsby* and some of his recent short stories, he seems to be entering upon a development in the course of which he may come to equal in mastery of his material those novelists whom he began by surpassing by vividness in investing it with glamor. Besides these, there are the other fabricators of fantasy, and the realists, satiric and plain; but the former, so far as I have read them, are either tawdry, like Ben Hecht, or awfully mild, like Carl Van Vechten; and the latter, though both in novel and drama they have learned to apply the formula of naturalism to almost every phase of American life and have, therefore, their local cultural importance, are otherwise especially uninteresting at a time when naturalism has run its course and is either being discarded or transformed everywhere except in America. And we have also had the Wellsian social novel, in various stages of mediocrity.

Sherwood Anderson is a different matter. In his novels, despite excellent pages, I become exasperated, before I have finished them, by the vagueness of the characters and the repetitiousness of the form. But his short stories and his symbolist prose poems have an artistic authenticity which neither Lewis's richer resources nor Miss Cather's technical study have been able to win for their possessors: without ever having learned the tricks of his trade, Anderson's artistic instinct in his best stories is almost perfect and the visions which fill his imagination have a freshness and a slightly discomfiting strangeness which seem to be derived from some more intimate stratum of being than our novelists usually explore. He could stand, however, to learn something from the methods both of Miss Cather and of Lewis: too much of his material has evaporated in his hands from his not knowing how to deal with it. And, in general, I believe that the new American generation has so far perhaps most distinguished itself in the short story rather than in the novel. Sherwood Anderson's short stories, Ernest Hemingway's *In Our Time* and Gertrude Stein's early nouvelles, to which should be added the best of Ring Lardner, constitute a remarkably satisfactory group and one quite free from the outworn conventions and the suggestion of second-rate imitation which render many of the novels suspect. It is interesting to note that all four of these writers have certain characteristics in common, that they may almost be said to form a school: remote from one another as they seem, there is really more direct relation between them than may obviously appear. Thus, Anderson has read Gertrude Stein and seems to have been deeply influenced by *Three Lives;* and Hemingway has evidently read and been influenced by all three of the others. Each of the four has developed what seems only a special branch of the same simple colloquial language based directly on the vocabulary and rhythm of ordinary American speech; and, if there can be said to be an American school of writing, aside from American journalese or from the mere use of American slang in otherwise conventional English prose, these writers would seem to represent it. It is a genre which has already produced one masterpiece in Mark Twain's *Huckleberry Finn,* a work to which Anderson, Lardner and Hemingway are all probably indebted.

As for the dramatists, there is still only O'Neill, who, for all his efforts to break away from naturalism, remains a typical naturalistic dramatist of something under the very first rank. He is a writer of the same school as Hauptmann, with very much the same kind of merits; but, where Hauptmann is as steady as Shakespeare, O'Neill is hysterically embittered. He forces his catastrophes and, at the same time, fails to prepare them; and, despite the magnificent eloquence of which he is capable, especially when handling some form of the vernacular, he has grave deficiencies of literary taste which allow him to leave great areas of his dialogue either crude or banal. John Lawson has a wit and a fancy which have found their proper vehicle in the theater; but, even more than his ally, Dos Passos, he is given to adolescent grievances and enthusiasms.

We come now to literary criticism. In my opinion, H. L. Mencken (who is perhaps a prophet rather than a critic) is ordinarily underrated as a writer of English prose. Belonging himself to the line of Butler and Swift rather than to that of Pater and de Quincy, he cherishes a rustic reverence for this latter and is never tired of celebrating the elegances of such provincial pretenders to its prestige as Cabell, Hergesheimer and Lord Dunsany, who have announced their high calling, in, I think, Mr. Cabell's phrase, of "writing beautifully about beautiful things." But, though Mencken's style lends itself to excesses and vulgarities, especially in the hands of his imitators, who have taken over the Master's jargon without possessing his admirable literary sense, I believe that his prose is more successful in its way than that of these devotees of beauty is in theirs. Mencken's ideas are neither many nor subtle and, even in his most serious writings, even in *The American Language,* he over-indulges an appetite for paradox; but he has succeeded in turning his ideas into literature: it is through the original color and rhythm of his prose that his opinions have become so infectious. He has now been saying the same things over and over again for a considerable period and I have become very tired of them. But I derive a certain literary satisfaction from even his editorials in *The American Mercury*. Consider the leaflet which he has recently circulated on the adventures of *The American Mercury* with the Boston Watch and Ward Society: this statement, of no literary pretensions, in which Mencken appears without war-paint or feathers, displays most attractive eighteenth century qualities of lucidity, order and force, for lack of which the youngest literary generation, who have thrown Mencken overboard, have so far proved rather ineffective. Another critic, much ridiculed by these latter, seems to me also an excellent writer. Though Paul Rosenfeld, too, is cursed with his jargon, which, in his case, takes the form of a weakness for writing French and German locutions in English, it is, none the less, precisely his command of a rich English vocabulary which is one of the things that makes him remarkable among American writers—who, in general, are handicapped by not having at their disposal a large enough variety of English words, or, if they have them, by not knowing what they mean. Rosenfeld, at his worst, is given to overwriting: receiving in his soul the seed of a work of art of some such tender plant as Sherwood Anderson, he will sometimes cause it to exfloreate into an enormous and rather rank "Mystic Cabbage-Rose." On these occasions, his prose seems coarse in quality and his color muddy; but, at his best, his prose is certainly among our soundest and his colors both brilliant and true. He is intelligent, well educated and incorruptibly serious; and he is perhaps the only American critic of his generation who has written anything really valuable about the contemporary artistic life of Europe. Van Wyck Brooks, who has also written good prose, but of a very different sort, I propose to speak of in another connection. George Jean Nathan is a wonderful humorous writer and a better critic of the theater than A. B. Walkley, in a recent article, gave him credit for being; but his prose, which superficially resembles Mencken's, is usually lacking in all the qualities which make Mencken's admirable. Willard Huntington Wright, some years ago, gave the impression of being some one important; and Lewis Mumford now gives the impression of some one perhaps about to be. Gilbert Seldes, through his activities as an editor of *The Dial* and his cultivation of the popular arts, has filled a rôle of considerable importance; but his principal literary quality is a kind of wit which tends to figure in his writings at the expense of accuracy, lucidity and taste. He has become addicted to esthetic editorial writing, a department for which his vivid and alert, but very glancing and volatile mind, is perhaps not well adapted. In my opinion, he is seen at his best in passages of straight description of some movie or vaudeville act which has aroused his imagination; and I am inclined to believe that he will prove better at dialogue than he has ever been at solid prose: his recent comedy, for all its unpopularity and its serious deficiencies, showed a real instinct of ironic comedy and a gift for conversation. Burton Rascoe has performed the astonishing and probably unprecedented feat of making literature into news. A master of all the tricks of newspaper journalism, which he has introduced into the Sacred Grove to the horror of some of its high priests, his career has yet, from the literary point of view, been singularly honorable; and the cause of letters has profited more from his activities than the proprietors of popular newspapers who have inevitably discovered in the long run that they would feel more comfortable with literary editors who did not find books so exciting. He has always written respectably and, at his best, with much intelligence and point. No one knows what his abilities might be outside the field of journalism, for he has never put them to any other test. Most of the younger generation of critics either are badly educated or have never learned to write, and many suffer from both disabilities. At best, we have produced no literary critic of the full European stature: the much abused Paul Elmer More remains our only professional critic whose learning is really great and whose efforts are ambitious. His prose is quite graceless and charmless, but always accurate and clear; his point of view, though a product of Puritan rationalism, is definitely formulated and possesses the force of deep and serious conviction; and, though hopelessly deficient in artistic sensibility, he has become, in so far as it is possible to be without it, a real master of ideas.

The modern method of biography, based on Strachey and psychoanalysis, has had many practitioners in America: Katherine Anthony, Brooks, Beer, Werner and others; but, though it has furnished a number of agreeable books, I have seen none, except Brooks's *Mark Twain* (I haven't yet read Krutch's *Poe*), of really first-rate importance. In the special departments of critical and expository writing, the general inferiority of our culture to that of France or Great Britain becomes particularly plain. Comparatively few university professors command the attention of the literary public. Professor Dewey writes much and usefully, but has not inherited William James's literary gift; Professor Cohen, who has a literary gift, publishes nothing but reviews, and not very many of them. In classical criticism, Professor Tenney Frank seems the only representative of a new generation; and Professor Frank, although interesting and bold and himself of an admirable literary competence, seems rather indifferent to the literary aspects of the classics. Professor Shorey is perhaps the only other scholar who writes readable books in this field. We have, in short, no university professor with a literary reputation equal to that of Garrod, of Gilbert Murray, of Mackail, of A. E. Housman, or of Whitehead or Bertrand Russell or Lowes Dickinson. I can remember no recent book by an American professor which has been widely read on its literary merits, except Professor Fite's *Moral Philosophy* and Professor Morison's *Maritime History of*

Massachusetts. In science, we have some effective journalists in the rousing modern manner, but they are mostly undistinguished writers: Doctor Fishbein, Doctor De Kruif and Doctor Dorsey. Edwin Slosson is rapidly becoming a sort of William Lyon Phelps of scientific culture. William Beebe, from the point of view of prose, writes a particularly degenerate form of journalese; but he is a man of some real literary ability, who deserves to be read by literary people: one of his assets is an extraordinary vocabulary which blends scientific with literary language in such a way that his scientific words become imbued with a new literary value. I doubt, however, whether the cable to the *New York Times* is a good school of writing. I am sorry not to be able to do the political writers justice: I believe that we are better off in this department than elsewhere; but it is the one in which I have recently read least.

As for poetry, the new movement of twelve years ago seemed at the time to assume impressive proportions. But who can believe in its heroes now? Edgar Lee Masters did one creditable thing. *The Spoon River Anthology;* but, except for a single fine poem called "Silence," I have seen nothing by him since that I could read. Vachel Lindsay's best poems, such as his "Bryan," are spoiled by the incurable cheapness and looseness which are rampant in the rest of his work. Carl Sandburg, unlike Masters and Lindsay, has a real instinct for language; with a hard-boiled vocabulary and reputation, he really presents perhaps the most attractive surface of any of the men of the group. But, when we come to read him, we are disappointed to discover how uninteresting he is—how meager appear his emotions and how obvious his ideas. The work of Amy Lowell is like a great empty cloisonné jar; that of Fletcher a great wall of hard descriptive prose mistaken for poetry. Conrad Aiken, except in a few lyrics, is one of those curious people, like William Vaughn Moody, who when we first glance at a volume by them, give the impression of high poetic gifts, but, when we eagerly set out to enjoy them, produce the effect of an involuntary imposture. Robert Frost has a thin but authentic vein of poetic sensibility; but he is excessively dull and writes abominable verse. In my opinion, he is the most generally overrated of this group of poets. Ezra Pound, who deserves all honor as a champion and pioneer, writes as one who understands very well, and as few of his contemporaries do, in what the highest poetry consists, but who has rarely been able to affect us as the highest poets do. His ambitious cantos, so full of fine passages, passages which, if we met them standing by themselves, might deceive us into thinking that the poem must be a masterpiece, seem only fragments in the patternless mosaic of a monument to poetic bankruptcy. And the other poets of the Left, though, like Pound, they have considerable literary interest, seem the victims of the same sterile blight. Marianne Moore is sometimes very fine; but, as she has herself shrewdly noted in choosing her title, the bulk of her work answers better to the description of Observations than to that of poetry: from a viscous slag of intellectual processes, intense and vivid images emerge, invested apparently with sharp emotional significance, but rarely precipitated out as poems. H. D. writes well, like Carl Sandburg; but, like Sandburg, there is little in her. Wallace Stevens has a fascinating nonsense gift of words, rather like that of Edith Sitwell, and he is a charming decorative artist. Alfred Kreymborg has his distinction but tends fatally toward insipidity. I think I prefer his frankly dry, prosaic and odd early work to his later more pretentious sonnets. E. E. Cummings possesses, in some respects, a more remarkable lyric gift than any of the poets reviewed above: his feeling is spontaneous and his words run naturally into music. But, as in his rather limp line drawings, his hand never seems firm: all sorts of ideas and images have come streaming into his head and he doesn't know how to manipulate them to make them artistically effective. W. C. Williams and Maxwell Bodenheim I have tried my hardest to admire but I have never been able to believe in them. Nowadays, the general appetite for poetry seems to have abated since most of the poets mentioned above made their reputation. Even the young poets of most promise find difficulty in getting their poems accepted, not only by the publishers, who have come to regard poetry as invariably unprofitable, but even by the magazines, which, having brought out two or three crops of poets, seem content to close the canon, and have no place for the new poetry of unknown men—even if so obviously gifted as Allen Tate or Phelps Putnam—who cannot be found in Mr. Untermeyer's anthologies or among the charter contributors to *The Dial.*

I have left the women lyric poets aside in order to discuss them as a group by themselves. On the average, though less pretentious, I think I find them more rewarding than the men: their emotion is more genuine and their literary instinct surer. Miss Reese, the dean of the guild, astonishes me by continuing to write, not only with the same distinction, but almost with the same freshness, as forty years ago. Sara Teasdale, the monotony of whose sobbing note rendered her rather unfashionable when a more arrogant race of young women appeared, has made real progress in her art since her earlier books of poems and has recently written some of her most charming lyrics. Miss Millay has now, in turn, grown so popular that she, too, is in danger of becoming unfashionable; but she remains the most important of the group and perhaps one of the most important of our poets. Like Mencken, the prophet of a point of view, she has, like him, become a national hero; nor, as in the case of certain other prophets, is her literary reputation undeserved. With little color, meager ornament and images often commonplace, she is yet the mistress of deeply moving rhythms, of a music which makes up for the ear what her page seems to lack for the eye; and, above all, she has that singular boldness, which she shares with the greatest poets and which consists in taking just that one step beyond one's fellows which, by bringing poetry in fresh contact with moral reality, has the effect of making other productions take on an aspect of literary convention. Elinor Wylie, in the best of her verse and in her novel *Jennifer Lorn,* gives expression to a set of emotions quite different from those of Miss Millay, but one which has also its intensity and its typical interest. Her literary proficiency is immense: she is never at a loss for a witty reference or for a brilliant image; she commands the finest fabrics, the richest sensations, the choicest works of art, the most amusing historical allusions and the most delicious things to eat. And, as a consequence, her inferior work is almost as well written as her best; and her best work has both a style and a splendor of a kind very rare in America—where, even when these qualities do appear together, as they did to some extent in Amy Lowell, they too often remain hollow and metallic from the lack of a heart at the core. Edna Millay's inferior work has no embroidery to disguise it; and, save in her vein of classical austerity, she has for her best only the sorrel or mullein-stalk of the barren and rocky pastures, the purple wild sweet-pea dragging drift-wood across the sand, the dead leaves in the city gutters, the gray snow in the city street, the kettle, the broom, the uncarpeted stairs and the dead father's old clothes—grown strange and disturbing now, to this reader's sense, at least, as the prison-window of Verlaine or the common cross-roads of Catullus. Louise Bogan plucked one low resounding theme on a tensely strung steel string, but they are its vibrations, rather than a development, which are still ringing in the air. Léonie Adams has published a most remarkable book, of which the language, seeming to branch straight from the richest English tradition of the seventeenth century, strikes music from the skies of the calm summer starbreak, the bright-washed night after rain and the blue translucence of evening, where a gull or a pigeon, rising alone, seeking freedom in that clarity and space, is lost in a celestial confusion of cloud and light. An anthology of these women writers of lyrics should contain, besides the poets mentioned above, the Cinquains of the late Adelaide Crapsey and the best of Miss Taggard, Miss Deutsch and a number of others, of whom the younger Laura Gottschalk may eventually prove one of the most interesting and in whose company Dorothy Parker, long known as a humorous writer, has recently, it seems to me, fully proved her right to belong.

I have left to the last the two poets whom, among the men, I admire most: T. S. Eliot and E. A. Robinson. T. S. Eliot, though heavily infected with the Alexandrianism of the Left, has been able to imbue with a personal emotional significance, not only his inveterate literary allusions and his echoes of other poets, but even the lines which he has borrowed from them. Both as poet and as critic, he deserves the position of influence which he now occupies. I deplore the mood of extreme fatigue and despondency which seems lately to have been drying up both his poetry and his criticism; but I cannot believe that so intense a passion for poetry—a passion scarcely to be matched among American writers—can be permanently stifled. E. A. Robinson is the last and, artistically (leaving the happiest flashes of Emerson aside), the most important of the New England poets. Though he has recently run much into the sands of long and arid blank-verse narratives, I believe that he is one of the poets of our time most likely to survive as an American classic. Both he and Eliot, despite the disappointing tendency of their poetic motors to get stalled, despite their exasperating hypochondrias of the soul, have had the authentic lyric gift and the artist's mastery of it.

Consideration of Mr. Robinson suggests some general observations. I have said that Mr. Robinson is the last of the New England poets and it is true that he belongs to an earlier period than ours and has really little in common with the writers in whose company the anthologists now place him. (He is closely akin to Henry James, and even to Hawthorne.) And when we look back on the literary era which preceded the recent renascence, we are surprised, after all that has been written about its paleness, its tameness and its sterility, to realize the high standard of excellence to which its best writers attained. When we consider Henry James, Stephen Crane, and such lesser novelists as Cable and Howells, with such critics as Babbitt, Brownell and Paul Elmer More, who belong essentially to the same era, we are struck with certain superiorities over the race of writers of today. These men, in general, with less liberal ideas, possessed a sounder culture than we; and, though less lively, were better craftsmen. They were professional men of letters and they had thoroughly learned their trade. Note the intense artistic integrity, the incapacity for careless writing, of even Stephen Crane, who passed for a clever newspaper man and an outlaw to respectable literature, but whose work astonishes us now by its quality, by no means incomparable—as how much of our present fiction is?—to the best European work in the same kind.

Another writer who, like Mr. Robinson, through her craftsmanship and her culture, is closely bound to this earlier tradition, but who, by reason of her point of view, forms a connecting link with our own, is Edith Wharton. Often described as an imitator of James, she was really, in her important novels, a writer of quite a different kind. James, except at very rare moments, was never a preacher or a bitter social satirist; but Mrs. Wharton was perhaps the first American to write with passion *against* American society and ideals, as they had come to present themselves by the end of the last century. Her recent books, since *The Age of Innocence,* have been of rather inferior interest; but, in her prime, she produced what I firmly believe are the best examples of this kind of fiction we have had, and some of our very best novels. She was soon followed by Van

Wyck Brooks, who represented the same civilization and expressed the same reaction against it: one of the chief prophets of the present generation, he belongs to the older literary tradition and, for better or for worse, has never learned any of the methods of the new.

Join these writers with the others I have mentioned and it will be seen that they fall together into a remarkably distinguished group, supplying both the history of a society and, with growing indignation toward the end, a criticism of it. Our own age will scarcely present so dignified or so solid a surface. We have the illusion of stronger vitality and of greater intellectual freedom, but we are polyglot, parvenu, hysterical and often illiterate. When time has weeded out our less important writers, those that are left will present a singular vaudeville: H. L. Mencken hoarse with saving souls in the manner of Billy Sunday; Edna Millay singing like a nightingale; Sherwood Anderson making up naïve but disquieting bed-time stories; Dreiser getting out newspaper copy in which the reporter astonishes the reader by having been rash enough to try to tell the truth; T. S. Eliot patching from many cultures a dazzling and variegated disguise for the timid and scrupulous soul of a hero out of Henry James. Let us remember, however, that vaudeville has always been a little an American specialty; and that our most important writers have not in general been such as I have mentioned as typical of the generation before ours. Emerson, Whitman, Poe; *Walden* and *Moby Dick:* they are all independent one-man turns, and who can say that we may not find their peers among the comic monologuists, the sentimental soloists, and the one-act melodramas of our present bill?

It is, however, true in our day, as it scarcely was to the same extent in theirs, that the popular appetite for literature gives rise to a serious temptation to be content, as the public are, with one's second-best work; and we may still feel a solicitude lest our writers, if they will not study more, will not at least bore deeper.

CAVOUR[1]

By P. W. WILSON

THE EARLY LIFE AND LETTERS OF CAVOUR, 1810-1848. *By A. J. Whyte. Oxford University Press, New York.*

IN THE minds of most of us there is a pigeonhole for Camillo Cavour. We schedule him as the Bismarck of Italy, the admirable Macchiavelli who lured the third Napoleon to the victories of Magenta and Solferino, and wove the red shirts of Garibaldi into the texture of Italian unity. At his appointed cue he walked to the center of the stage, the inevitable actor, perfect already in his part. He devoted ten thrilling years to restoring a long-shattered nation. And then, his work done, he died. On the flame of a genius that was consumed by its own intensity, the curtain fell.

In skimming thus the mere surface of biography we are apt too often to skip the juvenilia. It is the career itself, external and objective, which supplies the historian with his melodrama; the character, evolved from youth, is mere psychology. Yet in the miracle that was Cavour there must have been a method. It was during the '30s and '40s that somehow there developed the diplomat of the '50s. To unveil this hidden period has been the aim of a

[1] From *The New York Times Book Review,* July 12, 1925.

historical commission in Italy. Many hundreds of letters and other documents have been collected and arranged, and these are the documents which Mr. Whyte introduces to the English-speaking world. His narrative deals only with the prelude to the play. But it is so fascinating that it reduces the play itself to a mere sequel. The Cavour of obscurity overshadows the Cavour of fame. The man proves to be no more than the son of the boy.

In what sense, then, was Cavour the Bismarck of Italy? Both men were born of ancient families, feudal or Junker, with estates and a dependent tenantry. And both men were educated by the army, emerging therefrom at an early age. Both men studied agriculture and both men set themselves the task of achieving the national unity of their respective and divided countries. Indeed, both men believed in war. When Cavour was forming his opinions men talked, as they talk today, of "universal peace." He admitted that it would be "an immense blessing." But, said he, if you would be "delivered from this scourge of war," you must "civilize, educate." Ignorant nations would never coöperate. And as for arbitration, he asked the searching question: "Do you count much on the morality of Metternich if he had to decide whether the claims of Don Pedro or his brother were legitimate?"

Thus far, there was then a certain similarity between the two nation-builders. But, in all else, the contrast was complete. Behind Bismarck lay Prussia; Cavour could only rely on Piedmont, a province no more powerful than a single New England State, minus railways and commerce. What the German achieved with the big stick, the Italian had to win by his sole rapier. Nor did the difference end there. Bismarck was a Tory who upheld the divine right of Kings. It is to the everlasting renown of Cavour that he believed in liberty. An Italy united must be also an Italy of free citizens. "There is no great man," he declared, "who is not a Liberal." In his democratic faith, Cavour was thus poles asunder from the Prussian autocrat.

It meant that against Cavour, as patriot, were ranged not only Austria and Metternich, but Cavour's own family, his King, the Pope, and every other constituted authority within Italy herself. By the Royal family of Savoy, for whose court he was paving the path from Turin to Rome, he was regarded as little better than a traitor to the throne. The army records contain, among other items, the order that "the Signor Cavour will immediately be placed under close arrest for having books in his possession without leave from his superiors." For "grave disobedience in refusing to obey the general orders of the school" he was "confined with bread and water for three days, with the addition of a *nota rossa* (or bad mark) from the professor." The army was no place for him.

At court he was for a time a page, on which experience he remarked: "How do you think that we were dressed except as the lackeys that we were? I blush with shame at it." As a younger son, he was dependent on his father for an income and in any event did not come of age until his twenty-fifth year. "The poor child," wrote his aunt, "is entirely absorbed in revolutions. . . . He is wildly enthusiastic about political economy, this erroneous science which warps the mind and is of no use." Why could he not "become a great mathematician like La Grange"?—so asked a friend, Major Carlo Cappai. "This is no time for mathematics," replied Cavour. "It is necessary to study political economy; the world progresses. I hope to see the day when our country is governed by a constitution, and who knows but I may be a Minister in it!" Not bad for a boy of thirteen years! And the "erroneous science" of political economy, which included a firm belief in free trade, began to be respected, even by aunts, when its application to live stock rehabilitated the family estates.

Piedmont, then, was the cage where was hatched this soaring eagle. The political reaction of that small province was incredible in its folly. In May, 1814, the Napoleonic nightmare, as it was regarded, came to an end. The King returned in triumph to Turin, his capital, which city became once more "half barracks and half monastery." On the morrow of his restoration, this earlier Victor Emmanuel issued an astonishing proclamation:

> We recognize the validity of no law whatsoever between this our present edict and those of the Royal constitutions of 1770.

By one sweep of the scepter the clock was put back forty-four years. The civil service, being French, was disbanded. Education was suspended. Abuses were again legalized. And, "calling for the court almanac of 1798," writes Dr. Whyte, "the King proceeded to reinstate every official still living in the position which he had then occupied." Men, sixteen years older, resumed jobs that for sixteen years had been in abeyance.

The atmosphere so created was, in Cavour's word, "suffocating." The one daily journal, called the *Gazetta Piemontese,* was issued by the Foreign Office, and "the news which appeared of most interest to the editors of this production concerned China and Japan, European affairs and news from the United States being too dangerous for publication." Otherwise:

> The only newspaper of any importance was Brofferio's weekly sheet, the *Messaggiere Torinese.* In this, by dint of clever editing and a kind of parabolic use of ancient history and the suggestive adaptation of non-political modern controversies, such as that between the Classicists and the Romanticists, he contrived in spite of the censorship to give the paper a liberal flavor, though it was more by implication than expression that its true opinions were to be discovered. Journalistic efforts of a more pronounced kind, like Mazzini's *Indicatore Genovese,* had a short life, and the severity of the Government effectually restrained the literary-minded from indulging too readily in the risky business of Piedmontese journalism.

When Cavour started his famous journal, *Il*

Risorgimento, the very term Parliament was barred. "In a word," we read, "Piedmont at this time realized the ideal of the thoroughly reactionary Government, where 'under pain of death one does not speak of what it is forbidden to do.'" It is no wonder that "secret societies flourished" and that "illicit literature was published, circulated, and read." The "more respectable societies, like the Agrarian Society and the Whist Club of later date, were simply disguised opportunities for political discussion."

Forgetfully we suppose that Bolshevism is a phenomenon of our own day. But in the Europe of Cavour Socialists were already talking the language of Moscow. In Cavour's diary we find this account of a conversation with an extremist from Marseilles who anticipated Marx by a generation:

> He regards a social and political revolution as good only in so far as it forwards a complete social reformation. He despises the American Constitution as merely substituting a President for a King, without destroying the corrupt power of money or the domination of the poor by the rich. His social theories are almost those of Babeuf; to make the State by degrees the sole proprietor of all land and capital, with the obligation of hiring them to the best and most honest workers. The first step of the Republic will be the dictatorship and universal war.

All such counsels Cavour himself rejected. He stood clearly and consistently for what he called the *juste milieu,* the happy mean, which signified Italy united under constitutional monarchy as understood in England. "To be a useful statesman," he declared, "it is necessary before everything to have 'the tact of the possible.'" And to tact he added knowledge. There was nothing of France and Frenchmen that he failed to note in his papers. He absorbed like a sponge the life of England, including her poor law. He read de Tocqueville on the United States. He had no troops at his back. He held no office. His only chance of power was knowledge.

Fomenting no revolution, he waited. He was certain that his destiny would come to him. "I am a very, an enormously ambitious man," wrote the Unknown, "and when I am Minister I shall justify my ambition; for, I tell you, in my dreams I already see myself Minister of the Kingdom of Italy." It seemed an idle boast, but in its prophetic wisdom Cavour's vision was at times uncanny. Writing after the upheavals of 1830, he hazarded this forecast:

> Eighteen years from now the great crisis which has already begun will reach its climax and Europe will then decide for good upon one of the great principles which now stand before it.

And eighteen years afterward the revolutions of 1848 swept over the Continent.

His industry was as "enormous" as his ambition. But there were times when his emotions overcame him. To "gallantry and gambling" this bachelor was sadly addicted. Of his romances here described it is enough to say that he and the lady of the moment swore eternal devotion to one another with the passionate fervor of opera singers and then parted to find other consolation. Having said that Cavour was a man about town and that the ladies were entirely of his opinion, you have said all that need be said of these common proceedings. One charmer tried to tempt him to desert Piedmont for Paris. The essential Cavour replied:

And why, Madam, abandon my country? To come to France to make a reputation in letters? To run after a little renown, a little glory, without ever being able to reach the goal of my ambition? What good could I achieve for my native land outside my own country? What influence could I exercise on behalf of my unhappy brothers, strangers and exiles in a land where egotism fills all the chief social positions? What does all this crowd of strangers whom choice or misfortune have thrown far from their homeland do in Paris? Who among them has rendered himself truly useful to his fellows? Which of them has carved out a great career for himself or won an influence over society? Not one. Those that would have been great upon the soil that bore them vegetate obscure in the whirl of Parisian life.

So wrote "the Italian with a complexion like a rose and a smile like an infant." The lady kept a comb and returned a stud. The gentleman, discouraged by debts, talked of suicide.

In 1848 the revolution came. There, in Turin, the people paraded, Cavour as a journalist marching between the wine-carriers and the wood-carvers.

He was thirty-seven years old, below the middle height, and his face was not yet sallow. He was thus described:

> The dominating feature of his face was his eyes, blue in color, so bright and vivacious and full of changing expression that it was difficult to determine their permanent character. His habit of body was not full but robust, without as yet showing that tendency to extreme stoutness which afterward became apparent. His facial angle, his extraordinarily full forehead and his peculiar way of fixing objects he wished to study, indicated him at the first glance as one called to high destinies. His neck was short and thick, set between two massive shoulders already somewhat bent from the habit of contemplation. His legs were short and stout in proportion to his body. His carriage was instinctively aristocratic, without, however, any suggestion of vulgar pride. In speech quick and incisive, with a keen sense of humor, he was a most polite and attentive listener no matter to whom he was speaking, a quality he retained even after he became famous, and which often saved him from impetuous or hasty speech.

The Constitution was completed; a government was formed; and—bitter blow—Cavour was left out. Ever the constituencies—four in succession—rejected him for the Legislature. Literally, his only mouthpiece was the editorial column in *Il Risorgimento.* How shall we explain it?

The Italy of Cavour was the Italy of Mussolini and of d'Annunzio. It is a land of genius; never has it failed of pontiffs infallible in religion, in art, in science, and in song. But in an affair comparatively so simple as politics, this genius of Italy's sometimes lapses. Cavour was himself indignant over the folly of Italian emigrants in Paris. He wrote of them in terms scarcely quotable.

At Turin, with the Austrians at the gates of Milan, the Legislature surrendered itself to ten days of oratory. Then, suddenly, the people demanded a man. And the only man was Cavour. It was useless to denounce him as an aristocrat. It was useless to ridicule his unready rhetoric and French accent. He had to be trusted. He had to be obeyed. He was the man who had the facts. And it was the facts that had to be faced.

1000034425

WILKES COLLEGE LIBRARY